# Lotus Notes®

## Developer's Guide

Eric Rayl

SAMS
PUBLISHING

201 West 103rd Street
Indianapolis, Indiana 46290

SAMS Developer's Guide

*To my mother, Mary Ann Rayl. Without the quality upbringing and education that she gave me, I would never have been in a position to write this book. Thanks, Mom :-)*

**Publisher**

Richard K. Swadley

**Associate Publisher**

Jordan Gold

**Acquisitions Manager**

Stacy Hiquet

**Managing Editor**

Cindy Morrow

**Acquisitions and Development Editor**

Dean Miller

**Production Editor**

Cheri Clark

**Editorial Coordinator**

Bill Whitmer

**Editorial Assistants**

Carol Ackerman
Sharon Cox
Lynette Quinn

**Technical Reviewer**

Saeed Naderi

**Software Development Specialist**

Keith Davenport

**Marketing Manager**

Gregg Bushyeager

**Cover Designer**

Kathy Hanley

**Book Designer**

Alyssa Yesh

**Director of Production and Manufacturing**

Jeff Valler

**Manufacturing Coordinator**

Paul Gilchrist

**Imprint Manager**

Juli Cook

**Production Analyst**

Dennis Clay Hager
Mary Beth Wakefield

**Proofreading Coordinator**

Joelynn Gifford

**Indexing Coordinator**

Johnna VanHoose

**Graphics Image Specialists**

Clint Lahnen
Tim Montgomery
Sue VandeWalle
Teresa Forrester

**Page Layout**

Nick Anderson
Angela P. Judy
Ayanna Lacey
Stephanie J. McComb
Michelle Mitchell
Chad Poore
Dennis Wesner

**Proofreading**

Carol Bowers
Mona Brown
Cheryl Cameron
Elaine Crabtree
Greg Kemp
Brian-Kent Proffitt
Ryan Rader
SA Springer
Suzanne Tully

**Indexer**

Bront Davis

# Overview

# Contents

# Preface

When people talk about "groupware," more often than not, Lotus Notes is mentioned. Since its inception in 1989, Notes has become the classic example of groupware. For several years after its introduction, Notes was not much more than a curiosity to companies, but today, there are approximately 1 million users worldwide. Although this is not a huge number, no one else in the groupware marketplace has such an installed base, and every other vendor, including Microsoft, is scrambling to catch up. Although Notes is doing well in the marketplace, it is not doing nearly as well as it should.

The problem lies in the fact that many Information Systems executives have pigeon-holed Notes as groupware, and they are not quite sure what "groupware applications" are. Additionally, many executives "micro-manage" application development solutions, forgetting to look at the grand scheme of application development and communications within their corporation. These same executives then become impervious to hot new Notes-related products and technologies, such as Notes F/X, Lotus Notes Document Imaging, Phone Notes, and Video Notes, because they already have dismissed, or at least put on hold, the idea that Lotus Notes is software that their company could reap large benefits from.

Notes is one of the hardest software packages to sell to a corporation. I have tried time and time again to convince people that their companies could benefit by using Notes applications, but many IS executives "just don't get it." Lotus Notes is not at all like any other software in existence. It is part second-generation electronic mail, it is part an application development platform, and it is in many respects similar to a network operating system. How many other software products do you know that publish detailed, independent return-on-investment studies, from many types of corporations, such as Lotus does?

I wrote this book because I firmly believe that Notes can be of benefit and have a high return-on-investment within almost any organization, large or small. The problem is that most companies don't understand the value of shared information and the benefits involved in having critical information available throughout the organization, whether it is a 20-user office or a global conglomerate with many remote users that is constantly acquiring other companies.

Corporations need to start viewing Notes as an application development platform, in competition with the products from such companies as Microsoft, Borland, and Gupta. Although it takes planning and effort up front to get a robust, stable Notes infrastructure in place, the payback comes when applications can be developed and rolled out to users in a fraction of the time required with other systems. Additionally, development and training costs decline almost exponentially with the number of Notes applications that are used within the corporation, especially for corporations that use various operating systems (Windows, OS/2, Macintosh, and UNIX), running on various network operating systems and protocols.

A testament to my belief that Notes is the best tool for sharing information is the large number of companies that are using Notes to communicate with and distribute information to their customers. This trend is largely within the computer industry, but I expect that it will gain momentum as corporations gain an understanding of the CompuServe Lotus Notes Information Service (CLNIS) and as the AT&T/Lotus alliance produces products and services.

This book was written with the main intent to teach you how to design and develop robust Notes applications, but it also should give you ideas for applications that you have never thought of before. Notes, available since 1989, is a relatively mature product that is available *today,* complete with plenty of Lotus and third-party developed add-ons to suit your requirements. When considering application development languages/ tools for networks, especially for distributed or multiplatform applications, Lotus Notes must be considered as a viable contender for many types of applications.

# Acknowledgments

I am totally indebted to David Alison, the cofounder of Alison, Rayl & Associates, Inc., for believing in my capabilities and hiring me when he was the Director of MIS at Nantucket Corporation. He has taught me a multitude of skills and techniques on everything from writing the highest quality programs, to management techniques, and even lessons in life. Additionally, he introduced me to his friends at *PC Week,* which led to my first published article. David Alison is one of the highest quality people that I know, and I give him and his ideas the utmost respect.

My exposure to Notes would not have happened without the foresight of Barry ReBell, Larry Heimendinger, and Rob Clarke, who were forward-thinking enough to bring Notes into Nantucket Corp., and who placed their faith in my capabilities in being able to roll Notes out within the corporation. I wish to give my earnest thanks to all three of these gentlemen.

Several of the people at one of my major accounts were instrumental in allowing me to push Notes to its fullest. Larry Zeni and Marsha Lansman had a relentless drive to use Notes as THE application development platform, and it is an experience I'll never forget. Additionally, Richard Martinez and John Van Borssum were very supportive and patient during our development cycle, and I want to thank them for allowing me the freedom that they did.

I owe many thanks to Mark Whiteside, the consummate sales and marketing genius, who has helped me numerous times to understand how Notes is viewed from a "user's" perspective. (The funny thing is that, after my years of harping at him about how Notes applications could/should be developed and used, he has become one of the most advanced Notes developers that I know). Thanks, Mark, for giving me a different perspective on Notes when I needed it most.

Pat Doherty, Diane Horak, and Meryl Franzman were invaluable, because they put me in touch with the people I needed to talk to in order to get my questions answered in order to write this book, and they always made sure I had the latest versions of the Notes software as I was writing. Thank you sincerely for your help.

No Notes book is complete without an acknowledgment to the amazing Ray Ozzie and his team of "rocket scientists" that created and constantly evolved Notes. It's almost unheard of today to have a software program that has virtually no competition. But Notes has been in existence since 1989, and as of July 1994, there are still no true competitors to Notes. That is a testament to how advanced Mr. Ozzie's ideas and achievements are.

And last, but not least, I want to thank my friends who have stuck by me and tried to understand my reclusive behavior while I not only wrote this book but built my consulting company. Even though I sometimes would not return my friends' phone calls and would not show up at events when by all rights I should have, my friends, including Scott Armstrong, Eric Banghart, Tess Enriquez, Doug Murphy, Bob Ruhlman, Roger Schmutz, Brian Schwartz, Cynthia Soloman, and Craig White, have tried to put up with me and my relentless drive to be the best at Lotus Notes. Thank you for your patience, and hopefully now that this book is done we can spend more time together.

# About the Author

Eric Rayl has been involved with computers since he was 17 years old and writing dBASE programs for an Apple II computer, using a CP/M emulation card. In college at the University of Colorado, he took computer programming classes but majored in Engineering Physics.

Working in a nuclear missile silo did not seem like a very exciting proposition, so his first job out of college, in 1986, was as an industrial engineer/production manager at a manufacturing corporation. At the company, he promptly decided to overhaul the aging minicomputer-based system. He learned PC networking on his own and single-handedly replaced the aging minicomputer system with a Novell network. Next, he tackled communications problems and installed a WAN to link the corporate office and the plant. Shortly thereafter, he was fired for spending too much time on computers. (As it turns out, that company is still a client of his today.)

Next, he was hired by Nantucket Corporation (developers of the dBASE compiler Clipper), where he knew that his computer and networking skills would be more appreciated. His future partner, David Alison, hired him as the Network Manager, and it was under Mr. Rayl's direction (and Mr. Alison's supervision) that rapid changes were made to the corporate network. These changes included upgrading to NetWare 3.0, standardizing on Windows 3.0 within three months of its release, and converting from thin-net to a fault-tolerant 10BASE-T topology. Additionally, a global WAN was designed, although not fully implemented.

During this same period, Mr. Rayl began writing computer articles, first by performing comparative reviews and "first looks" for *PC Week*. Shortly thereafter, he was granted a position as a Contributing Technical Editor at the periodical. Eventually, ZD-Labs was created to perform in-house comparative reviews, at which point Mr. Rayl was commissioned to write reviews and "how to" articles for publications such as *Network Computing*, *Windows*, and *Data Based Advisor*.

It was at Nantucket that Mr. Rayl was first exposed to Lotus Notes. In early 1990, the company decided to buy into the Notes concept wholeheartedly, and Mr. Rayl was charged with implementing the Notes infrastructure, along with developing the necessary applications. Notes was a huge success at Nantucket. Unfortunately, however, Nantucket was sold to Computer Associates, which really did not understand Notes and decided to not support its internal use, so Mr. Rayl resigned.

Within a week, by exceptional luck, Mr. Rayl was offered a job by Symantec Corporation, as the Network Supervisor for its Peter Norton Product Group. (Even luckier, Mr. Alison had started work at the Peter Norton Group a week earlier, as a Senior Software Engineer.)

This job was offered with the idea that Symantec would soon be standardizing on Notes, corporation-wide, and Mr. Rayl would be in charge of the Notes implementation. Although Mr. Rayl was able to help with several pilot projects within different Symantec organizations, Notes was never supported from the upper echelons within Symantec. After a year at the company, Mr. Rayl resigned to form his own Notes consulting organization, and Mr. Alison soon joined him to form Alison, Rayl & Associates, Inc.

Since the inception of the Alison-Rayl corporation, Mr. Rayl has personally been involved with Notes implementations at more than 20 corporations, including Bank of America, The Southern California Gas Co., Delrina Corporation, Digitalk, and KPMG Peat Marwick. His company is located in Manhattan Beach, California, and he can be reached at 1-800-255-3575, extension 2.

# Introduction

## This Book's Audience

This book should prove useful not only to all ranges of Notes applications designers, but also to Notes users and to managers responsible for Notes implementations. New Notes developers will get an idea of how powerful the Notes environment can be, and they might get ideas for Notes applications they had not thought of before. Advanced Notes developers should see some techniques they can incorporate into their Notes applications.

Notes is a very empowering tool, especially because its development environment is integrated into the program. In many corporations, Notes "power users" become the Notes application developers for their workgroup, and this book should help these power users support their workgroup.

Managers responsible for Notes application development and deployment should find that the chapters in Section I, "An Overview of Lotus Notes as an Application Development System," and the first two chapters in Section III, "Architecting, Developing, and Deploying Complex Notes Applications," can help them understand how Notes application management is different from traditional application development management.

Although this book can be useful for people deciding what applications to develop in Notes, it is not intended for developers who are not familiar with the Notes environment. Notes is a *very* deep product, especially when you consider its very robust security, remote access capabilities, and multiplatform, multiprotocol capabilities. Asking even a very experienced C programmer, but inexperienced Notes user, to develop Notes applications is like asking a DOS programmer who has barely used Microsoft Windows to develop Windows-based applications. Before embarking on Notes application development, developers really need to use Notes for a time, if only to explore the example applications that Lotus ships with Notes.

Additionally, this book does not cover the Notes Application Programming Interface (API). A book much larger than this one could be written on how to use the Notes API, because it has hundreds of functions. The Notes API is very useful for commercial software developers who are trying to create, read, and edit documents in Notes databases, but most corporate Notes developers will not need to access Notes documents at the API level, and doing this could be counterproductive to the Notes application development process. In my experience, many seasoned C programmers, when first exposed to the Notes development environment, immediately decide they need to order the Notes API toolkit from Lotus. In reality, many of the tasks that they are trying to accomplish can be done in the standard Notes environment, with a little creative thinking.

# How to Use This Book

This book should be used in conjunction with the manuals and online help that come with Lotus Notes. The manuals and help databases that ship with Notes version 3.x are very thorough and useful, and I have made no attempt to rehash the information and function references that are included in these resources.

Instead, this book should help you create new types of Notes applications that you might not have thought of, using techniques that are not explained in either the manuals or the example databases. Don't dwell on the exact syntax of every statement or formula, but try to understand the overall concept, and then think about how the concept can be of use in your applications.

You should also be aware that the three sample applications that come with this book are "real world" applications. As I mention several times in the book, the best Notes applications that I know continually evolve to meet a changing business environment. By the time you read this book, these applications will probably have changed many times, and you should not try to implement these applications within your organization as-is. Because Notes is such a rapid application development system, I believe that almost every corporation should develop its own Notes applications primarily from scratch—learn and get ideas from my examples and the examples that ship with Notes, but create your own applications in-house. In the overall scheme of things, this technique will not add a lot of time to your application development efforts (especially when compared with traditional application development systems), but the system will be much more maintainable by you or your developers.

# I

## An Overview of Lotus Notes as an Application Development System

# 1

## Notes: "Groupware" or Development Platform?

"Groupware" has become one of the biggest buzzwords of the software industry, but it's a very nebulous concept. Countless articles and reviews have appeared that talk about Notes as groupware. (I even authored an article that the editors decided to title "Develop Groupware Apps with Lotus Notes 3.0"—I still cringe when I see the title.) The problem with pigeonholing Notes as groupware is that many Information Systems (IS) people don't consider the option of using Notes when they are deciding how to meet their users' requirements.

With the release of Notes 3.0, I firmly believe that Notes became an application development platform. For many types of applications, the Notes environment can be considered an alternative to using development tools from vendors such as Borland, Gupta, and PowerSoft. Certainly, Notes has many limitations when compared with an application that is built with a system such as PowerBuilder or SQL Windows. But when you are evaluating which system to choose for the development platform, there are many factors to consider.

For example, I once worked at a software company that needed a bug-tracking system. The company decided to use a PowerBuilder/Microsoft SQL Server solution. It took three developers nine months to complete the system. Although the system was fairly robust, it lacked several key items, such as a way to distribute the data to remote development sites, remote access for dial-up users, and a Macintosh interface for the Mac developers. Additionally, the system was not mail-enabled.

Several months later, using similar specifications, I developed a system in Notes in less than a month, and the system was immediately a multiplatform, distributed database with remote access. Of course, the Notes-based system could never handle hundreds of thousands of bug reports, but there are different ways of solving this problem, such as having separate databases for each product line, or archiving bugs that have been fixed or are for older versions of the software. Solving application development problems with Notes just requires a little creative thinking.

In the real world, a Notes application will probably never meet 100 percent of the system's requirements, but I doubt that you will ever find an application development system that exactly meets all the requirements. Additionally, when evaluating the cost of a Notes-based application versus a traditional database approach, you must factor in the opportunity cost of not having a system in place. For instance, how much valuable data and history was lost in the nine months while the software company was developing the bug-tracking system in PowerBuilder?

Notes most definitely is groupware, because it enables information to be dynamically shared between individuals, and it can be used to design workflow systems. But categorizing Notes as groupware is actually a disservice to the product, because it is much more. IS professionals need to start thinking of Notes as an application development platform.

And the press needs to start thinking about including Notes in development systems reviews and "application development shootouts" to see who can develop the most robust application in the least time. Reading this book should compel you to think more and more about how Notes can solve your application development requirements.

# 2

# Why Use Lotus Notes as an Application Development Platform?

# Overview

Although companies can benefit greatly from just using a Notes discussion-type database to increase communications and the flow of information within the organization, the companies that create Notes applications to be used in their core business processes will get the greatest returns. The combination of Notes features and its capability to prototype and develop applications quickly give it an edge over competing application development systems in many instances. In addition, training time becomes minimal if Notes is used as more of an "environment" in which employees do most of their work, rather than as a platform for one "killer" application.

# Major Features

Feature by feature, Notes has no true competition. It would take products from several vendors to come up with the same kind of functionality that Notes has built in.

Of course, cost is an issue, and Notes will probably cost more initially, on a *per-user* basis, than other systems. But when you consider that it can be used to create many applications that your users will work with daily, I think you'll find that the cost *per application* is much lower than with other systems.

The most important Notes features are covered in the following sections.

## Notes Is Multiplatform, with a Very Consistent Interface

Lotus Notes applications can be developed and run on four platforms: Windows, Macintosh, OS/2, and UNIX. Some people might criticize the interface, but the good part is that the interface is very consistent from platform to platform. This consistency makes developing training materials easier and enables developers to use their platform of choice while designing an application that can be used on another platform. Because the "code" is actually part of documents in the database, no changes or recompiling is required to use an application on a different platform.

## Excellent Security Tools

Lotus Notes uses both public- and private-key encryption schemes that you as a developer can use to ensure that your applications are secure. Its RSA-licensed encryption is built into the mail system, so any of your applications that use Notes mail routing can automatically have the documents encrypted, with no extra work. Additionally, individual fields of documents can be selectively encrypted, and encryption keys can be given to individuals who need access to the data.

# Integrated E-mail

The electronic mail system that is part of Lotus Notes is very robust, customizable, and maintainable. Additionally, Notes applications can use the built-in mail engine to move documents between databases, for workflow or archiving purposes.

Granted, the Notes mail's interface might be a little clunkier than that of some other packages. But it is very customizable, by both application developers and Notes users themselves. Custom forms and views can easily be added to a user's mail database. Mail-in macros or "filters" can be written that cause certain actions to occur based on the contents of a mail message.

Notes mail might not be as intuitive to use as other electronic mail systems, but I believe that the consistent interface between a Notes mail database and other Notes applications is really a plus in the long run, especially when training is considered. After a user is trained on Notes mail, it is easy to add new functionality to the mail system with little or no training required for the user. For instance, a company might roll out Notes using the standard mail database template. Then after a user has been trained on Notes mail, for example, a well-designed "MIS Help Request" form could be added to the user's mail database. The user would immediately understand how to use the new "MIS Help Request" workflow system because it would use the same metaphor as Notes mail.

I think that Notes mail administration and management is as easy as any mail system I have used. I personally have managed and evaluated many E-mail systems, including large cc:Mail and MHS-based mail systems, and I definitely had to fight to keep these other mail systems running smoothly.

When you consider the variety of client operating systems, network operating systems, and protocols that Notes mail supports, it's hard to argue that it's not a robust electronic mail package.

# Integrated Remote Access

One of the key features in Lotus Notes is remote access for users. Additionally, the remote access in Notes does not require that users be online while they are working, as with a traditional remote-access package such as Symantec's PC Anywhere or Microcom's Carbon Copy. This feature makes Notes an ideal platform for applications that will be used by people who are out in the field a lot, such as salesmen.

# Server-to-Server Connectivity Without a WAN

The Notes replication engine can efficiently use dial-up lines to synchronize databases between servers. Although it is nice to have the luxury of a fast leased-line link between your sites, this is not mandatory for Notes. For example, if your company buys or merges with another company, you can get the company online with Notes very quickly by putting Notes servers at that company's locations and using the public phone lines for the servers to replicate over—no waiting the three to six months for leased lines to be installed and configured.

## Rapid Application Prototyping and Development

When compared with applications created through traditional application development systems, Notes applications can almost always be prototyped and developed much quicker. In many cases, the Notes prototype can easily be changed into the production database with little modification.

## Wide Variety of Notes Add-On Products

Lotus has several key Notes add-ons that make Notes a particularly strong application development platform. These products include inbound and outbound fax gateways, Lotus Notes document imaging, Phone Notes, and the forthcoming Video Notes. Additionally, there are gateways to other mail systems, and third-party products are available that can be used to acquire data from various online news and financial services. Notes FX (Field eXchange), although not an add-on product per se, is an integral part of all the Lotus core applications (123 for Windows, Improv, Approach, and Freelance). Notes FX allows a very tight integration between Notes and the other Lotus products, and it should be seriously examined by any Windows-based shop deciding which vendor's "SmartSuite" to standardize on.

> **TIP**
>
> When picking Notes add-on products, be very careful when selecting third-party products (those not directly from Lotus). I personally do not use any third-party Notes products—Lotus Notes is a very complex product in terms of operating system and network support. It's hard to guess how long it will take a third-party product that is an integral part of your application that worked in a specific Notes 3.x environment to work when Notes 4.0 ships.

# Summary

Lotus Notes is a very robust platform for developing distributed database applications. Its feature set is unmatched by any other single application development system.

Companies that will benefit most from Notes are large multisite organizations that will adopt the Notes electronic mail system, but almost any company should be able to get a solid return-on-investment from implementing Notes when all costs are considered. Notes (and its related add-on products) provides a very strong base for an IS department to build on and to allow it to be responsive to the organization's applications and information needs.

# 3

## What Applications Could Be Considered for Lotus Notes?

For every conceivable computer application specification, one or more combinations of software (languages, databases, CASE tools, and perhaps special security and remote-access software) could be used to create exactly the application as it is specified.

When deciding to use Lotus Notes as an application development platform, you must also consider whether you are already using Notes within your organization. If Notes has already been deployed to a particular group, you should strongly consider the use of Notes for developing other applications for use within that group. In this situation, minimal training would be required for the current Notes users, and there would be a synergistic effect of building a work environment in Notes, where many of a user's daily activities take place. Many applications, when considered alone, would not be good candidates for Notes applications. But when they are evaluated in the context of an IS organization that has already deployed Notes, the applications become stellar candidates for Notes applications.

For example, Notes has never been an especially strong platform for group scheduling and calendaring applications. If an organization has already deployed Notes for other applications, however, a calendaring/scheduling application in Notes makes plenty of sense. Again, Notes's distributed database design, along with its remote access and security features, gives it an advantage over many LAN-based group scheduling packages, not to mention the $100 to $200 per user that is saved on software licenses, and the hidden costs of MIS implementing and supporting a new program.

Of course, there are many data- and transaction-intensive applications that will never make good Notes applications. High-volume, distributed reservation systems could not be designed effectively in Notes. Real-time data acquisition, in a manufacturing or research environment, could easily overwhelm a Notes database.

Many companies implement Lotus Notes just for its discussion and document library types of applications, and Notes does a great job with those basic "groupware" applications. I have developed the following applications that fall into this groupware/forms routing genre:

■ Heavily modified discussion-type databases that contain other important group-related documents, such as status reports, meeting agendas and minutes, and "red flags" or problem reports (see Figure 3.1 and Figure 3.2).

**FIGURE 3.1.**

*A modified discussion database showing the Status Report view, along with the various types of documents that can be created.*

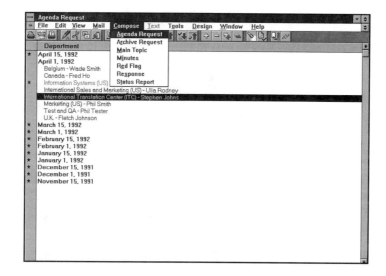

**FIGURE 3.2.**

*The various views that can be easily made available in a modified discussion database.*

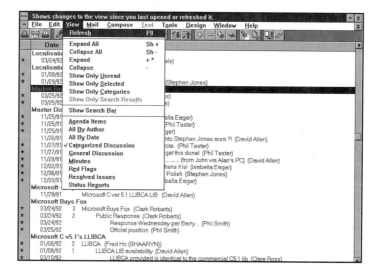

■ Document libraries, such as an HR policies-and-procedures database that includes a form enabling employees to ask questions of the HR department, enabling other employees to benefit from the questions and answers (see Figure 3.3 and Figure 3.4).

**FIGURE 3.3.**
*A view of an HR policies database.*

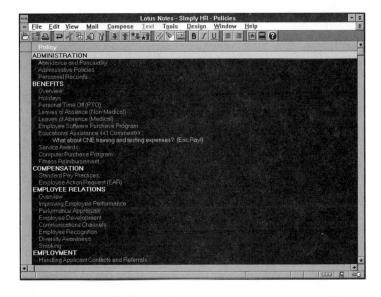

**FIGURE 3.4.**
*An HR policy document with an embedded flowchart.*

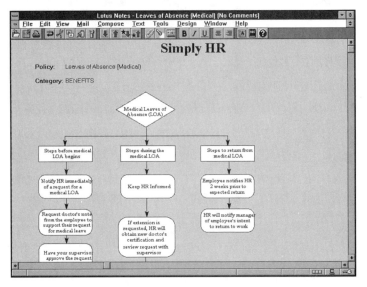

■ Forms-routing applications, such as a purchase requisition/approval/ordering system that enables users to compose electronic requisitions from their mail database and route these forms to the appropriate managers for approval, with the form ultimately ending up at the purchasing agent, where an order confirmation is generated (see Figure 3.5 and Figure 3.6).

**FIGURE 3.5.**

*A purchase requisition form that is part of a user's mail database.*

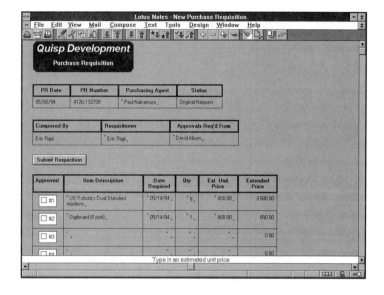

**FIGURE 3.6.**

*A view of a purchase requisition tracking database.*

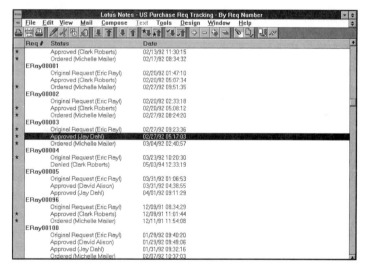

■ Notes databases make good "object repositories"—that is, Notes documents can be used as holders for various files (either attachments or OLE-objects), such as bitmaps, sound and video clips, software drivers, or even complete programs. For a software developer, we effectively used a simple discussion-type database as a place to store the latest versions of the software under development, as well as international versions and documentation (see Figure 3.7 and Figure 3.8).

**FIGURE 3.7.**
*A database used as a repository for various files and programs.*

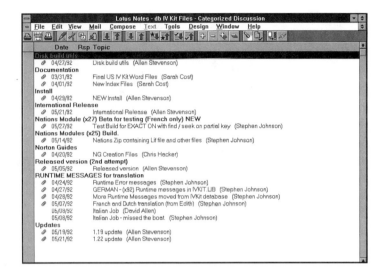

**FIGURE 3.8.**
*Bitmaps (icons) saved in a Notes document, where they can be cut and pasted to other applications.*

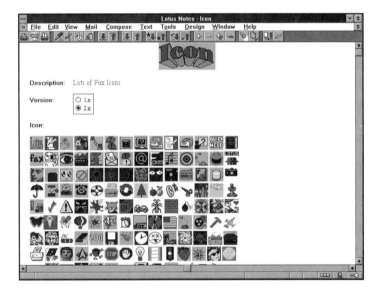

I have also used Notes to build many successful systems that are more similar to traditional database systems, including the following applications:

■ A trademark tracking application for use within the legal department at a software company (see Figures 3.9, 3.10, 3.11, and 3.12). Not only did the database provide a way of globally tracking the status of its various trademarks, but it enabled users to create action items to remind them of important deadlines and potential problems, along with documents detailing important discussions or letters.

**FIGURE 3.9.**

*A view of a trademark tracking database by country and trademark name.*

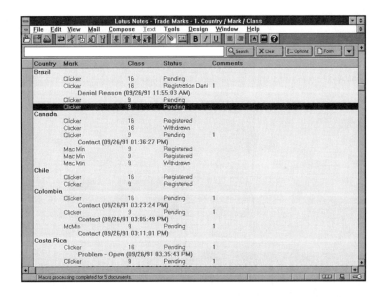

**FIGURE 3.10.**

*The Pending Items view in the trademark tracking database.*

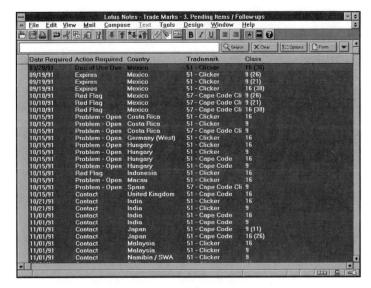

**FIGURE 3.11.**

*A comment form in the trademark tracking database. Note the keyword options for the Type of Comment field.*

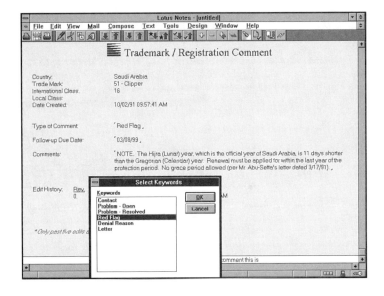

**FIGURE 3.12.**

*A main trademark document.*

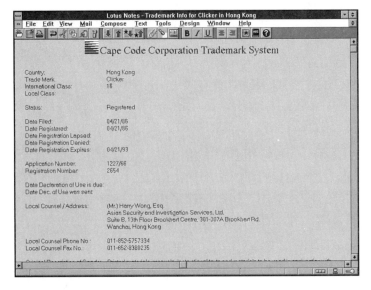

■ A system to track all aspects of the various tradeshows that a software company was involved with (see Figures 3.13, 3.14, and 3.15). This included tracking the requirements for the booths and all the associated equipment, along with tracking the staff associated with the tradeshows. The system also had provisions for creating action items, such as phone calls, shipments, and so forth.

**FIGURE 3.13.**

*The tradeshow tracking database's view by event name.*

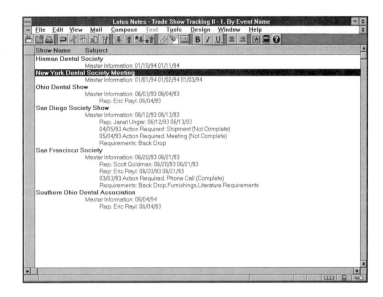

**FIGURE 3.14.**

*A view of the tradeshow database's action items.*

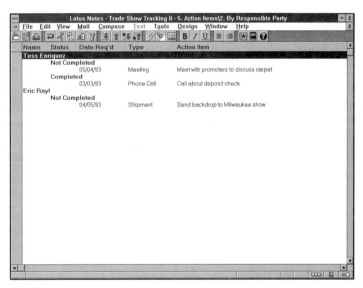

**FIGURE 3.15.**

*The Resources view in
the tradeshow tracking
application.*

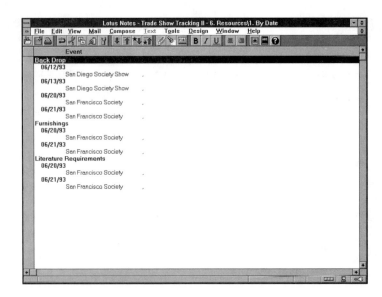

■ A system of Notes databases that automated a human resource department. An Applicant Tracking database was used to track job candidates and rank their skills and interview results. A master HR database was used to track all employee information in all divisions, including salary reviews, vacation days taken, benefits eligibility, EEO-reporting, and so on (see Figure 3.16). This database consolidated all salary information for the overseas units and converted the salaries to U.S. currency using a variable exchange rate, which made for interesting reports of salaries by country and department. A Job Evaluation system assigned a point value to each of the company's job titles, based on four factors (knowledge and skill, experience, contacts with others, and mental effort). The total of the points of the four factors was used to help adjust compensations among the various departments and to determine job grades (see Figures 3.17, 3.18, and 3.19).

**FIGURE 3.16.**

*The **C**ompose menu in an HRIS application, with the EEO view in the background.*

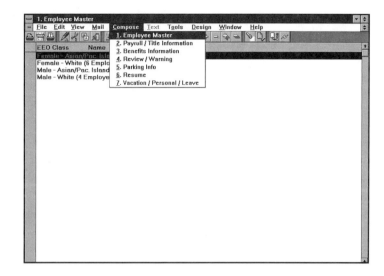

**FIGURE 3.17.**

*The HR job evaluation system's view by department/title.*

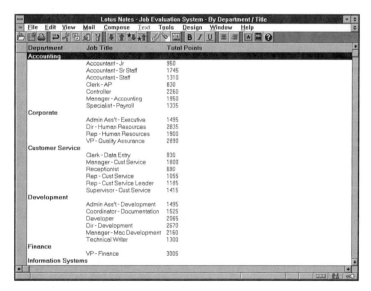

**FIGURE 3.18.**

*The HR job evaluation system's view by department/points.*

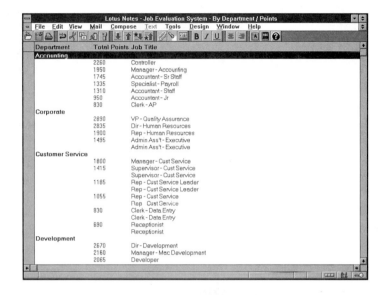

**FIGURE 3.19.**

*The HR job evaluation system's Job Title document, where points are assigned to a job title based on four factors.*

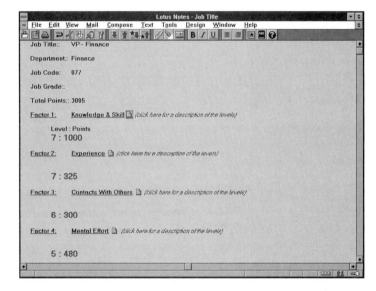

■ A collection tracking system that I designed for a manufacturing/direct marketing company to help the company reduce its overdue accounts receivable. A Notes document was composed for each past-due account, which in turn was used to generate a mail-merged letter seeking payment. The status and effectiveness of the collection effort could then easily be tracked by management (see Figures 3.20, 3.21, and 3.22).

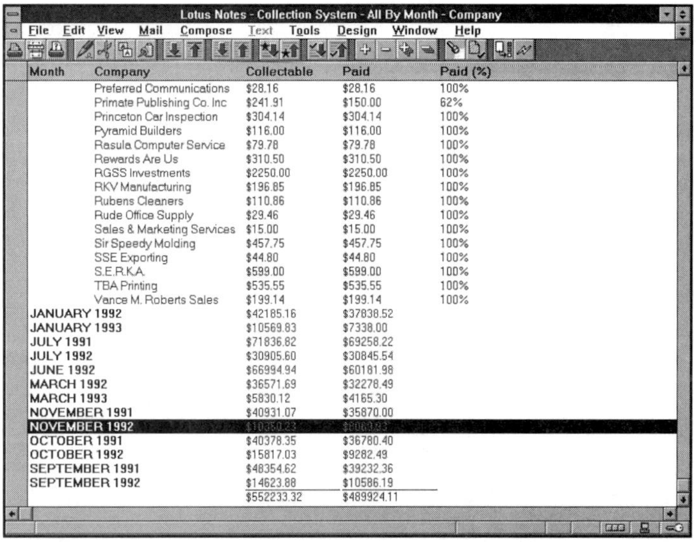

**FIGURE 3.20.**

*The collection application's view of delinquent accounts by month.*

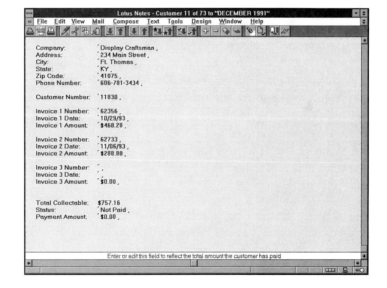

**FIGURE 3.21.**

*A delinquent account document showing where the invoice information is entered.*

**FIGURE 3.22.**

*The form letter generated by the collection application using Notes's form override feature when printing.*

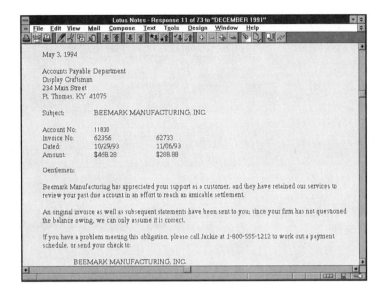

■ A crime and investigation tracking system. The system consisted of main case documents, in addition to suspect documents, loss recovery documents, and investigator status report documents. One of the major benefits of using Notes as the application development platform was that investigators could easily work from the field, completing case documents and status reports and then replicating their updates to the Notes servers. Notes views, combined with its full-text search capabilities, enabled users to find out whether suspects had any involvement in previous cases. Additionally, the statistical capabilities of Notes views were used to produce informative management reports. Figures 3.23, 3.24, and 3.25 show some sample views from this application.

**FIGURE 3.23.**

*One of the master views in the crime tracking system, showing all the documents related to a case.*

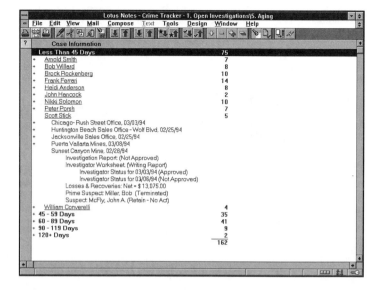

**FIGURE 3.24.**

*A management reporting view of crimes during a given period, categorized by the type of criminal activity.*

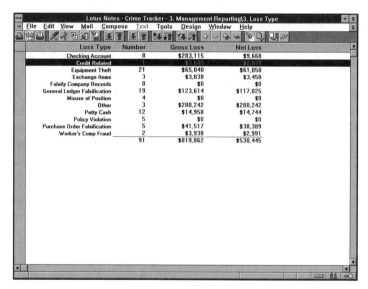

**FIGURE 3.25.**

*The crime tracking system's regional reporting view, showing loss amounts and percentages for the given period.*

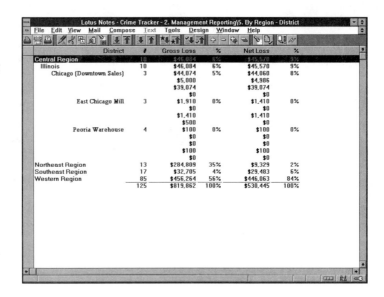

# Summary

As you can see, there are many opportunities for using Notes as an application development system. The main idea is that when deciding whether to use Notes for a specific project or application, you need to step back and look at the big picture, noting how Notes could solve other problems within your organization. In many instances, you can justify Notes based on one "killer" application, but it's much easier to justify implementing Notes based on multiple uses and applications. The most successful Notes projects I've been involved with have viewed Notes as an "environment" that encompasses many of a user's daily activities. After Lotus Notes has been purchased and installed, and after users have been trained in Notes fundamentals, the incremental cost of adding applications is minimal. This chapter should have given you some new ideas on how Notes could be used within your organization.

# II

## Notes Application Development Basics: Forms, Fields, Views, Formulas, and Macros

# 4

# Creating an Application:
# A Personnel/Event Tracker

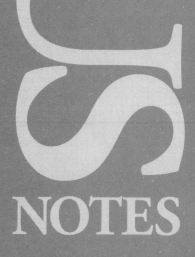

# Overview

Many times the easiest way to learn a new application development system is to identify a particular problem and then try to create a program/system to solve the problem. In this chapter, I will present a problem that is common at many medium to large companies, and then I will walk you through the creation of a Notes database that can solve the problem. If you are new to Notes database design, I strongly recommend that you follow through this exercise to get an exposure to Notes database design.

Additionally, this event tracking database will be used extensively in the rest of this section for demonstration purposes. Therefore, if you don't want to create it now, you should copy the completed Event Tracking database (SCHED.NSF) from the sample disk included with this book into your Notes data directory (usually C:\NOTES\DATA).

Many concepts, including inheritance, multivalue fields, date/time ranges, and response documents and hierarchy, will be introduced in this tutorial. Don't spend time concentrating on one particular step or concept, because the issues that are only touched on here will be dealt with in detail in the chapters that follow.

# What Corporate Problem Does This Database Address?

Many companies have the need for, or can benefit from, Notes databases that serve as calendars of personnel schedules, as well as corporate or industry events that are of general interest. Although a Notes database does not make as robust of a scheduler as a dedicated scheduling program installed on a LAN, there are many benefits to using a Notes-based solution, such as these:

- The ease with which the scheduler can be distributed and used globally on a Notes network
- The capability for remote personnel and offices to be kept informed of corporate events and happenings
- Support for Windows, Macintosh, OS/2, and UNIX clients
- The capability to rapidly develop a system that is customized to the exact need within the company

The Personnel/Event Tracker is not an application that would cause a corporation to buy Notes, but these types of applications are the ones that can easily be created and rolled out to existing Notes users with little pain or training. Users can reap great benefits from databases that increase the availability of and ease of access to calendaring/scheduling information.

# Creating the Database

Choose the **N**ew Database option on the Lotus Notes **F**ile menu. This causes the New Database dialog box to appear (see Figure 4.1). You will not be basing this new application on one of the design templates that Notes ships with; therefore, leave the design template listed as -Blank-.

**FIGURE 4.1.**

*The Notes New Database dialog box.*

In the **S**erver: selection box, you might have several Notes servers listed. Because you will create this database on your local hard drive, leave the default as Local.

In the **F**ilename: box, type

DEVELOP\SCHED

This entry causes a database with the filename SCHED.NSF (.NSF is the default Notes file extension) to be created in the DEVELOP subdirectory under your Notes data subdirectory. (Use the T**o**ols|**S**etup|**U**ser menu option if you are unsure of where your Notes data directory is.) Additionally, if the DEVELOP subdirectory does not already exist, it is automatically created.

In the Ti**t**le: box type

Personnel/Event Tracker

Click the **N**ew button, and the default (untitled) view is opened. Press Esc and you return to the Notes workspace, with the icon for the new database highlighted.

# Creating the First Form

Double-click on the icon of the new database to open it. At this point, there are no fields, forms, or macros in this database (there is one default view, however).

You will now create the first form for this application. This form not only is what people will use to enter information about their schedule or a particular event, but it also will be used to display this same information, in read-only mode, to other users.

Select the **F**orms... option on the Notes **D**esign menu to pop up the Design Forms dialog box. Notice that no forms are currently listed. Click the **N**ew button. This causes a new, completely blank form to be opened in design mode.

# Adding and Formatting Fields on the Event Form

Your cursor will end up in the left corner of this new form. Press Enter a couple of times to position the cursor down a couple of lines on the blank form. Type the static text

```
Event Name:
```

and then press the Tab key. Now select the New Field option from the **D**esign menu, and leave the default option, Create field to be used only within this Form, selected (see Figure 4.2). Throughout this example, we will always use this option when creating a new field.

**FIGURE 4.2.**
*The Notes Design New Field dialog box.*

In the **N**ame: box in the Field Definition window, type

```
EventName
```

and in the **H**elp Description: box, type

```
Type in the name or type of the event
```

Leave the **D**ata Type as Text, and the Field Type as **E**ditable, as shown in Figure 4.3.

**FIGURE 4.3.**
*The Field Definition window showing the details of the EventName field.*

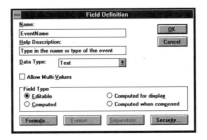

Click the **O**K button to create the field.

Position the cursor at the end of the EventName field, and press Enter twice. Type the static text

```
Event Location:
```

Then press the Tab key. Again, select the New Field menu option on the **D**esign menu, and select the option Create field to be used only within this Form from the Design New Field dialog box.

In the Field Definition dialog box, in the **N**ame: box type

```
EventLocation
```

and in the **H**elp Description: box type

```
Where the person/event will be
```

As before, accept the default **D**ata Type (Text) and Field Type (**E**ditable). The Field Definition dialog box should appear as shown in Figure 4.4.

**FIGURE 4.4.**
*The field definition for*
*the EventLocation field.*

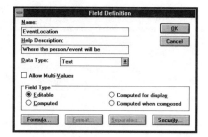

Click the **OK** button to create the field.

Now press Enter a couple of times to move the cursor down two lines, and type the static text

```
Event Description:
```

Then press the Tab key. Again, create a new field using the New Field option on the **D**esign menu, and again, select the option to use the field only on this form from the Design New Field dialog box.

Type

```
EventDescription
```

into the field **N**ame: box, and type the **H**elp Description

```
A complete description of the event, activity, or meeting
```

For this field, use the **D**ata Type Rich Text, which enables the images of brochures and flyers that have been scanned in to be pasted into this field. The dialog box should look like the one shown in Figure 4.5.

**FIGURE 4.5.**

*The field definition for the EventDescription field.*

Click the **O**K button to create the field.

At this point, your form should look like Figure 4.6.

**FIGURE 4.6.**

*The new form with the three new fields and corresponding static text.*

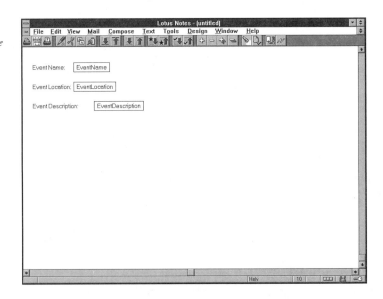

Now you should start adding a little aesthetic design to your form layout. First add a descriptive line to the top of the form. Move the cursor to the first line of the form, and type

`Schedule/Event Details`

Now change the font to make this line stand out. Highlight the text you just typed ("Schedule/Event Details"), and then select the **F**ont... option from the **T**ext menu. Make this text 14 point bold Helv by selecting the appropriate choices and then clicking the **O**K button. Next, center this text on the form by using the **A**lignment option on the **T**ext menu. Select the **C**enter Alignment option, and then click the **O**K button.

Next we need to set some tab stops to make the fields line up correctly, and we need to set the default paragraph margins for the rich text field (EventDescription) so that the text in that field will wrap correctly.

The easiest way to set tab stops is to use the Ruler, which you turn on by selecting the Show **R**uler option on the **V**iew menu. Next, highlight all the text on the lines that contain fields. After you have highlighted these lines, you can create a tab stop on all of them at once by left-clicking on the ruler. Click on the 2½" mark on the ruler to create a tab stop at this location. Notice that all the fields line up now, as in Figure 4.7.

**FIGURE 4.7.**

*Aligning fields using tab stops and the ruler.*

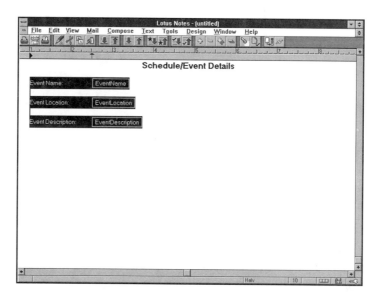

We also want to change the indent of the second line of text on each line so that the text in the second and subsequent lines of a field wraps to the 2½" point. First highlight the lines to format (in this case, all three lines with fields). Then left-click on the bottom half of the diamond shape that appears at the 1" point on the ruler, and drag it to the 2½" point. The ruler should now look as shown in Figure 4.8.

**FIGURE 4.8.**

*Setting the margins using the ruler.*

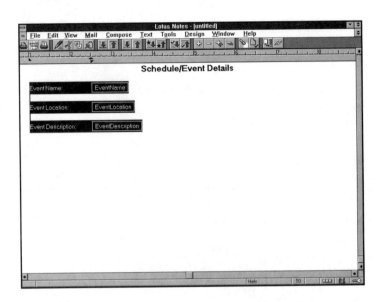

At this point, you need to add some fields to the form that will enable users to specify the dates and times for the event, along with which persons will be involved. Position the cursor at the end of the EventDescription field, and press Enter twice to move to where we will create the new fields. Type the static text

```
Date(s) of Event:
```

Then press the Tab key to move the cursor to the 2½" tab stop. Use the New Field option on the **D**esign menu to create a new field that will be used only on this form. In the **N**ame: box, type

```
DatesEvent
```

In the **H**elp Description: box, type

```
Type in the dates of the event, separated by commas
```

For the **D**ata Type, select Time, and check the Allow Multi-**V**alues box (see Figure 4.9).

**FIGURE 4.9.**

*The field definition for the DatesEvent field.*

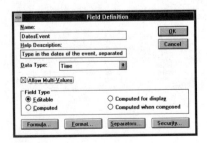

Now we want to format how the dates will appear on-screen, so click the **F**ormat button. Change the **O**verall Format to the first option, the one that does not include the hours, minutes, and seconds, as shown in Figure 4.10.

**FIGURE 4.10.**
*Using the Design Time Format window to select how the DatesEvent field should appear.*

Now click the **OK** button to exit and save the date format, and click **OK** again to save the field definition.

This form now needs a way for the users to enter the starting time and ending time for this event. This could be two separate fields, TimeStart and TimeEnd, for example, but we will use the Notes Time Range feature to combine both times into one field. Additionally, we want to have an easy way for users to rapidly schedule an event for "All Day" (such as when entering a person's vacation day) rather than having to type "12:00 am - 11:59 pm," which is cumbersome to enter and not as intuitive to display as the text "All Day."

To accomplish these objectives, we will add two new fields. Press Enter twice to move the cursor two lines below the DatesEvent field, and type the static text

```
Times of Event
```

Press the Tab key. Now create a new field named AllDay using the New Field option on the **D**esign menu, and this time, make its **D**ata Type Keywords. In the **H**elp Description: box, type

```
Select "All Day" to block out the entire day for this event
```

Keyword fields enable users to select from a list of possible values. The keyword field can have the Notes standard keyword user interface, a radio button interface, or a check box interface. The intricacies of these different interfaces will be discussed later in detail, but for now, we will just format this keyword field with the radio button interface. Click the **F**ormat button to access the Design Keyword Format window, and then select Radio button from the **U**ser Interface: picklist.

The Design Keyword Format window is also where you enter the allowable values for this keyword field. In the Allowable **K**eywords: box, type

```
Time Range:
```

Then press Enter to move to the next line, and type

`All Day`

Leave the default Text button selected, as in Figure 4.11.

**FIGURE 4.11.**

*The Design Keyword Format dialog box, where keyword choices are defined.*

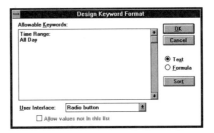

Click **OK** on the Design Keyword Format dialog box to close the window. Now we want the value of this field to default to Time Range:. Click the Formula... button, and in the Default Value Formula: box, type (in quotation marks, because the value should be interpreted literally)

`"Time Range:"`

as shown in Figure 4.12.

**FIGURE 4.12.**

*Using the Design Field Formula window to set a field's default value.*

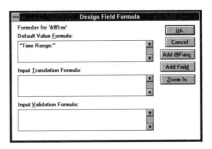

Click the **OK** button to create the field, and then space over a couple of spaces from the AllDay field in preparation for adding a new field. Create a new field (using the **D**esign|New Field menu option), and name the field TimesEvent. Make this field's **D**ata Type Time, make its Field Type **E**ditable, and check the Allow Multi-**V**alues check box. Click the **F**ormat button, and select the **T**ime Format to display only hours and minutes, and change the **O**verall Format to display only times, not times and dates (see Figure 4.13).

**FIGURE 4.13.**

*Setting the TimesEvent field to display time information only.*

The final field that we need on this form is the one that will contain the names of the people who will be at or involved with the event or meeting. To add this field, press Enter a couple of times, and then type the static text

```
Person(s) Involved:
```

Press the Tab key, and then create a new nonshared field (again, using the New Field menu option on the **D**esign menu). Name this field PersonsInvolved and type the **H**elp Description

```
Type in the name(s) of the people involved, separated by commas
```

For now, leave the field as an editable text field, but click on the Allow Multi-**V**alues check box. Set the field to default to the current user's name (contained in the user's Notes ID file) by clicking the Formul**a**... button and typing the formula

```
@UserName
```

into the Default Value **F**ormula: box (see Figure 4.14).

**FIGURE 4.14.**

*Setting the default value of the PersonsInvolved field using the Notes function @UserName.*

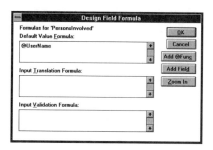

Click the **O**K button on the Design Field Formula window, and then click the **O**K button on the Field Definition window to create the field. Your form should now look like Figure 4.15.

**FIGURE 4.15.**

*The Schedule/Event form as it should appear now.*

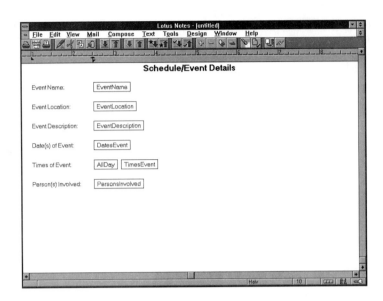

We now have completed creating the fields for the Appointment/Event form, but the form still needs to have its Attributes and Window Title set.

# Setting Form Attributes

Select Form Attributes from the Notes **D**esign menu to access the Form Attributes window. In the **N**ame: box, type

```
1. Appointment/Event ¦ frmEvent
```

The use of the vertical bar symbol (¦) creates a form name synonym. The actual underlying form name is what is to the right of the vertical bar (frmEvent), but "1. Appointment/Event" will be what appears on the Notes **C**ompose menu. This capability enables you to easily customize the appearance of the form names of the application on the **C**ompose menu without having to change any underlying formulas that depend on the form name.

Leave the form **T**ype: as Document, and accept all the other default values as they appear in Figure 4.16.

**FIGURE 4.16.**
*The Design Form Attributes window for the form.*

# Adding the Window Title to the Form

The Window Title is the text that will appear in the uppermost border of the form's window when it is open. Although a Window Title is not necessary for a form, a meaningful, consistently used Window Title gives your Notes applications a polished look and promotes a consistent user interface for your Notes applications.

To access the Design Window Title dialog box, select the **W**indow Title option on the **D**esign menu. The Window Title Formula can be as simple as a text string enclosed in quotation marks, such as "Event Description", but you will use the Notes function @IsNewDoc to dynamically change what is displayed in the Window Title.

In the **W**indow Title Formula: box, type this formula:

```
@If(@IsNewDoc;  "New Schedule/Event";  "Schedule/Event Description for " + EventName)
```

Make sure that you have typed the formula exactly as shown, including spacing and punctuation, and then click the **O**K button to close the Design Window Title window.

What this formula does is dynamically compute the form's Window Title. If the document is new (which means that the document has not been saved), the window's title will be "New Schedule/Event"; otherwise (that is, if the document has been saved), the window title will be the concatenation of the static text "Schedule/Event Description for " and the contents of the document's EventName field.

# Saving the Form and Exiting Design Mode

Close this form and save it by pressing the Esc key and selecting Yes when prompted as to whether you want to save the form. You should now be back at the default, untitled view of the database.

# Testing the New Form

It's time to compose a document with this new form to verify how it works. Select the new form that you just created, 1. Appointment/Event, from the **C**ompose menu. Notice that the form's window title reflects that it is a new document. Fill in the fields on the new form with some sample data, similar to the data in Figure 4.17. Notice the field help text that appears in the form's bottom border as you move from field to field.

**FIGURE 4.17.**

*A new Appointment/ Event form being composed, with some sample data added.*

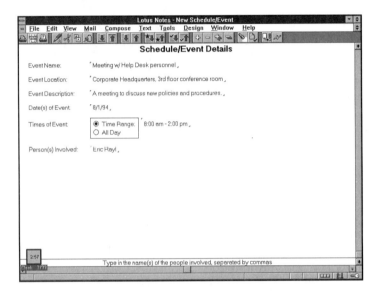

Now save this form and close it by pressing Esc; then click on Yes to save the document. Notice that the view now contains a "1" in the # column, signifying document number 1. To reopen the document you just created, double-click the "1" row, or press Enter when the "1" row is highlighted. Notice that the form's Window Title has changed since the document has been saved. Close this document to return to the default view.

# Adding a View

We need to create a couple of views that will enable users to easily find pertinent scheduled events. We will design three ways to present this information to users in views: sorted by the names of the persons involved, sorted by date, and sorted by event name. We'll quickly create these three views and see how our sample document appears in each of the views.

Create a new view by selecting the **Views...** option on the Notes **D**esign menu. Because this is the first view you are creating, the only view listed in the Design Views dialog box is the default view, *(untitled). Click the **E**dit button to modify this default view.

This view will be used to display events sorted by the persons involved, so the first column should contain the contents of the PersonsInvolved field. Double-click on the only existing column—the one with the "#" title—and change the field Form**u**la: from @DocNumber to PersonsInvolved. (Hint: You can click the Add Fiel**d** button and select the field name from the list of field names currently defined in this database.) Also change the column's **T**itle to Person, and change the **W**idth: to 25 characters (see Figure 4.18).

**FIGURE 4.18.**

*The Design Column Definition dialog box.*

Additionally, click the **S**orting... button. Select the Sort and Categorize check boxes, and leave the other values to their defaults. Click the **O**K button to close the Design Column Sort dialog box.

Because we are categorizing this column, we will follow one of my suggested database design standards and make entries in this categorized column appear in bold type. Click the **F**ont button, select the Bold check box, click **O**K to close the Font window, and then click the **O**K button on the Design Column Definition dialog box to change the column definition and return to the view in design mode.

Notice that the Refresh Question Mark appears in the upper-left corner of the view. Either click on the Refresh Question Mark or press F9 to refresh the view and see your changes. Depending on what sample data you entered into the first document that you composed, you should see a view similar to Figure 4.19.

**FIGURE 4.19.**

*The new view in design mode, showing the contents of the Person column.*

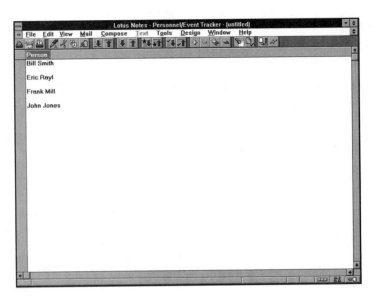

Notice that this view displays only the one document that currently exists in the database but that the document is falling into four Person "Categories." This happens because we designed the Schedule/Event Description form with a field (PersonsInvolved) that had the Allow Multi-**V**alues check box selected in its field definition, and then we created a view with a column that is categorized on this field. This technique is very useful for displaying one document under several different labels or categories in a view and for making views easier to navigate.

Now that this column is categorized, it does not need to be 25 characters wide. Resize the column to 5 characters wide by double-clicking on the column and changing the **W**idth: to 5 characters.

Now we need to display the date and time of the event. The next column we create will have the formula `DatesEvent` that we will sort and categorize to help eliminate screen clutter. Select the undefined column heading next to the Person column, and create a new column either by using the Notes menu option **D**esign|**N**ew Column... or by double-clicking anywhere on the undefined column header.

Create the column heading by typing `"Date"` in the **T**itle: box, and type `DatesEvent` in the For**m**ula: box. Click the **S**orting... button. Select the Sort and Categorize check boxes, but also change the sort order to Descending (this order puts older dates at the bottom of the list, which should help users find pertinent dates more quickly than if old dates came first in the column). Click **O**K to close the Design Column Sort dialog box. Again, because this column is categorized, we should make this column's font bold to give the user a visual clue that it is a category. Click the **F**ont button and select the Bold check box. Click **OK** to close the Font window, and then click **OK** to close the Design Column Definition dialog box and create the new column. After you refresh the view (by using the Refres**h** option on the **V**iew menu or pressing F9), the view should look similar to the one shown in Figure 4.20, but with your own data.

**FIGURE 4.20.**

*The new view in design mode, with a categorized Date column.*

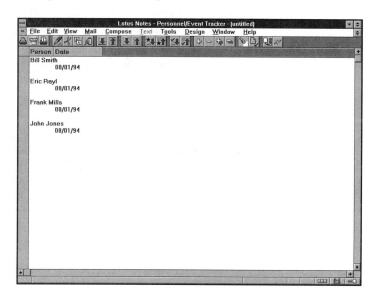

Now we will create a column after the Date column to display the times of the event. Additionally, we want a quick, intuitive way to show the user that a person/event is scheduled for all day, rather than having to display "12:00 am - 11:59 pm" in the column. Create a new column to the right of the Date column, and title the column Time. In the column's Form**u**la: box, type

```
@If(AllDay = "All Day"; "All Day"; TimesEvent)
```

The literal translation of this formula is "If the contents of the AllDay field are equal to "All Day" (that is, the AllDay radio button is set to "All Day"), then place the text "All Day" in the Time column; otherwise, place the value contained in the TimesEvent field into the Time column."

Click the **S**orting... button, and select the Sort check box. Leave the sorting order as Ascending, and do not categorize this column. Click **OK** to close the Design Column Sorting dialog box.

Now click the Ti**m**e... button on the Design Column Definition dialog box. We want to display time values only to the nearest minute, so change the **T**ime Format to show only hours and minutes, and change the O**v**erall Format to reflect only the time, not the date (see Figure 4.21).

**FIGURE 4.21.**

*The Design Time Format window for a view's column definition (exactly like for a field).*

Close the Design Time Format dialog window by clicking **O**K, and then complete the creation of the column by clicking **O**K on the Design Column Definition dialog window. Refresh the view (either by clicking on the Refresh Question Mark or by pressing the F9 key). The view should now appear similar to that shown in Figure 4.22.

**FIGURE 4.22.**

*The new view in design mode as it appears with the Time column.*

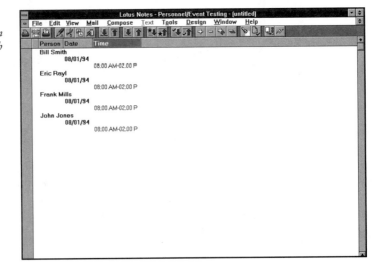

Notice that the Time column is not wide enough. Resize this column either by dragging its right boundary or by double-clicking on the column title and changing its width to, say, 12 characters. While you are at it, resize the Date column to be approximately 6 characters wide.

We need to add one more column to this view that will display the event's title. Create a new column to the right of the Time column, type Event Name in the Title field, and type EventName in the Formula field. Additionally, change the column's width to 25. Now create this new column by clicking the **O**K button.

We are ready to save this view, but we need to name it first. Select the **D**esign|View **A**ttributes... menu selection, and in the **N**ame: field type 1. Schedule by Person ¦ vwLookupByPerson, as shown in Figure 4.23. This step creates a *synonym* for the view name; the view's real name is vwLookupByPerson, but it appears on the **V**iew menu as **1. Schedule by Person.** (The reason for using view-name synonyms is discussed later when I describe how to enhance this application by using a dynamic keyword list for the PersonsInvolved field.)

**FIGURE 4.23.**

*The Design View Attributes window.*

On the Design View Attributes window, click the **C**ategories... button. Change the Categories to being Initially Collapsed when the view opens—this makes it quicker for users to navigate to the schedule for the individual they are concerned about. Click **OK** to close the Categories dialog box. Click **OK** to close the Design View Attributes window. Then save this view by pressing Esc to close the window and selecting Yes when prompted to save your changes.

Test the view by composing several new documents. Try composing an All Day type of event, such as a person's vacation schedule, as in Figure 4.24, for instance.

**FIGURE 4.24.**

*A Schedule/Event details form with the All Day keyword selected.*

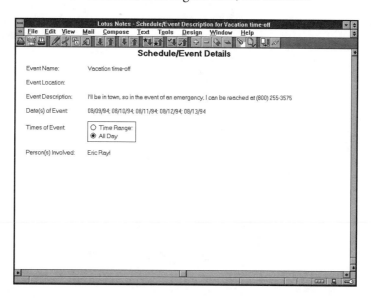

Also try composing an event for an individual on the same date as another event, but during a different time period. Expand the categories in the view using the Expand All option on the **V**iew menu, and verify that the document appears and sorts correctly in the view (see Figure 4.25 and Figure 4.26).

**FIGURE 4.25.**

*Another sample schedule document.*

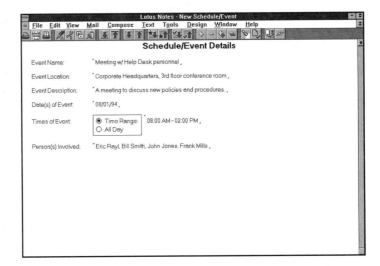

**FIGURE 4.26.**

*The schedule document from Figure 4.25 as it appears in the Schedule by Person view.*

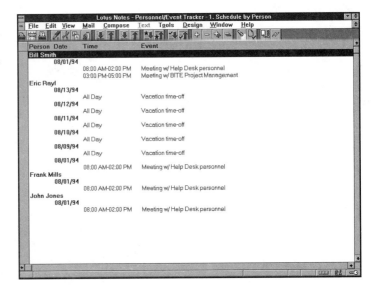

## Creating a View by Event Date

We need to create a view that is very similar to the view by the person involved, except that we want it sorted first by date and then by the individual involved. Because this view contains the same columns as the preceding view, we can rapidly design the new view by making a copy of the first view and then modifying it.

Select **V**iews... from the Notes **D**esign menu, and with the *1. Schedule by Person view highlighted, click the New **C**opy button.

Now we will quickly reorganize the view's columns by cutting and pasting them. Highlight the Date column by clicking on its header, and then use the Notes menu command **E**dit|**Cu**t. Now highlight the Person column, and use the **E**dit|**P**aste command. Notice that the Date column now appears before the Person column. Refresh the view by using the F9 key or by clicking the view Refresh Question Mark button, and its contents should appear similar to Figure 4.27.

**FIGURE 4.27.**

*The rearranged Schedule by Person view.*

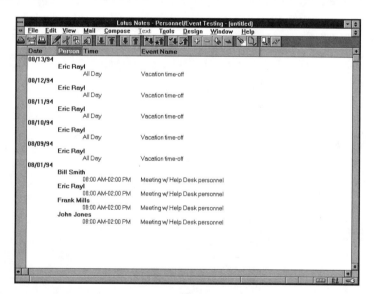

Select the **V**iew... Attributes from the **D**esign menu, and type 2. Schedule by Date/ Person in the **N**ame: box. Click **O**K and then press Esc to close the Design View Attributes window. Select Yes when prompted to save the changes. You should now have two views available under the Notes **V**iew menu.

## Adding a Comment Form

Many Notes databases will benefit from having a comment form where a user can compose a general comment or question regarding a specific document. There are many different ways a comment form could be used with our current database. For example, a user could compose a comment to a meeting that he has been scheduled for, noting that an emergency has come up and he will not be able to attend. (Of course, if he had editor access, he could just take his name out of the list of attendees. However, this action risks a replication conflict and does not convey as much information to his coworker, such as the concept that his omission from the list of attendees was not an oversight.)

When the database is used for a corporate-wide event calendar, a comment might be useful to ask for more information on the event, and the comment form can also be used for the response to the preceding question. This technique is much more efficient and useful than traditional E-mail because the information is shared by more people. Figure 4.28 shows a few comments that illustrate the previous ideas.

**FIGURE 4.28.**

*Comment documents as they could appear in a view.*

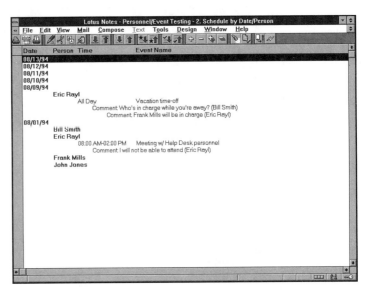

To create a simple comment response form, select **Forms...** from the Notes **D**esign menu, and then click the **N**ew button. This new form contains only five fields: ComposedBy, DateComposed, Subject, Details, and EventName. Type

```
Comment
```

on the first line of the form, and then press Enter several times to insert a few blank lines. Highlight the static text you just typed, and format its font to be 14-point bold

Helv by using the **F**ont... option on the **T**ext menu. Additionally, center this heading using the **P**aragraph... option on the **T**ext menu and selecting **C**enter Alignment.

Next, move the cursor down a couple of lines, and type the static text

```
Composed By:
```

Press the Tab key. Now add a new field to the form, and name the field ComposedBy. Additionally, select the Computed when com**p**osed option for the field type. We do not need to have any **H**elp Description for this field because it will not be editable, but we must enter a formula for this field. Click the Formu**l**a... button, and type

```
@UserName
```

Click the **O**K button on the Design Field Formula window to accept the formula, and then click **O**K again to create the field.

We will now set the tab stops and margins for this area of the form. With the cursor located somewhere on the line you just added, use the **P**aragraph... option on the **T**ext menu. Type 2.5 in the Tabs box, and additionally set the left margin at 2½" (leave the First line margin at 1", however). Click **O**K to reformat the paragraph.

Now we need to add the other three fields. With the cursor at the end of the ComposedBy field, press Enter twice to move down two lines. (Having the cursor at the end of the Composed By line ensures that the new lines will have the same paragraph format as the Composed By line.)

Type the static text

```
Composed On:
```

and press the Tab key. Add a new field, name it DateComposed, select Time as the **D**ata Type, and select the Computed when com**p**osed field type. Click the Formu**l**a... button, and type the formula

```
@Now
```

Click the **O**K button on the Design Field Formula window to accept the formula, and then click **O**K again to create the field.

With the cursor at the right of the DateComposed field, press Enter twice to move down two lines, add the static text

```
Subject:
```

and press the Tab key. Add a new field here, and name it Subject. In the field **H**elp Description, type

```
Type in a brief summary of your comment
```

and then click **OK** to create the Subject field.

We need to add another field, the Details field, which will enable users to type lengthy descriptions of their comments. With the cursor to the right of the Subject field, press Enter twice, type the static text

```
Details:
```

and press the Tab key. Add a new field called Details, and select Rich Text as its **D**ata Type. In the **H**elp Description: box, type

```
Type in the details of your comment
```

and then click the **O**K button, creating the new field.

We need to add one last field, EventName, which will contain the name of the event that the comment relates to. The data that is contained in the EventName field will then be used to create the Window Title for this Comment form.

With the cursor to the right of the Details field, press Enter a couple of times, type the static text

```
Hidden Fields:
```

and press the Tab key. Now add a new field called EventName that is computed when composed, and set the formula of the field to be

```
EventName
```

Click the **O**K button on the Field Formula window, and then click **OK** again on the Field Definition window to create the new field.

Now we are going to hide this new line from displaying by using the **H**ide when option on the **T**ext|**P**aragraph... menu. With the cursor positioned anywhere on this new Hidden Fields line, select **P**aragraph... from the **T**ext menu, and then click the Reading and Editing check boxes under the **H**ide when area (notice that the Printing box automatically checks when you select the Reading check box). Click **OK** to close the Text Paragraph window.

At this point, the new Comment form should look like Figure 4.29.

**FIGURE 4.29.**

*The Comment form in design mode.*

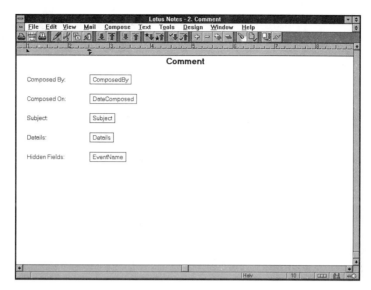

Now we need to set the form attributes for the Comment form. Click on the Form **A**ttributes... option on the **D**esign menu. For the Form Name, type

```
2. Comment ¦ frmComment
```

Change the form type from the default to make it the Response to response type. Additionally, select the **I**nherit default field values check box (see Figure 4.30). Click the **O**K button to close the Design Form Attributes window.

**FIGURE 4.30.**

*Using the Design Form Attributes window to set the form name and type.*

To add the final touch to this new form, we need to specify its Window Title Formula. Under the **D**esign menu, select the **W**indow Title option. Type the following formula:

```
@If(@IsNewDoc; "New comment for " + EventName; "Comment for " +
  EventName + " by " + ComposedBy)
```

Click the **O**K button to save the Window Title Formula. Then save the Comment form's design and exit design mode by pressing the Esc key and selecting Yes when prompted to save this new form.

Notice that the new form now appears on the Notes **C**ompose menu as "2. Comment," but we now need to modify the existing views to correctly display documents created with the Comment form.

## Modifying the Views to Display Comments

First we'll compose a Comment document so that you can see the necessity of modifying the view, and additionally you'll have sample data to help you see how the views change as you redesign them.

From the view 1. Schedule by Person, highlight the first document in the view, and then select 2. Comment from the **C**ompose menu. On the Comment form, type a simple subject such as this:

```
Who's in charge while you are away?
```

No details are necessary for this comment, so just press the Esc key and save the new document. Notice how this new response document appears in the view (if you do not see the document, use the Expand All option on the **E**dit menu to fully expand the view). As the view stands, it is not very useful for displaying documents created with the Comment form. But we can easily modify the views so that they are more useful.

Select the **V**iews... option on the **D**esign menu, select the view *1. Schedule by Person, and then click the **E**dit button. This action opens the view in design mode. Highlight the Time column heading, and select the **N**ew Column... option from the **D**esign menu.

In the For**mu**la: box in the Design Column Definition window, type the following formula:

```
"Comment: " + Subject + " (" + ComposedBy + ")"
```

Leave the column **T**itle: box blank, change the **W**idth: box to 1 character, and select the **R**esponses Only check box (see Figure 4.31).

FIGURE 4.31.

*Setting the column's definition to display the Comment document.*

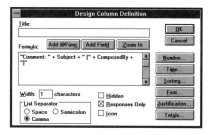

One other change we'll make to this view is to add a visual cue of expandable documents (that is, documents that have responses to them). Highlight the Person column, and select the **N**ew Column... option on the **D**esign menu. Again, this column will have no title, and the width should be set to 1 character. For the formula, type

```
@IsExpandable("+"; "")
```

This formula puts a "+" in the first column whenever the document or category is not fully expanded. This symbol lets users know that there are more documents collapsed under that document.

Now save the view and exit design mode by pressing the Esc key and saving the changes to the view. The view should look similar to Figure 4.32.

**FIGURE 4.32.**

*The Schedule by Person view showing a new Comment document and the expandable visual cue ("+").*

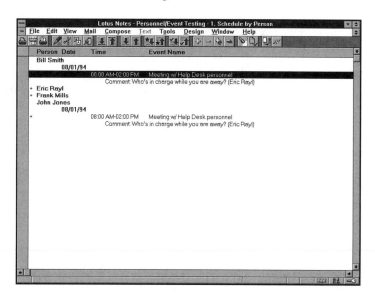

Now we'll quickly make similar changes to the view 2. Schedule by Date/Person by copying and pasting columns from the view you just created. Select **V**iews... from the **D**esign menu, select the view 1. Schedule by Person, and click the **E**dit button. Now we also want to open the view 2. Schedule by Date/Person in design mode, so again select **V**iews... from the **D**esign menu. Select the second view and click the **E**dit button. Now you should have both views open in design mode, and you can use the Notes **W**indow menu option to switch between the views.

Use the **W**indow menu now, and switch back to the view 1. Schedule by Person. Highlight the first column in the view, the one with the formula `@IsExpandable("+"; "")`. Select **C**opy from the **E**dit menu. Then, using the **W**indow menu, switch to the view 2. Schedule by Date/Person, and highlight the first column (Date). Now select **P**aste from the **E**dit menu, and the column and its definition will be copied from the first view. Repeat this procedure for the other column that you added to the view 1. Schedule by Person, the responses-only column, but this time have the Time column highlighted when you paste in the new column so that it is located in the proper location. Now close both of the design mode windows for the views, saving your changes to the view 2. Schedule by Date/Person.

You now have a fully usable application that illustrates how quick and easy it is to design a functional Notes application.

# What's Next?

In the next chapters in this section, we'll fully explore all the concepts that were introduced in this application, and I'll use this application as the basis for many of the design examples in the following chapters.

# 5

## Starting Out: Setting Up a Database

# Overview

Notes applications might be complex systems that involve many Notes databases on different servers, but the underlying application structure begins with a single Notes database. Notes databases can come in three basic varieties:

- Databases that are based on a Lotus-supplied database design template
- Databases that start out as either a database design template or another Notes database and then are modified to suit a particular application
- Databases that are created from scratch

Creating a Notes database for the first time can be confusing, and you might be left with the nagging feeling that you've forgotten to do something important. A Notes database can have many attributes, but in this chapter, I'll discuss the "nuts and bolts" of creating Notes databases, as well as how to set the important attributes, such as the basic security and design template settings.

# Creating the Database

In many Notes shops, a limited number of people are allowed to create databases on a given Notes server. Some sites have servers that are specifically development servers where developers can "play" and create databases at will. Other sites might require developers to submit requests for database creation to the Notes administration group, who in turn creates the database and sets the ACL. Of course, you can always create a database locally, on your hard drive, and have the Notes administrator move it to the server later.

To create a Notes database, select the **N**ew Database option on the Notes **F**ile menu. You are presented with the New Database window, shown in Figure 5.1.

**FIGURE 5.1.**

*The New Database dialog box.*

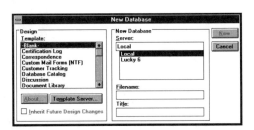

In the New Database window, the default server is always Local, which means that you will be creating the database on your local hard drive, generally in a subdirectory of your

Notes data directory (more on this in a moment). The names of any other Notes servers you are currently connected to, either on a LAN or via modem, are listed in the **S**erver: box.

If you are not authorized to create a database on a given server, you receive an error message similar to the one in Figure 5.2.

**FIGURE 5.2.**

*The error message that is generated when an unauthorized user tries to create a database on a server.*

> **TIP**
>
> The capability to create databases (and replicas) is controlled server-by-server by two fields on a given server's Server document in the Notes Name & Address Book. These two fields, called CreateAccess and ReplicaAccess, generally contain the names of one or more Notes groups. As a developer, you must have your name listed in one of the groups for you to be able to create databases or replicas on a given server.

When you are creating a new database, the filename is an important attribute; this is a *pathed* filename relative to the server's Notes data directory. For example, if you type the pathed filename

`APPS\PROJTRAK`

a file called PROJTRAK.NSF is created in the APPS subdirectory of the server's Notes data directory (you don't have to specify an extension; Notes assumes an .NSF extension for all Notes databases). A Notes server's data directory is the directory specified in the Notes server's NOTES.INI file (generally C:\NOTES\DATA). Therefore, in reality, the fully pathed filename of the database on the server would be C:\NOTES\DATA\APPS\PROJTRAK.NSF.

> **TIP**
>
> Be careful when entering a Notes database filename. If you have rights to create databases on the Notes server, you also have rights to create directories (or folders, for Macintosh users) on the Notes server. The **F**ilename: dialog box

does not display the current directories, so you must type a pathed filename; if you spell a directory name incorrectly, you will end up creating a new subdirectory. Additionally, Macintosh users should stick to the conventional DOS "eight-dot-three" naming convention, using .NSF as the filename's extension.

# What Are Design Templates, and Why Use Them?

When you are creating a new database, you have the option of using a design template (see Figure 5.1). A Notes design template is basically just a Notes database with no data, just forms, views, and macros. Design templates are files in the Notes data directory that end with an .NTF extension. By default, Notes looks to the user's local Notes data directory for these templates, but a Notes server can be selected by clicking the Template Server... button and then selecting a server.

Clicking the **A**bout... button displays the text of the template's "About Database" document, which generally describes the purpose of the template.

Lotus ships Notes with various design templates. Several of the templates are for databases that are fundamental to the Notes system, such as the Name & Address Book, the Notes Log, and the Mail Router Mailbox. Other templates can be used to create applications that can used immediately within your organization.

Of the templates that Lotus ships, I have used the Discussion template the most. This template, although useful for creating actual discussion-type databases, can also be used as the basis for very complex Notes applications that do not resemble discussions at all (see Chapter 11, "Two Techniques for Rapid Notes Applications Development").

Some fairly robust templates come with Notes, such as the Status Reports, Things To Do, and Customer Tracking templates. I strongly recommend that you use the templates only to get some ideas about how a particular application could be developed. Additionally, even though you could use one of these templates as a starting point for your application, in the long run you'll be better off if you create your database from scratch, from the -Blank- template. That way, the application will more closely match your requirements, and its fields, forms, and views will adhere to any corporate Notes application standards that you might have established.

If you are creating a database from a template (other than the -Blank- template), you have the option to **I**nherit Future Design Changes. On Notes servers, a nightly process updates the designs of all databases that are based on design templates. This is a very powerful feature of Notes that enables companies to easily maintain a great number of Notes databases that are based on a single design template. For example, you can easily add a new form to all of your users' mail databases by adding the form to the mail template on a Notes server. By default, users' mail databases are based on the mail template MAIL.NTF, so any changes made to MAIL.NTF are passed on to the users' mail databases the next time the nightly designer process runs on the Notes server.

> **TIP**
>
> Be careful when creating an application that is based on a design template; any changes you make to the database will be removed when the nightly designer process runs. For example, you might want to create a custom discussion database that has a new field to indicate whether the issue is open or closed. When you create the database, be sure to deselect the **Inherit Future Design Changes** option; otherwise, the new field will be removed by the server's designer process. If you are unsure of whether a database is based on a design template, or if you want to change its status, select the **Database|Information** option on the **File** menu, and then click the **Design Template...** button. The Design Template Options window appears (see Figure 5.3). In this window, you can deselect the database's design template if you want.

**FIGURE 5.3.**

*The Design Template Options window enables you to see the design template options for a database.*

An advanced feature worth mentioning here is that selected components (forms, views, and macros) of a database can be based on components in a design template, and you can also selectively "lock" a form, view, or macro from having its design refreshed by the design template. This capability is covered in the upcoming forms, views, and macros chapters.

# The Database's Access Control List

One of the first tasks you should attend to after you create a Notes database is setting up the Access Control List (ACL). The database's ACL is the fundamental security tool that you use to control who can do what with a given database.

To set up a database's ACL, you either highlight the database's icon or have it open, and then use the **D**atabase|**A**ccess Control... option on the **F**ile menu. This selection opens the Database Access Control List dialog box, shown in Figure 5.4.

**FIGURE 5.4.**

*The Database Access
Control List dialog box.*

People, Groups, and Notes Servers can be listed in a database's ACL, and each can be assigned one of seven Access Levels:

- ■ *Manager:* The manager of a database has complete control of the database and its design, including the ability to set the database's ACL.

- ■ *Designer:* People, groups, or servers that are listed in the ACL with Designer access can change the design of the database's form, views, and macros. They can't, however, change the database's ACL. Only Managers and Designers can affect the database's design.

- ■ *Editor:* A person with Editor access in a database not only can create new documents, but can edit and (possibly) delete documents that were composed by another person.

- ■ *Author:* An Author can compose new documents but is limited to editing only documents that he or she composed.

- ■ *Reader:* A Reader cannot compose or edit any documents but can only read them.

- ■ *Depositor:* Depositors can only compose (or mail in) documents in the database. After the document is in the database, it cannot be viewed by people with Depositor access.

- ■ *No Access:* Persons, groups, or servers listed as No Access cannot do anything with the database.

Several of these access levels have the additional attributes **C**an Delete Documents and Can Create Documents, as in Figure 5.4. For instance, an individual could be given Editor access to the database so that he could edit documents composed by other individuals, but he could be restricted from deleting documents by deselection of the **C**an

Delete Documents check box. The Can Create Documents option can be used with the Author access level to limit who can compose new documents in a database.

The **R**oles... button on the Database Access Control List dialog box allows security to be fine-tuned and controlled at the form and view level. Many databases will not need Roles, but their use is discussed in Chapter 15, "Advanced Security Issues."

**TIP**

When setting a database's ACL, you want to use groups as much as possible to reduce the administrative headache of having to specify users individually. You might want to create some groups that are specific to the application (look at the ACL in Figure 5.4, for example). Additionally, be careful with what access level you grant the -Default- user because this access is granted to all users who are not specifically listed in the ACL. Many of the Lotus-supplied templates have the -Default- user listed as a Designer, which can cause security problems if it is not changed immediately.

When setting up the ACL, you should also confer with the Notes administrators because if the application is to reside on more than one Notes server, or if it will be accessed by users remotely, the server's name needs to appear in the ACL (or at least a group that the server is in, such as LocalDomainServers, needs to appear).

What access level should you grant the servers? This issue is covered in more detail in the advanced security chapter, but generally, you want to grant the Notes group LocalDomainServers Manager access to your applications. With all the servers in your local Notes domain having Manager access to your database, not only design changes but also ACL changes will "filter" from server to server as the database replicates between them.

# Creating Help Documents

All Notes databases can have two different help documents associated with them. Every database has both an "About..." document and a "Using..." document that can be created by the Notes developer. These documents can be accessed by users from the Notes **H**elp menu (see Figure 5.5).

**FIGURE 5.5.**

*The Notes **Help** menu, showing the About... and Using... help documents for the Expense Reports database.*

The About... document is what the user sees the first time he opens the database. Additionally, this document is listed in the Notes database catalog that is automatically maintained on Notes servers. This document is traditionally used to convey information about what a database's purpose is, who should use it, and how it is intended to be used. The Using... document normally contains detailed information on how to actually use the database. One item to remember is that although a user might not have access to a particular database, the database's About... document does appear in the database catalog, so it should not contain any sensitive information.

Creating a Notes help document is as simple as selecting **H**elp Document from the Notes **D**esign menu, then selecting either **U**sing Database or **A**bout Database from the submenu.

You then are presented with a completely blank Notes document, where you can type the necessary information and instructions. Additionally, you can paste in any explanatory bitmaps such as diagrams and flowcharts. When you have completed the document, you save it just as you do any other Notes document (by closing the document window and selecting Yes when prompted to save the changes).

> **TIP**
>
> The example Notes databases that ship with Lotus Notes (usually found in the EXAMPLES subdirectory on a Notes server) contain robust examples of how to write a Notes database help document. You should look at these documents and use them as templates for your application's help documents.

# Designing the Database Icon

Notes database icons are not actually standard Windows-type icons, so you cannot just use commercial or shareware icon tools to create database icons. Notes does, however, come with a simple icon designer you can use to create and customize your database's icon. To change the icon, you select **I**con... on the Notes **D**esign menu, and you are presented with the Design Icon dialog box (see Figure 5.6).

**FIGURE 5.6.**

*The Design Icon dialog box.*

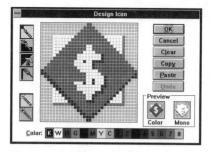

When you are designing an icon, pressing the F1 (Help) key brings up a dialog box explaining how each of the icon design tools can be used. As mentioned, these tools are not as robust as in other icon designers you might be used to.

> **TIP**
>
> Notice the Copy and **P**aste buttons on the Design Icon dialog box shown in Figure 5.6. Many times it's easiest to find an icon that is similar to what you want on another Notes database and then copy and paste the icon to your new database, where you can then modify the icon to suit your needs.

# Tweaking the Database

As mentioned earlier, there are myriad settings that affect how a given Notes database behaves. Many of these settings are geared for either remote users (such as the Replication settings) or for Notes administrators (such as the options in the Database Settings dialog box). For many types of Notes applications, you will not need to concern yourself with all of these settings. In this section, I'll discuss the important database settings that you should be aware of as a beginning developer.

Most of a given database's attributes are set by clicking buttons on the Database Information window, which is accessed by either selecting or opening a database, and then selecting **D**atabase|**I**nformation from the **F**ile menu (see Figure 5.7).

The **D**esign Template... button allows access to the Design Template Options window (see Figure 5.3). For most applications, you probably won't want to use either of the design template options.

**FIGURE 5.7.**

*The Database
Information window.*

The **R**eplication... button brings up the Replication Settings dialog box, shown in Figure 5.8. Many of these replication settings are more applicable for remote users because they control how much of a given database will be replicated. But as an application developer, you should be aware of the ramifications of selecting a particular replication priority (High, Medium, or Low). The Notes administrator controls how often the various priorities replicate between servers. For example, high-priority databases might be replicated every hour, whereas low-priority databases might replicate only once a day. Be sure to confer with your Notes administrator when deciding what priority to select because too many high-priority databases could impact a server's performance.

**FIGURE 5.8.**

*The Replication
Settings dialog box.*

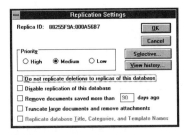

The **U**ser Activity... button on the Database Information window enables any user with access to the database to view a usage log for the database, as shown in Figure 5.9 (assuming that the **R**ecord Activity check box is selected). As an application developer, you can use this log to help you keep track of how much a given database is being accessed by users.

**FIGURE 5.9.**

*The User Activity
window.*

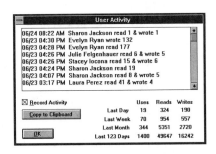

Clicking the Other **S**ettings... button on the Database Information window allows access to the Database Settings dialog box (see Figure 5.10).

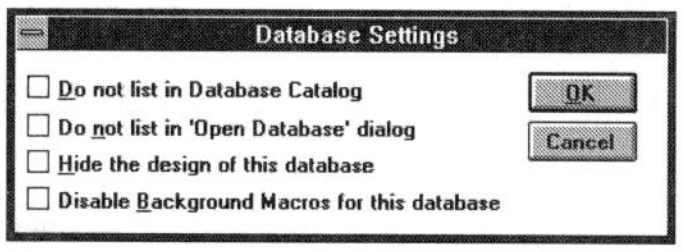

**FIGURE 5.10.**
*The Database Settings dialog box.*

The first two options, **D**o not list in Database Catalog and Do **n**ot list in 'Open Database' dialog, are useful for sensitive databases and databases that are under development. Note, however, that even if a database does not appear in the 'Open Database' dialog, a user can still gain access to it by typing the database's filename in the File Open Database dialog box. The last option, Disable **B**ackground Macros for this database, is not terribly useful, but the third option, **H**ide the design of this database, is actually quite dangerous.

---

**TIP**

The **H**ide the design of this database feature *does not* work properly! Although it does suppress most of the Design menu options, the design options can easily be returned to the menu by creating a new replica of the database. Additionally, this feature also makes maintaining a database very difficult because even the database's designer or manager cannot design macros to maintain the database. Additionally, the **D**esign|Document Info option is not available when a design is hidden, which is also a very useful tool for maintaining an application. My advice is to not use this option.

---

The **S**how Usage button on the Database Information window displays the percentage in use—that is, the percentage of the disk space that is actually occupied by documents in the database (notice the "80.5%" in Figure 5.7). If you have Manager access to the database, you can reclaim the unused disk space by selecting **D**atabase|Com**p**act on the Notes **F**ile menu. Databases should occasionally be compacted to ensure their reliability, especially if the database usage drops below 80 percent.

# Using the Full Text Search Capability

A very powerful feature of Notes is its capability to index the documents in a database so that they can be searched for words or phrases anywhere within a document's fields. Creating a full text index for a database is as easy as selecting **F**ull Text Search|**C**reate

Index... from the Notes **F**ile menu, which opens the Full Text Create Index dialog box (see Figure 5.11). You must have at least Designer access to the database to create a full text index.

**FIGURE 5.11.**

*The Full Text Create Index dialog box.*

For most applications, you will just use the default values when creating the index.

When a database is full text indexed, there is a subdirectory created with the database's filename plus the .FT extension. For example, a Notes database called ARTRACK.NSF that is full text indexed would have an associated subdirectory called ARTRACK.FT that would contain all the incremental full text indices for the database. Because of these files, full text indexing a database can use approximately 50 to 75 percent more disk space. Also be aware that full text indexes must be created and maintained server-by-server; a database can be full text indexed on one server while its replica on another server is not full text indexed.

# Summary

Although many options are available when you are creating a database and setting the various database options, a couple of important attributes of the database include what template it was created from and how its ACL is set up. Additionally, when creating databases on a server, you should be careful when you specify the filename of the database because you can create directories "on the fly." This will not make your Notes administrator happy because the administrator probably has a standard directory structure he or she would like to maintain.

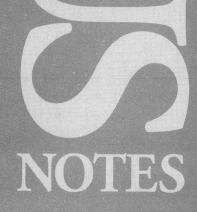

# 6

## Forms: Creating Data-Entry and Display Windows

# Overview

In Lotus Notes, forms are very similar to their paper-based counterparts. Forms contain a mixture of static text and fields. The static text on a form remains the same on all notes displayed with that particular form. The fields on the form are what contain information that is entered by users or computed by the application, and this information generally varies from note to note.

A form can be thought of as a "window" into a note. Although a document can contain many fields, a form can display or modify only the fields contained on the form. (An exception to this rule is when a form contains a computed field that sets the value for another field in the note, but the field itself does not actually exist on the form—this technique is covered in the advanced forms design section.)

# Form Layout

Designing a Notes form is very similar to using a word processor: you type static text and format its font, point size, color, and paragraph characteristics. The tools available when you design a Notes form include tables, paragraph styles, a spell-checker, and a ruler. Additionally, Notes forms can contain buttons that perform certain actions, as well as embedded objects, such as bit maps, drawings, or even spreadsheets or templates.

Although many users are tempted to design Notes forms to look exactly like a similar paper-based form, doing so is generally not a good idea, and it could make data entry and editing cumbersome. Also, designing a Notes application using traditional applications development concepts, such as getting all of a given form's fields on one screen or not leaving a lot of blank area on a form, might create awkward Notes forms, especially on the Macintosh platform due to the default size and position of the Notes "windows" that open.

In Notes, a linear form design usually is the best approach, at least for forms that are used for data entry and viewing. This is because of the way Notes wraps text to accommodate various window sizes and screen resolutions.

For example, look at the design of the Appointment/Event form in the Personnel/Event Tracking sample application. When the Schedule/Event Details form is viewed full-screen under Windows, it appears that the screen "real estate" is not being used very efficiently, particularly on the right side of the form (see Figure 6.1).

**FIGURE 6.1.**
*The Schedule/Event form full-screen.*

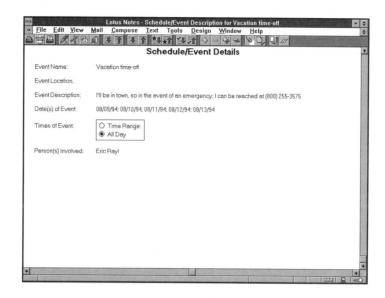

Many users, however, particularly on the Macintosh and UNIX platforms, work with windows that are not full-screen, as in Figure 6.2.

**FIGURE 6.2.**
*The Schedule/Event form in a window.*

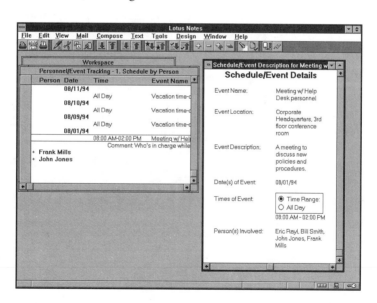

If the form had been designed with more fields side-by-side, as in Figure 6.3, the form would look better and print nicer under a full-screen window. But some users, particularly those on Macintoshes, UNIX computers, or standard VGA laptops, might have problems with the lines wrapping in the windows, which is confusing (see Figure 6.4).

**FIGURE 6.3.**

*The redesigned Schedule form.*

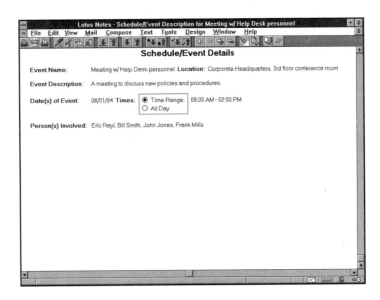

**FIGURE 6.4.**

*The redesigned Schedule form, windowed.*

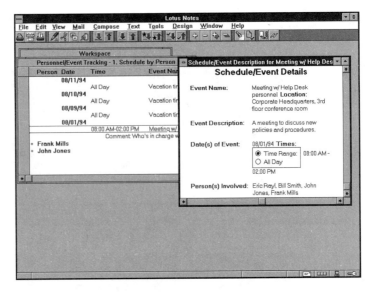

Note, however, that using techniques such as hidden tables can help alleviate text- and field-wrapping problems, and the form-override technique can be used for designing a form that prints differently than it displays on-screen. These techniques are described in Chapter 14, "Advanced Techniques."

# Creating a New Form or Editing an Existing Form

To create a new form in a database, the **F**orms... option is used on the **D**esign menu. (If the database already has one or more forms, you can edit one by selecting the form in the Design Forms window and clicking the **E**dit button.)

To create new forms or modify existing forms in a database that is on a Notes server (as opposed to your local hard drive), you must have your name listed as either a designer or a manager in the database's Access Control List. If you do not have the appropriate access level, the **N**ew and **E**dit buttons are grayed out on the Design Forms window.

# Adding, Editing, and Formatting Text on a Form

Formatting text on a form when in design mode is exactly like formatting text in a rich text field when composing a Notes document, and all the tools that you have available when composing a form are available at design time. I won't go into great detail here about all the menu options and shortcuts that can be used for formatting text and paragraphs because this information is covered in great detail in both the *Notes Application Developer's Reference* and the online Help database.

On a new form, the cursor will be at the upper-left corner of a blank screen. As with word processors, you can just begin typing the static text at this point, using the Enter key to insert hard paragraph breaks as necessary, and letting the text naturally wrap on the screen where you want the text to wrap to fit the window (unfortunately, there is no "show paragraph marks" or similar feature in Notes).

When you are just beginning a new form, you don't need to worry about the fields right away. You can just lay out and format the static text first, then add the fields after you are satisfied with the look of the static text. One item worth mentioning here is that a Notes form must have at least one editable field on it to allow it to be saved. A quirk of Notes is that it will not allow a form with purely static text and/or computed fields to be saved.

We'll use the Appointment/Event form in the Personnel/Event Tracking sample database and explore how the text and paragraphs could be modified to suit you. First, open the Appointment/Event form in edit mode using the **E**dit button on the Design Forms window. When you are designing a form, it is often easiest to have the ruler visible, so select the Show **R**uler option on the **V**iew menu (see Figure 6.5).

**FIGURE 6.5.**

*The Appointment/
Event form in design
mode.*

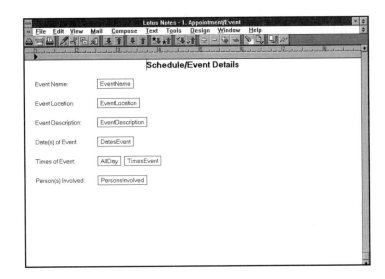

By default, text is 10-point Helv on a new form, and that is the font used for all the static text on this form. The font can easily be modified, either by selecting the text and bringing up the Font window (see Figure 6.6) using the **F**ont option on the **T**ext menu, or by using the shortcut keystroke Ctrl+K. Additionally, there is a font and point menu on the status bar at the bottom of the screen, and some font attributes, such as bold, italic, and underline, are available as smart icons on the toolbar.

**FIGURE 6.6.**

*The Font window.*

There's really nothing tricky about using the Font window to select an appropriate font, size, and attribute for the selected text. As with traditional form design and desktop publishing, I suggest that you keep the number of font types and styles to a minimum to avoid having a cluttered or "busy" screen.

**TIP**

Notes ships with two cross-platform fonts, Helv and Tms Rmn, that are very useful for designing cross-platform applications. Helv is converted to the closest sans-serif font, and Tms Rmn is converted to the closest serif font that is available on the operating system where the form is displayed. For example, Helv is converted to Arial on a Windows computer, but it maps to Geneva on a Macintosh. For the most predictable results when designing applications that will run on multiple platforms, stick to these two fonts.

In this example, we'll change the format of the static text to be 8-point bold Helv. Highlight each line of static text (but not the field), and then change its format to 8-point Helv using the point size menu on the status bar (see Figure 6.7).

**FIGURE 6.7.**

*Setting a font's point size using the status bar.*

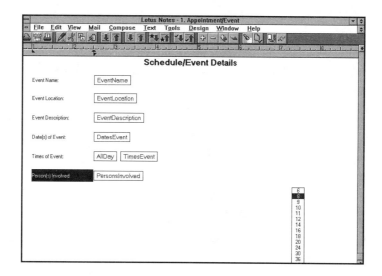

Additionally, changing the font attributes of fields is exactly like changing the attributes of static text; you just highlight the field or fields and then select the font attributes. We'll make all the fields bold text. The quick way is to first highlight the field, then press Ctrl+B. Repeat this step for each field on the form.

# Formatting Paragraphs: Margins, Justification, and Tab Stops

Formatting paragraphs in Notes is, again, very similar to using a word processor. There are two main exceptions: the right margin of a paragraph applies only when the form is printed (on-screen, the text wraps at the window's edge, regardless of where the right paragraph is set), and the Notes Paragraph **S**tyles... (on the **T**ext menu) feature is very primitive and quirky compared with similar features in most word processors.

By default, all Notes paragraphs have both their left and first-line margins set at 1", and no right margin is set. Additionally, tabs are set by default every ½".

Changing margins, justification, and tab stops can be accomplished either by using the **P**aragraph... option on the **T**ext menu or by using the shortcut Ctrl+J. (Although the **T**ext menu also has the **A**lignment option, I often find it more convenient to use the **P**aragraph... option because more formatting options are available.) The ruler is also very useful for setting margins and tabs. You can click on the ruler to set a tab stop in the currently selected paragraphs, click on an existing tab stop to delete it, or click on and drag a tab stop to a new location. The left margin, first-line margin, and right margin can also be set by clicking on and dragging the small black triangles on the ruler.

Because we just modified the font size of the static text on the Appointment/Event form, we'll move the tab stop for the fields and the left margin to move the fields closer to their labels. First, highlight all the lines with static text except for the first centered line; then drag the tab stop "arrow" on the ruler from 2½" to 2". Then drag the small triangle on the ruler that represents the left margin from 2½" to 2" (see Figure 6.8).

**FIGURE 6.8.**

*Setting tab stops and margins using the ruler.*

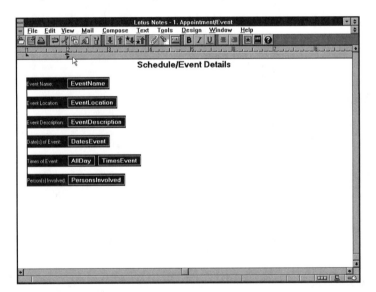

# Adding Headers and Footers

When a form is in design mode, a default header or footer can be added to the form. This header or footer is only a default value, however. A user with Editor access can override its contents when printing a document created with the form by adding a header or footer. Notes headers and footers are useful, but users accustomed to the powerful header and footer features found in high-end word processors will be frustrated by the many limitations of the Notes counterparts.

To add a header or footer when designing a form, select the **Header/Footer...** option on the **Edit** menu. The Edit Header/Footer window appears (see Figure 6.9).

**FIGURE 6.9.**

*The Edit Header/
Footer dialog box.*

Static text can be typed directly into the header or footer box, and it should not be enclosed in quotation marks. Unfortunately, there is no way to use the contents of a form's field in the header or footer.

The **P**age, **T**ime, **D**ate, and **Ti**tle buttons are used to insert the page number, the time or date that the document was printed, or the form's window title into the form's header or footer. The limitation here is that you cannot control what page number to begin numbering with.

The **Fo**nts... button is used to set the font for either the entire header or the entire footer, depending on which box the cursor is located in when the button is clicked. The whole header or footer is formatted with the selected font, even if only a portion of the text was highlighted.

The Ta**b** button inserts a | symbol. Its use can be a little confusing because these tabs have no relationship to where the tab stops are actually set on the form. There are three predefined tab stops for headers and footers: left, center, and right. Listed here are a few examples of how the header and footer tabs work:

| | |
|---|---|
| Confidential | "Confidential" appears left-justified |
| \|Confidential | "Confidential" appears right-justified |
| \|Confidential\| | "Confidential" appears centered |

# Adding Page Breaks

Page breaks can be "hard coded" into Notes forms by using the **Insert**|**Page** Break option on the **Edit** menu. Note that a page break is signified by a line across the entire form. This line appears on the form when a document created with the form is being read by a user.

# Using Paragraph Styles

The Paragraph **S**tyles... menu option is more of an end-user word processing feature, but I also recommend using paragraph styles for designing complex forms. This option's behavior is a little quirky, however, and will frustrate developers accustomed to the robust paragraph styles in many word processing programs. For one thing, a Notes paragraph style does not affect font attributes, as in many word processors. Additionally, if you are not careful, you can end up with several styles with the same name but different definitions on one form—a confusing situation. The main problem crops up when you're cutting and pasting text from different forms that have been formatted with the same style name, but the styles have different attributes. For example, if you routinely use the style name "Normal" on your forms, if you cut and paste fields or static text from one form to another, you will end up with two Normal styles in the Text Paragraph Styles window, and each might have a different definition. You'll just have to live with this problem with Notes 3.x.

# Adding Bitmaps and Graphics to Forms

There are many instances in which the appearance and functionality of a form can be enhanced by adding a graphics image or bitmap, such as a company logo, to the form at design time. Any image that can be copied to the clipboard can be pasted into a Notes form while it is being designed. There are two caveats to doing this: (1) the loading and scrolling of forms, particularly on slow computers, might be affected, and (2) if the form attribute **S**tore form in documents is selected, the amount of disk space that each document occupies might be prohibitive.

To see how a graphics image can be pasted onto a form at design time, we will paste the icon for the Personnel/Event Tracking database into the Appointment/Event form. First, select **I**con... from the **D**esign menu, click the Copy button in the Design Icon window, and then click the Cancel button to close the Design Icon window. Now position the cursor to the immediate right of the "Schedule/Event Details" static text heading, press Enter to insert a new line, and select **P**aste from the **E**dit menu (see Figure 6.10). Press Esc and save the changes to the form when prompted.

**FIGURE 6.10.**
*A form that has a bit pasted into it in design mode.*

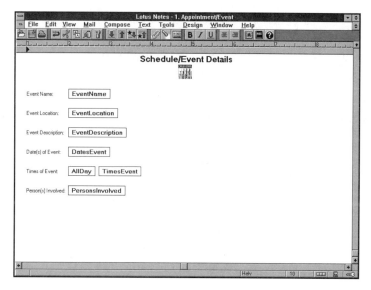

# Using Tables

The table creation and manipulating tools in Notes are very primitive when compared with the table design tools found in word processors and true forms-design software. But using tables when designing Notes forms not only can add to the aesthetics of the form, but can solve many text- and field-formatting problems.

## Adding a Table to a Form

Notes forms have tables inserted during form design by using the **I**nsert|**T**able option on the Notes **E**dit menu. This selection opens the Edit Window dialog box (Figure 6.11).

**FIGURE 6.11.**
*The Insert Table dialog box.*

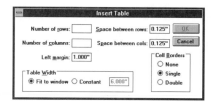

In the Appointment/Event form, we'll insert a two-row by three-column table to help control the way fields wrap within a window. Position the cursor to the left of the "Event Name:" static text, press Enter twice to insert two blank lines, and then move the cursor back up two lines. Change the paragraph's formatting back to the default. To do so, you can select the **P**aragraph... option on the **T**ext menu, changing the left margin to

1" and deleting the tab stop at 2", or you can use the ruler, deleting the Tab stop by clicking on it and dragging the left margin marker from 2" to 1". Changing the left margin of a table that has already been inserted into a table can be a little tedious; it's easiest to have the paragraph's margins set correctly before a table is inserted.

Now select **Insert | Table** from the **Edit** menu. Type 2 in the Number of **r**ows: box, type 3 in the Number of **c**olumns: box, and leave all the other defaults alone for now. Then click OK to create the table (see Figure 6.12).

**FIGURE 6.12.**

*The Schedule/Event form with a new table added.*

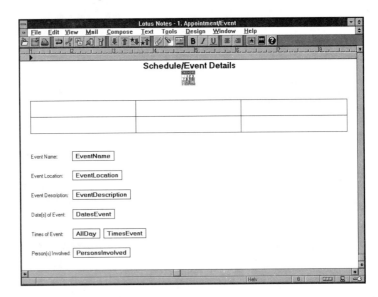

We will now move the static text items "Event Name:," "Event Location:," and "Event Description:" into the elements of the first row by cutting and pasting the text. Select the text "Event Name:" using the mouse, and then select **Cut** on the **E**dit menu (or use the keyboard shortcut Ctrl+X). Move the cursor to the cell in the first column and row of the table, and select the **P**aste command from the **E**dit menu (or use the keyboard shortcut Ctrl+V). Repeat this process for the other two static text strings, creating a table that looks similar to the one in Figure 6.13.

**FIGURE 6.13.**

*The Schedule/Event form with static text moved inside the new table's cells.*

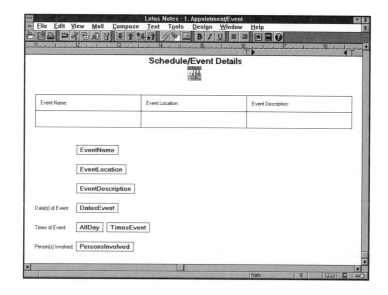

Now we need to move the fields into the table. We'll use the cut-and-paste process just as we did with the static text. Highlight a field, select the **Cut** command on the **Edit** menu, position the cursor in the appropriate cell, and then select **P**aste on the **Edit** menu.

---

**TIP**

If you inadvertently delete a field while cutting and pasting, or if you overtype it by mistake, immediately use the **U**ndo command on the **Edit** menu.

---

## Formatting and Justifying Text Within Tables

Notice that the font size and style of the fields has changed because, as in a word processing program, the font of a particular string is governed by the formatting of the paragraph into which the text (or field) is pasted. Change the field's font size and style to 10-point bold Helv by highlighting each field individually and then selecting the appropriate choices from the Format Text dialog box, or by using the status bar and the tool-bar tools.

**TIP**

Because you can change the text formatting (and justification) in a table only one cell at a time, try to have the font style and point size correct *before* you insert a table in a Notes form. If you make a mistake by inserting a large table into an improperly formatted area, you can save time by deleting the table, formatting the text font and size correctly, and reinserting the table.

Now delete the extra paragraphs where the fields used to be located. Then format the table's static text as bold, as in Figure 6.14.

**FIGURE 6.14.**

*The table on the Schedule/Event form with the appropriate fields moved into the table's cells.*

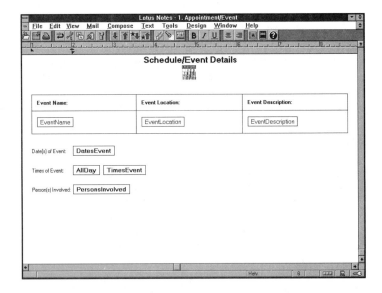

Now save the form and open one of the schedule documents to see how the data is displayed in the table (see Figure 6.15).

**FIGURE 6.15.**

*The modified Schedule/
Event form with the
table.*

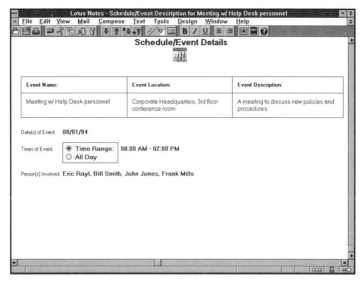

## The Table Option Fit to Window

Minimize the form into a window, and notice how the table sizes itself to fit the window (see Figure 6.16). This happens because you left the **F**it to window check box selected on the Edit Table Format dialog box when you created the table. If you had deselected the **F**it to window check box, the form would appear as in Figure 6.17.

**FIGURE 6.16.**

*How a table appears
when the design option
**F**it to window is
selected.*

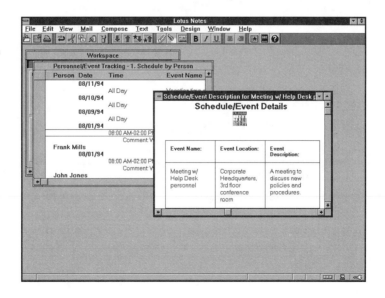

**FIGURE 6.17.**

*The same table as in Figure 6.16 but with the **Fit** to window option deselected.*

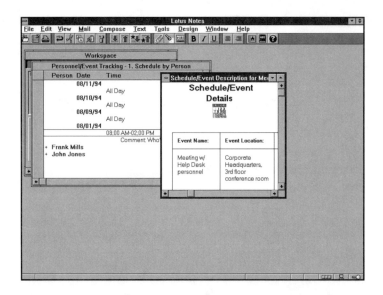

---

**TIP**

Note that the widths of the columns vary when **F**it to window is selected, which makes the form fit the screen nicely but causes havoc when the form needs to be printed consistently (that is, with the table at the same location on a page, with page breaks at predefined locations). This is one of the first form design dilemmas you'll face—deciding whether you want the form to look best when printed or when viewed on-screen. An advanced feature, called Form Override, can help solve this problem. This feature is discussed in the advanced section of the book.

---

## Changing the Format of an Existing Table

Formatting a table in a form can be an exasperating experience. To illustrate some of the problems you might encounter when designing a form with a table, open the Appointment/Event form in design mode again (by using the **F**orms... option on the **D**esign menu). To edit a table that already exists on a form, place the cursor anywhere within the table, and select the Ta**b**le|**F**ormat menu option on the **E**dit menu. Notice that the row and column number of the cell that the cursor was in when you selected the Ta**b**le **F**ormat command are what appear as the current cell in the Edit Table Format dialog box (see Figure 6.18).

**FIGURE 6.18.**
*The Edit Table Format
dialog box.*

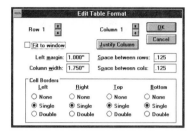

First, we'll put a double border around the cells in the first row of the table. Again, as with changing the fonts for an entire table, there is no way to format multiple cells all at once—you must individually select them and then apply the format. Make sure that you are in Row 1, Column 1 (if not, use the up and down arrows to change to the correct cell), and select Double for the cell borders for **L**eft, **R**ight, **T**op, and **B**ottom. Now go to the second column by clicking the up-arrow button next to the Column number, and again select Double for all the cell borders for this cell. Repeat this process one last time for the third column, and then click **O**K; the form should look similar to the one shown in Figure 6.19.

**FIGURE 6.19.**
*Adding double borders
to a table's cells.*

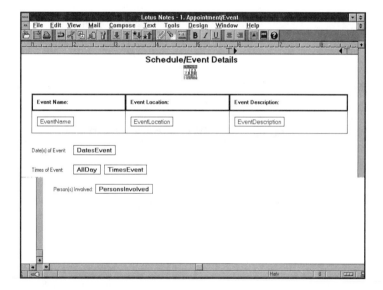

> **TIP**
>
> Because each cell's border has to be formatted individually, on large tables try to plan ahead for what most of the cell borders will be when you create the table. This will save you from spending a lot of time reformatting cells.

Now we'll resize the cell widths and fix the total width of the table to be 6", with a 1" margin on either side for printing purposes. With the cursor located in the upper-left cell, select Table|Format from the **E**dit menu. For Row 1, Column 1, change the **Col**umn **w**idth to be 1.75". Now click the up-arrow button next to the Column indicator to move to column 2, and then change its width to 1.75" also. Repeat this process for column 3; then click **OK** and look at the table's new dimensions (turn on the ruler if you don't have it visible using the **V**iew|Show **R**uler menu option). Notice that the actual table is 6" wide, even though there are three 1.75" columns. This is due to the .125" of "padding" between the column's border and the text or field within the column. To make the spacing closer between the columns or the rows, select Table|Format from the **E**dit menu, and then change the values in the **S**pace between rows: box and the S**p**ace between cols: box. Try entering .075" for both values; then click **OK**. Notice how this setting makes the columns and rows move tighter together, and how this in turn affects the overall width of the table.

Another limitation of Notes forms is that individual rows cannot have different column widths—the column width applies to all rows within the column. Column widths can be changed by using the ruler to drag the "T" indicator to a new location.

> **TIP**
>
> Notes will not allow column widths to be any narrower than the width of the name of the field within a given cell. This means that field names within a given table might have to be very short, and formatted in a small point size, to create tables with tightly spaced columns.

While in the Edit Table Format dialog box, you can change the justification of the contents of each cell by clicking the **J**ustify Column button and selecting either Left, Right, Center, Full, or None. Note, however, that this is the equivalent of highlighting a cell and using the **A**lignment option on the Format Paragraph dialog box.

# Adding and Deleting Rows and Columns in a Table

Adding and deleting columns or rows in an existing table is an easy process. Just put the cursor in the table at the location where you want to insert a row or column, and select either **I**nsert Row/Column or **D**elete Row/Column from the **E**dit—Ta**b**le menu. This action brings up a dialog box that prompts you for the number of rows or columns to add or delete.

For example, we'll add a column to the table on the Appointment/Event form. This column will contain the field with the date(s) of the event and will be located in the far-right column of the table. With the form in design mode, position the cursor in the extreme-right column of the table, and select **I**nsert Row/Column from the **E**dit—Ta**b**le menu. This action causes the Insert Row/Column dialog box to appear (see Figure 6.20). Select the **C**olumn(s) radio button; then click the **A**ppend button to add one column to the end of the current table.

**FIGURE 6.20.**

*The Insert Row/Column dialog box.*

Next, cut and paste the static text "Date(s) of Event:" into the column's heading, and cut and paste the field DatesEvent into the table. Format the static text as bold, and resize the width of the column to approximately the same width as the static text, as in Figure 6.21.

**FIGURE 6.21.**

*The Schedule/Events form with the added column Date(s) of Event.*

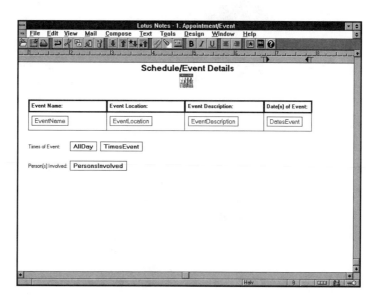

Additionally, reset the table format to Fit to window by selecting **F**ormat from the **E**dit—
Ta**b**le menu option and checking the Fit to window box. Now save the changes to the
form, and open a schedule/event document to see how the form appears now (see Figure 6.22 and Figure 6.23).

**FIGURE 6.22.**

*A Schedule/Event
document with a
four-column table,
maximized.*

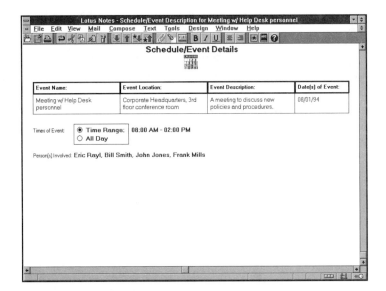

**FIGURE 6.23.**

*The Schedule/Event
document in Figure
6.22, but displayed in a
window.*

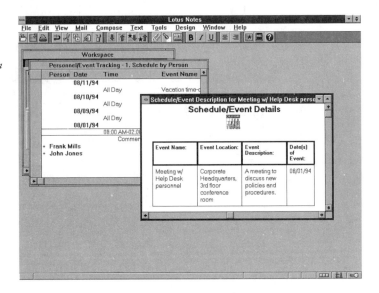

## Table Usage Caveat

Although tables are useful for formatting data and aesthetically enhancing forms, they should be used sparingly because they impact the speed at which forms open, particularly when the table is large and is located in the part of the form that is visible when the form opens. Many times, tab stops are a better solution for formatting data into columns.

# Form Attributes

One of the most important parts of designing a form is setting the form's attributes. When a form is open in design mode, the Form **A**ttributes... option is available on the **D**esign menu. Selecting this option opens the Design Form Attributes dialog box (see Figure 6.25). Some of these form attributes that are considered advanced options are only briefly described here but are covered in detail in Chapter 15, "Advanced Techniques."

**FIGURE 6.24.**

*The Design Form Attributes dialog box.*

## Form Name

The form name serves two purposes; it's what appears on the Notes **C**ompose menu when the database is selected or open, and it's what appears in the document's Form field (if the **S**tore form in documents attribute is not selected). Form names can (and generally should) have *synonyms*—that is, the form name that appears on the **C**ompose menu can be different from the name that is used internally by Notes.

### Synonyms

The vertical bar (|) symbol is used to separate synonyms. What appears to the far left of the | is what appears on the **C**ompose menu, and what appears to the far right of the | is the name used internally by Notes. If the form name was Main Topic | Document | MainTopic, then "Main Topic" would appear on the Compose menu, but documents composed with the form would have "MainTopic" stored in the Form field. Documents with "Document" in the Form field would be displayed with this form also.

> **TIP**
>
> The main reason to use form-name synonyms is so that you can change the way the form name appears on the Compose menu without having to change any formulas that reference the form name.

To try to make sense of how synonyms work, look at the form attributes of the Appointment/Event form in the Personnel/Event Tracking sample database (Figure 6.24). Because the form name is 1. Appointment/Event | frmEvent, "**1.** Appointment/Event" appears on the **C**ompose menu, but the internal Form field contains "'frmEvent'." Suppose that you want to change the way this form appears on the **C**ompose menu. In the form name box, type the name 1. Acme Corporation Event ¦ frmEvent, and then click **O**K to save the form. Now look at the **C**ompose menu. As shown in Figure 6.25, the **C**ompose menu now reflects the changes you made to the form name. Also notice that you can still open event documents that were created with the form when it was named 1. Appointment/Event | frmEvent—this is an important point.

**FIGURE 6.25.**

*The **C**ompose menu in the Personnel/Event Tracking sample database.*

As a second example of what can go wrong if you don't use form-name synonyms, consider the following example using the Personnel/Event Tracking database. Open the 2. Comment form in design mode, and open the Design Form Attributes dialog box (by selecting the Form **A**ttributes... option on the **D**esign menu). Type the form name 2. Response, with no synonym, and then click **O**K to save the form.

Notice that the **C**ompose menu now reflects the new form name, but if you try to open a document that was previously created with the Comment form, you receive an error message, as in Figure 6.26. (You also receive the error message "Cannot locate Default Form," which is explained in the Default Database Form section later in this chapter.)

**FIGURE 6.26.**

*When a form of a given name cannot be found to display a document, an error message similar to this one will appear.*

To help you understand a little more about what's going on here, highlight a Comment document, and then select the menu option Do**c**ument Info... on the **D**esign menu. The Design Document Info dialog box appears, as shown in Figure 6.27.

**FIGURE 6.27.**

*The Design Document Info dialog box.*

Notice that "frmComment" is the content of the Form field.

> **TIP**
>
> Use the Do**c**ument Info... option on the **D**esign menu to see what fields are contained in a given document, and the data types and data contained in the fields. It's important to remember that this menu option is available to any user, and therefore users can see the contents of any unencrypted fields on a document, regardless of whether the field is hidden or not present on a particular form.

What this means is that when a user tries to open this document, Notes looks for a form named "frmComment" to display the document with. Because there is no form with a name or synonym that matches "frmComment", Notes displays the error message "Cannot locate Form: frmComment." Because Notes can't find the correct form to display the document with, it next looks for a default form in the database to display the form with. The Personnel/Event Tracking database does not have a default form specified, so the second error message, "Cannot locate Default Form," is generated.

## Cascading Form Names

The form names listed on the **C**ompose menu in a Notes database can cascade one level, as shown in Figure 6.28. The backslash (\) symbol, when used in a form name, produces a second menu level on the **C**ompose menu. For example, the **C**ompose menu in Figure 6.28 was produced with forms that were named as shown in Figure 6.29.

**FIGURE 6.28.**

*A Notes cascading Compose menu.*

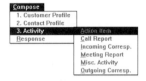

**FIGURE 6.29.**

*The form names that create the cascading Compose menu shown in Figure 6.28.*

Notes allows only nine form names to appear on the main **Compose** menu before it creates a menu option called **O**ther..., as in Figure 6.30. Therefore, it's a good idea to cascade your form names to avoid having more than nine form names appear on the main **Compose** menu.

**FIGURE 6.30.**

*If more than nine items appear on the main level of the Compose menu, an **Other...** option is added to the menu.*

## Accelerator Keys

The form name also controls the *accelerator* key—the underlined key that Windows and OS/2 users can use to access the form via keystrokes rather than the mouse. Usually the first unique letter in the form's name is used as the accelerator key, but you can force Notes to use a different key by placing an underscore (_) character before the desired letter in the form name. For example, the form name Main _Topic would cause the "T" to be the accelerator key for the form on the **Compose** menu.

> **TIP**
>
> I suggest always starting form names with either a numeral or a letter, and then adding the desired text for the form name. This method enables you to determine how the forms will be sorted on the **Compose** menu, and it sets the

accelerator key to be the number, as long as there are nine or fewer options on the main **Compose** menu. Additionally, by convention, I start form synonyms with "frm" to make formulas that reference form names more readable.

# Form Type

One of the most fundamental form attributes is the form type. The form types are Document, Response, and Response to response. It's very important to understand what these form types mean, because their names can be misleading. It's easier to think of the form type Document as actually meaning "Main document" or "Parent document," and to think of the two Response types as "Children" or "Children-of-children" documents. Notes builds an internal relationship or pointer between Main documents and Children documents, and likewise between Children documents and Children-of-children documents. This is one of the most fundamental concepts of Notes.

For example, in the Personnel/Event Tracking sample application, there is a Notes-created relationship between a specific note that was created with the Comment form (a response-type form) and the note created with the Appointment/Event form (a Document-type form) that it is a comment for. The relationship between these documents was determined by what Event was highlighted when a Comment was composed.

> **TIP**
>
> Applications that use the Notes "response hierarchy" will be much more powerful than applications that do not effectively use Response-type forms.

Many newcomers to Notes development think that a Response-type form seems to imply that it is used in discussion-oriented databases, but response documents are much more useful than just in discussion databases. Here are a few examples of a much broader way to think of the use of main and response documents:

- In a project management application, each project could be a main document, the tasks associated with each project could be response documents, and the resources required for each task could be responses-to-responses.

- In a management application, there could be a Meeting Notice main document, and there could be response documents for Agenda Requests, as well as response forms used to contain the minutes of the meeting after it is held.

- In a crime- and investigation-tracking application, each investigation could be a main document, and each suspect for a given investigation could be a response document related to the main case document.

## Include in Compose Menu

This option determines whether a form will be available for users to compose documents with. Many times, applications will require forms that are used for displaying documents but that should not appear on the Compose menu. Another method for removing a form from the Compose menu is to include the leftmost part of a form's name in parentheses. For example, (1. Acme Corporation Event) | frmEvent would cause the Event form not to appear on the menu in the Personnel/Event Tracking sample database.

## Include in Query by Form

This feature is relevant only in databases that are full-text indexed. If this option is selected, users can access this form via the Form button on the Search Bar to create field-specific queries.

## Default Database Form

As discussed earlier in this chapter in the Form Name section, when a user opens a document, Notes displays that document using the form that is referenced in the document's Form field (unless the document was created with a form that had the Store form in documents attribute set when it was composed). If Notes cannot find a form with the given name, it displays the document with the database's Default form, if there is one.

Many Notes applications do not require default forms. Default forms are most useful when you cut and paste documents between dissimilar databases, but even then their usefulness is limited. A database's default form name is listed in the Design Forms dialog box with an asterisk to the left of the form name, such as the Memo form in a standard Notes mail database (see Figure 6.31).

**FIGURE 6.31.**

*The Design Forms dialog box for the Notes standard mail template. Notice the asterisk next to the default form.*

To see how the default form works, try copying an event document from the Personnel/Event Tracking database to your personal mail database (by highlighting an event document from a view, selecting **C**opy from the **E**dit menu to copy the document to the clipboard, and then opening your mail database and selecting **P**aste from the **E**dit menu). Now try to open the event document in your mail database. You first receive the error message "Cannot locate Form: frmEvent." Then the document is displayed with your mail database's default form, Memo. Because there are no field names in common between the Event form and the Memo form, the memo will be, for the most part, blank (the From and Date data are computed).

## Automatically Refresh Fields

Many Notes forms have computed fields whose values are based on the content of other fields on the form, such as on a spreadsheet. For example, a Purchase Requisition form might have a computed field that is the product of an item's unit price times the quantity ordered. In general, computed fields on a Notes form are not automatically computed or "refreshed" until either the document is saved or the user forces a refresh by selecting the Refres**h** Fields option on the **V**iew menu (or use the F9 shortcut key).

When the **A**utomatically refresh fields form attribute is selected, Notes refreshes computed fields as a user moves from field to field on a form. Although this action provides the user with a sense of confidence because he can see the contents of fields change in response to his input, it usually becomes annoying due to the performance impact of refreshing computed fields every time a user moves to a different field. I discourage use of this attribute unless absolutely necessary. I feel it's much better to train users to properly use the Refres**h** Fields menu option or shortcuts if they need to verify the correctness of computed fields.

## Store Form in Documents

This Notes feature is perplexing to most beginning Notes developers. By default, a form is part of a database's design, and the proper form for displaying the document is selected either by the contents of the internal Form field or by a view's Form Formula (see Chapter 8, "Views: Organizing Notes Documents"). Sometimes you might want to have the actual form's design stored entirely within each document that is composed with the form. Generally, this action is necessary when you will be mailing or cutting and pasting documents between databases, and a form to display the document correctly might not exist in the target database.

Do not use this feature too often because each document consumes much more disk space than usual because the document contains all the forms design details. Additionally, documents composed with a form that has this attribute set will not reflect later changes to the form's design, which can cause many problems. If possible, do not use this feature but make a copy of the necessary form available in the target database's design.

> **TIP**
>
> Be careful when turning this option on and off in databases that have existing data. If you have existing documents and you decide to store forms in documents, you'll have to refresh the fields of the existing documents for them to store the form in the document. On the other hand, if you have documents that have the form stored in them, you need to run a macro to initialize and set the contents of the Form field to the name of a form. Additionally, you might want to create a macro to delete the fields $TITLE,$INFO, $WINDOWTITLE, and $BODY to conserve space in the database. (These macro techniques are discussed in Chapter 10, "Macros.")

## Inherit Default Field Values

Inheritance is a powerful and important Notes concept. Inheritance is the way that data can be transferred from one Notes document to another. When a note is composed, a field can get data from the document that is either open or highlighted in view. It's important to remember that inheritance happens only once, when a document is composed. Many Notes applications use this form attribute to transfer data between documents at compose time.

> **TIP**
>
> A user can cause a form to not inherit data by pressing the Ctrl key when selecting the form from the Compose menu.

## Mail Documents When Saving

This option alters the normal Notes document-save dialog box (shown in Figure 6.32) and adds the options to **M**ail, **Si**g**n**, and **E**ncrypt the document when saving it (see Figure 6.33). If the form is to be mailed when it is saved, you'll need to know about several important fields that control how the form is mailed (see the section on mail-enabled forms in Chapter 15, "Advanced Notes Design Techniques").

**FIGURE 6.32.**

*The standard Lotus Notes dialog box for saving a document.*

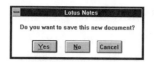

**FIGURE 6.33.**

*The Document Save dialog box that appears when a form has the **Mail** documents when saving attribute set.*

## Updates Become Responses

If a document was created with this form attribute selected, any changes to the document become completely new documents that are responses to the original document. This form attribute can be used as a method of version control because the original document always remains unchanged.

## Prior Versions Become Responses

This form attribute is similar to the preceding one, except that the most current document is always the parent document, and all previous edited versions of the document are responses.

## Color

The background color of a form can be selected from the Design Form Attributes dialog box. Unfortunately, Notes does not offer a very wide range of color options, and if users might have monochrome displays, care must be taken to select colors for forms and text that will be readable on their machines.

## Read Access..., Compose Access..., and Encryption... Buttons

Generally, the security of documents and fields in a Notes application is controlled by the database's Access Control List. Some applications, however, require a more advanced security scheme that allows certain forms to be read or composed only by selected users. Additionally, certain fields on a form can be encrypted with a specified encryption key, making the contents of those fields readable only by users who possess the encryption key. These concepts are covered in Chapter 16, "Advanced Security Issues."

## Object Activation... Button

This form attribute is an advanced feature that works in conjunction with Object Linking and Embedding (OLE). Basically, an object from an application that supports OLE, such as a Lotus 1-2-3 spreadsheet or an Ami Pro document template, can be embedded in a Notes form when it is designed. Then when a user composes documents using the form, the embedded spreadsheet or document can be opened in its native format. This option, along with an example of its usage, is covered in Chapter 15, "Advanced Notes Design Techniques."

# Window Titles

Window titles are the text that is displayed in the top border of a window when a document is open. To specify a form's window title, the **W**indow Title option is selected on the **D**esign menu when the form is open in design mode. Although a window title is not necessary for a form, it is a nice finishing touch, and if it is not specified, the title defaults to "(untitled)."

Window titles can be simply static text, such as "Schedule Information," or they can be more complex formulas that cause the window title to vary depending on whether the note is new and how many response documents it has.

# Summary

Records (or "notes") in a database are created, displayed, edited, and printed using forms. Notes forms serve as the window into a note or document.

Because of the way Notes wraps lines of text that do not fit completely on the computer's screen, thought must be given to the form's layout, and forms used for displaying and entering data might not be designed to look similar to their paper-based counterparts.

Tables are useful for formatting data and creating borders around paragraphs, but large tables should be used sparingly on forms that are used for data entry and editing because they impact the speed at which the form loads.

# 7

# Creating and Manipulating Fields on a Form

# Overview

Fields are the most basic components of a Notes document. In a Notes application, usually the contents of a Notes field are set by either an editable or a computed field located on a Notes document. The relationship between a Notes field and a Notes form that contains the particular field name is therefore very important.

To fully understand some of the concepts that are discussed in this chapter and the upcoming chapters, you should have access to a computer running Notes that has a copy of the Personnel/Event Tracker database on it. Either make a copy of the database that you created in Chapter 4, "Creating an Application: A Personnel/Event Tracker," or copy the database from the sample disk to your Notes data directory.

# The Relationship Between Fields and Forms

The way the data contained in a particular field of a document is displayed is mainly controlled by the form that is used to create and view the document. In most instances, when a document is composed, a special field called Form is created by Notes. (The exception is when the Form has the attribute **S**tore form in documents selected.)

It is also important to mention that contents of Notes fields can also be set or changed in a couple of other ways. Notes automatically creates several special fields that control the way documents behave, and macros can be written that create or modify the contents of fields. This chapter discusses the fields that Notes automatically creates, but creating and modifying fields with macros is covered in a later chapter.

## Shared vs. Nonshared Fields

Fields can be added to, modified, and deleted from a form when the form is open in design mode. With a form open in design mode, a field can be added at the cursor's insertion point by selecting the **N**ew Field... option on the **D**esign menu. This selection causes the Design New Field window to appear (see Figure 7.1), prompting you to indicate whether this will be a shared field.

**FIGURE 7.1.**
*The Design New Field*
*dialog box.*

What is a shared field? This designation concerns only the field's *definition* and has nothing to do with the data that is contained within the field. Shared fields can be re-used on multiple forms within the same database, which makes maintaining the field's definition easier because it needs to be changed in only one place, even if the field is used on five forms within the database.

It has been my experience that there are very few instances in which using a shared field is desirable. Although the concept sounds good and is something I dearly wanted in my Notes 2.x development days, several other features in Notes 3.0 (particularly the capability to use @DbColumn to generate keyword lists for fields) have made this feature less than attractive. I suggest that as a beginning Notes application developer, you stay away from using shared fields until you more fully understand Notes application development. For the rest of this chapter, all examples assume that when you create a new field, you will select the option Create field to be used only within this Form.

## The Field Definition Dialog Box

When you select **N**ew Field... from the **D**esign menu, and after you select whether to create a shared field, you are presented with the Field Definition window (see Figure 7.2).

**FIGURE 7.2.**

*The Field Definition dialog box.*

### Field Name

The first option on the Field Definition window is the field's name. Field names can be up to 32 bytes long (usually 32 characters) and can contain numbers and the under-score symbol.

Many Notes developers follow the convention of beginning field names with a capital letter and using a pseudo-"Proper Case" format, capitalizing the first letter of each word of multiword field names. For instance, you will see that most Lotus-developed Notes applications have field names such as CompanyName, CompanyAddress, and ContactPhoneNumber. I suggest that you adhere to this naming convention because it makes Notes formulas much more readable. Additionally, I suggest that you use very descriptive field names when possible—don't be afraid to use long field names such as DateAccountOpened, VerifyInheritingFromCorrectForm, or TotalLossAmount. These field names help Notes forms and formulas to be almost self-documenting, and they are a lot more comprehensible than names such as acctopndt, chkform, or ttllsamt.

> **TIP**
>
> In many programming languages, there are "reserved words" that cannot be used for variable or object names. In Notes, the field name Form is the most important reserved word and should not be used as a field name within a form. Most other reserved Notes field names are related to mail-enabled forms, such as the field names SendTo, CopyTo, and ReturnReceipt, or they begin with the character $. You should refrain from using the field name Form or any field name that begins with the $ symbol.

## Help Description

The next box on the Field Definition window is the **H**elp Description: box. The help description is the line of text that appears in the bottom border of a form's window when a user is entering or editing data in a field. For example, in Figure 7.3, the text at the bottom of the screen, "Type in the dates of the event, separated by commas," is the help description for the DatesEvent field.

**FIGURE 7.3.**
*A field's help description as it appears to a user. Note that the user must have the View\Show Field Help option selected.*

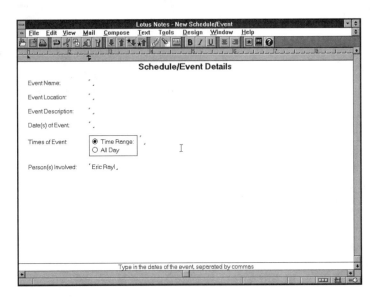

If help descriptions are consistently and effectively used within an organization, they go a long way toward helping users become familiar with new Notes applications as they are rolled out.

## Data Types

The next box on the Field Definition window is the **D**ata Type: box. The entry in this box controls what type of data can be placed in or displayed within a given field. Notes supports nine data types: Text, Number, Time, Keywords, Rich Text, Names, Author Names, Reader Names, and Section. The uses of these data types are detailed here:

| | |
|---|---|
| Text | Text fields can contain letters, numbers, spaces, and punctuation, and they can contain up to 15K of data. The fonts and colors of data in text fields are controlled by the formatting that is applied by the application designer when the field is placed on the form, and they cannot be changed by users. |
| Number | Number fields generally contain data that will be used mathematically. The only non-numeric characters that can be entered into a Number field (without generating an error message) are the +, −, $, ., and E (exponential) symbols. |
| Time | Time fields can contain both time and date information. In addition to standard formats such as "11:45 AM 12/23/94" and "23:15:30 09/23/94," Notes supports using the words "Today," "Tomorrow," and "Yesterday" in time fields. |
| Keywords | Keywords fields present a selection of choices to the user, and they enable the user to select one or more choices from the list. The list of the values to be displayed in a Keywords field can be either "hard coded" into the field definition or dynamically looked up from a Notes database. |
| Rich Text | Rich Text fields contain text that can have the font and paragraph formatting determined by the user. Rich Text fields can contain objects that are pasted in or embedded by the user, such as spreadsheets, graphics, doc links, files, and sounds. |

| | |
|---|---|
| Names | Names fields provide a way for controlling how Notes users' names are displayed in a Notes document. This data type is useful only in organizations that are using Notes hierarchical names, such as "CN=Eric Rayl/O=Alison, Rayl & Associates/C=US," because it allows control over how this distinguished name is displayed. |
| Author Names | The Author Names data type is used to control edit access to a particular document. See Chapter 15, "Advanced Security Issues," for an explanation on how and where to use this field. |
| Reader Names | The Reader Names data type is used to control reader access to particular documents in a database. The use of this data type is covered in Chapter 15. |
| Section | Section fields are used to subdivide a form and its fields into various areas that can be accessed by only a subset of the form's regular editors. Although this is not truly a security tool, its use is discussed in Chapter 15. |

If the data that is entered into a field is inconsistent with the field's data type, Notes does not allow the document to be saved, prompts the user with an error message, and moves the cursor to the offending field.

> **TIP**
>
> Macintosh users are generally used to entering dates in the format "08-22-94," using the "-" separator, but the hyphen character generates the Notes error message "Unable to interpret Time or Date." Be sure to instruct your Macintosh users to use the "/" separator.

## Field Types

The next area of the Field Definition window specifies the field type. Every data type except Rich Text can be one of four types (editable, computed, computed for display, or computed when composed). Rich Text fields can have only the field types editable or non-editable. It's important to understand how these field types behave, particularly the computed types, because the time it takes for forms to load and recalculate can be affected by the choices you make.

| | |
|---|---|
| Editable | This field type allows data to be entered and edited freely. Additionally, you can provide default values to the field, and validate and translate data that is entered into these types of fields using the Formula... button, discussed shortly. |
| Computed | The data in computed fields is not editable but is calculated every time the document is edited and saved or has its fields refreshed. |
| Computed for display | The value in computed for display fields does not actually exist in the Notes document but is computed every time the document is opened for reading or editing. This is an important distinction between this type of field and a computed field because the computed field can be recalculated only by a person who has the rights to edit the document. Additionally, data in computed for display fields is not available for use in views because the data does not actually exist in the document. |
| Computed when composed | Data in a computed when composed field is calculated only once, at compose time, the moment a new document is opened. This field type is most useful for fields that will inherit data from other documents because inheritance occurs only one time, at compose time. |
| Non-editable | Rich Text fields can be only editable or non-editable. Non-editable Rich Text fields are generally used for displaying data that was entered via an editable field on another form. |

## Allow Multi-Values Check Box

The Field Definition window also includes an Allow Multi-Values check box. Notes fields can contain multiple values, which is a very powerful feature. This feature, when used with the **S**eparators... button, can allow fields to contain and display multiple names, dates, and so on.

> **TIP**
>
> Developers familiar with traditional programming languages might find it useful to think of multivalue fields as *1 by n* arrays of variable-length values, in which the number of elements, *n*, is not fixed.

For example, in the Personnel/Event Tracking sample application, this feature is used in two fields. Both the DatesEvent and the PersonsInvolved fields have the Allow Multi-**V**alues check box selected. To see how multivalues are stored internally in the Notes document, select one of the event documents, and then select the Do**c**ument Info... option on the **D**esign menu. Now select the PersonsInvolved field, and notice that its data type is a Text list, as in Figure 7.4. (Note that to see the multiple values contained in that field, you'll have to scroll down, as in Figure 7.5.)

**FIGURE 7.4.**

*The Design Document Info dialog box showing a Text list data type field.*

**FIGURE 7.5.**

*Scrolling down on the Design Document Info dialog box reveals the complete contents of the PersonsInvolved field.*

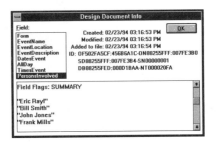

## Formula... Button

Clicking the Formula... button on the Field Definition window causes the Design Field Formula dialog box to appear. Its contents vary depending on whether the field is editable or one of the computed field types, and whether the field is a Rich Text data type.

Although writing formulas is discussed in much greater detail in the following chapters and in the advanced section, the different *types* of formulas are discussed here, and some example formulas are explained.

Editable fields can have three types of formulas associated with them: the default value formula, the input translation formula, and the input validation formula (see Figure 7.6).

**FIGURE 7.6.**

*The Design Field Formula dialog box for an editable field.*

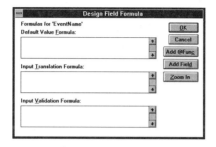

Additionally, three special buttons are available on any formula definition dialog box: Add Fie**ld**, Add @Fun**c**, and **Z**oom In. The Add Fie**ld** and Add @Fun**c** buttons are just shortcuts that allow a field name or Lotus Notes @Function to be pasted into the formula window. Clicking the Add Fie**ld** button causes a list of the currently defined field names to appear, along with the buttons **P**aste and Cancel (see Figure 7.7). Clicking the **P**aste button just pastes the selected field's name into the formula dialog box, helping to eliminate spelling errors.

**FIGURE 7.7.**

*The Paste Field dialog box.*

Clicking the Add @Fun**c** button causes a list of the Notes @Functions to appear (see Figure 7.8), along with a **P**aste and a Cancel button. This feature is most useful because the user can highlight a function's name and press the F1 key, bringing up the online help for that function. This feature is very useful in helping avoid syntax errors.

**FIGURE 7.8.**

*The Paste Function dialog box.*

An editable field's default value formula describes what information will be present in the field at compose time, or the first time a document is composed. This formula is not ever reevaluated, so the contents of any fields that are referenced in this field must be available at compose time. For example, suppose that a form for creating purchase requisitions has two editable fields, RetailPrice and DiscountedPrice, and the RetailPrice field has no default value. Many developers would be tempted to write a default value formula for the DiscountedPrice field that references the RetailPrice field, but this formula would always return a null value (that is, the DiscountedPrice field would be blank) because the RetailPrice field is empty at compose time.

Some simple examples of default value formulas, and a simple explanation of them, follow:

| | |
|---|---|
| `"All Day"` | Defaults a text field to the text string All Day. |
| `0` | Defaults a numerical field's value to 0. |
| `@Today` | Defaults the field's value to the date when the form is composed. |
| `@UserName` | Defaults the field's value to the name of the user (from the user's Notes ID) who is composing the form. |
| `RetailPrice` | Defaults the field's value to the value of the RetailPrice field. If the form has the Inherit Default Values attribute set, the contents of the RetailPrice field could be on the form that is either highlighted or open when the form is composed, causing its contents to be inherited to the new document. If there is no field called RetailValue on either the form that is being composed or the document from which data is being inherited, the field defaults to the null value. |
| `RetailPrice * .85` | Defaults the field's value to the contents of the RetailPrice field times .85. |

The input translation formula is used to convert the data that appears in a field into a particular format, and the formula is invoked every time a document is saved. This feature is most useful in making certain that data is entered consistently by users, because capitalization and spacing are very important in Notes.

A couple of examples of input translation formulas, and a description of what they do, follow:

```
@Trim(@ProperCase(Subject))
```

Formats the contents of the Subject field in proper case (capital letters at the beginning of words, the rest lowercase), and strips out any extra spaces at the beginning or end of the text string or between words (that is, PROBLEMS WITH ACME ACCOUNT becomes Problems With Acme Account when the document is saved).

```
@Left(PersonsInvolved;1) + @Right(PersonsInvolved; " ")
```

Takes the first letter of the name contained in the PersonsInvolved field and concatenates it with the last word of the PersonsInvolved field (that is, everything to the right of the last space). If the PersonsInvolved field contains the multiple values Eric Rayl ; Frank Mills, it would be translated to ERayl ; FMills.

Input translation formulas should always have a reference to the current field's name to work correctly. For example, if you are defining the input translation formula for the Subject field, Subject would normally be referenced in the formula.

Input validation formulas are used to ensure that the information a user enters into a field meets certain conditions. This feature is often used in conjunction with the Notes `@If`, `@Success`, and `@Failure` functions to make sure that a certain field is not left blank. Input validation formulas are evaluated when a document is being saved unless the form has the attribute **A**utomatically refresh fields enabled.

A couple of examples of input validation formulas follow:

```
@If(Subject = "" ; @Failure("You must enter a subject for this document"); @Success)
```

If the Subject field is blank, the user is prompted that a subject is required, and the cursor is moved to the Subject field. The user must enter a value in the Subject field before Notes will enable the user to save the document.

```
@If(Price < 1000; @Success; @Failure("You are not authorized to order items
  costing $ 1000 or more))
```

If the content of the Price field is greater than or equal to 1000, Notes prompts the user with an error message, and then moves the cursor to the offending field, when the user tries to save the document. The user must correct this problem before the document can be saved.

As with input translation formulas, input validation formulas generally have a reference to the current field's name. But they can also reference the values in computed fields and not allow forms to be saved if the value is incorrect (this technique is covered in Chapter 14, "Advanced Techniques").

Computed fields and non-editable Rich Text fields have a different Design Field Formula dialog box, as in Figure 7.9. Only one type of formula is available for computed and non-editable Rich Text fields, the formula that computes the field's value. Writing the formula for a computed field is very similar to writing the default value formula for an Editable field. Formulas are covered in detail in Chapter 9, "Basic Formulas and @Functions."

**FIGURE 7.9.**

*The Design Field Formula dialog box for a computed field.*

## Format... Button

The **F**ormat... button on the Field Definition window is active only for Time, Number, and Keywords data types, and it controls the appearance of data contained in these fields.

If the field's data type is Time, clicking the **F**ormat... button causes the Design Time Format dialog box to appear (see Figure 7.10).

**FIGURE 7.10.**

*The Design Time Format dialog box for Time data types.*

Most of the options on the Design Time Format dialog box are self-explanatory. The most important idea to remember is that in this dialog box you indicate whether your field will display a date only, a time only, or a mixture of a time and date. Additionally, you have the option of displaying fields that contain both time and date values using the words "Today," "Tomorrow," and "Yesterday."

One of the more interesting features of the Notes Time data type is its capability to display Time Zone information and adjust times to a user's local time zone. In applications that are used globally or across multiple time zones, this is a very handy feature that helps users avoid the confusion associated with mentally converting times from distant parts of the world. Of course, each user's time zone must be set correctly (and in the case of a roving person, maintained), but this is one of the unique features of Notes that adds a nice touch to widely distributed applications.

If a field's data type is defined as Number, clicking the **F**ormat... button causes the Design Number Format dialog box to appear (see Figure 7.11).

**FIGURE 7.11.**

*The Design Number Format dialog box for formatting Number data types.*

Notes uses four number formats, along with several optional characteristics, for displaying numbers.

The **G**eneral format is the default for number fields. It displays numbers as they were entered but deletes any zeros to the right of the decimal place. Selecting the **G**eneral format causes the Decimal **P**laces: option to not appear in the Design Number Format dialog box.

The **F**ixed format enables the developer to specify how may zeros to display after the decimal place.

Numbers formatted as **S**cientific are displayed in exponential format, with an E followed by the number of exponent places (for example, 1.00 E2 is the equivalent of 100).

Selecting the **C**urrency format causes all numbers to be displayed with a dollar sign ($) preceding them.

Additionally, several other options are available for formatting numbers: **P**ercentage, **Pa**rentheses on negative numbers, and **Pu**nctuated at thousands.

If a field is defined as a Keywords data type, clicking the **F**ormat... button displays the Design Keyword Format dialog box (see Figure 7.12).

**FIGURE 7.12.**

*The Design Keyword Format dialog box for formatting the appearance of keywords.*

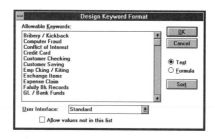

In the Allowable **K**eywords: box, you type the list of words or text strings that will be presented as keyword choices to the user. (Formulas can also be typed here, if the **F**ormula radio button is selected rather than the T**e**xt radio button—more on this topic in a minute.)

Keywords fields can have one of three types of user interfaces: Standard, Radio button, and Check box.

The Standard keyword interface is the Notes default. It offers the user three methods of selecting a value from a list and entering it into the field. The user can press Enter, and a Select Keywords window presents the user with a list of allowable keyword values, as in Figure 7.13.

**FIGURE 7.13.**

*The Select Keywords dialog box.*

Additionally, when a user's cursor is positioned in a keyword field, the user can press the first letter of the keyword choice desired or press the Spacebar to cycle through all the choices. If the Allow Multi-**V**alues option is selected for the field, the user can choose multiple keyword values from the list.

The Radio button user interface displays the keyword list as in several of the fields in Figure 7.14. The user can select only one keyword, even if the Allow Multi-**V**alues option is enabled.

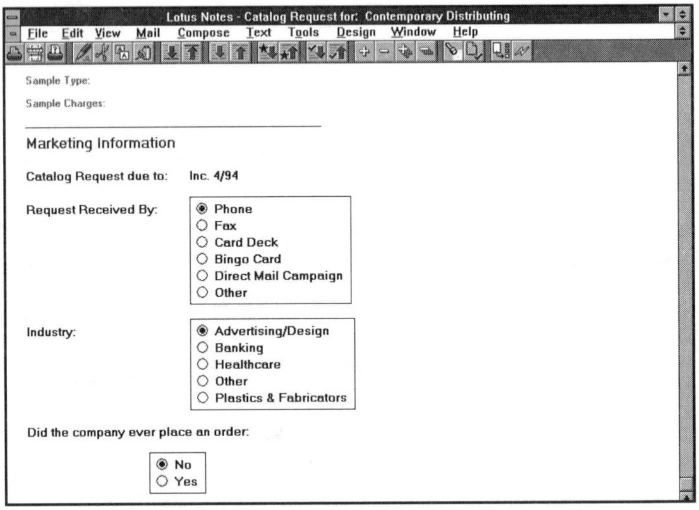

**FIGURE 7.14.**

*Keywords fields, as they display with the Radio button interface.*

The Check box user interface is similar to the Radio button interface, except that it enables users to select multiple keywords, even if the Allow Multi-**V**alues attribute is not selected (see Figure 7.15).

**FIGURE 7.15.**

*A keyword field with the Check box interface, which allows multiple keywords to be selected.*

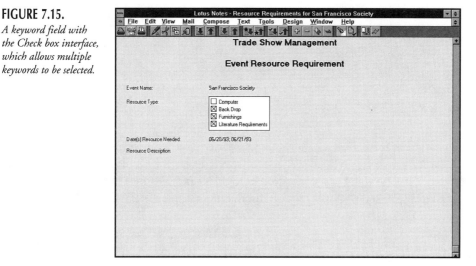

The Allow values not in this list option is available only for Standard interface keywords. If this option is selected, the Select Keywords dialog box presented to the user has an extra entry box at the bottom of the window where the user can type a new keyword (see Figure 7.16).

**FIGURE 7.16.**

*The Select Keywords dialog box, with a place for the user to enter a new keyword.*

> **TIP**
>
> New keywords that a user enters into the **N**ew Keywords: box *are not* dynami-
> cally added to the Keywords dialog box. That is, if a user enters a new keyword
> when composing a document, the next time a user composes a document, the
> new keyword will not appear in the keyword list. For the keyword list to be
> dynamic, the Allowable **K**eywords: list must contain a formula that describes
> how to populate the keyword list that the user sees.

Notes defaults the keyword list to Text, but if a dynamic keyword list is desired, the
developer must select the **F**ormula radio button, as in Figure 7.17. Then a Notes formula can be entered in the Allowable **K**eywords: box. This formula is evaluated each
time the keyword list is created for a user. For example, the formula in Figure 7.16 builds
a keyword list from entries in the first column of the current database's view named
vwLookupByPerson. This technique is discussed in Chapter 14, "Advanced Techniques."

**FIGURE 7.17.**

*Using a formula to*
*define the list of*
*keywords in the Design*
*Keyword Format*
*dialog box.*

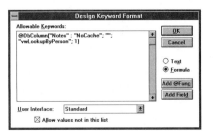

Although Radio button And Check box interfaces are pretty, they present some interesting form layout problems due to their lack of formatting options and the way in which
text wraps around these fields. Many times, however, it's desirable to present a Radio
button or Check box interface to the user who is composing the document, and then
present the user's selections in a Standard, computed when composed text field when
the document is being viewed or printed.

## Separators Button

If the Allow Multi-**V**alues option is selected in the Field Definition dialog box, the **S**eparators... button will be active. Separators are the characters that Notes uses to distinguish the different elements of a multivalued field, for both data entry and display.
Clicking the **S**eparators... button brings up the Design Field Separators dialog box,
shown in Figure 7.18.

**FIGURE 7.18.**
*The Design Field Separators dialog box.*

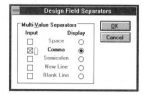

Input Separators are what a user types to signify the end of one value and the beginning of another value. There can be multiple types of Input Separators. For example, a RequiredResources field can have both the comma and the new-line characters defined as separators, which would mean a user could type either

```
LCD Projection Panel, PA System
```

or

```
LCD ProjectionPanel <Enter>
PA System
```

to signify two values.

There can be only one type of display separator. This is the value that is inserted between the values of fields that contain lists when they are displayed on-screen or printed. Figures 7.19, 7.20, and 7.21 show how the PersonsInvolved field can be displayed differently just by selecting the display separator to be comma, new line, or blank line.

**FIGURE 7.19.**
*The results of having the display separator for the PersonsInvolved field set to Comma.*

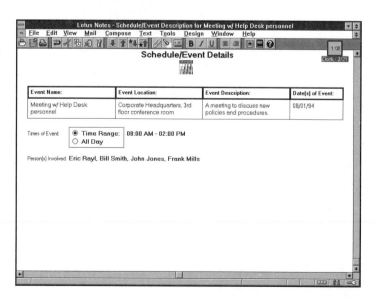

**FIGURE 7.20.**

*The results of having the display separator for the PersonsInvolved field set to New Line.*

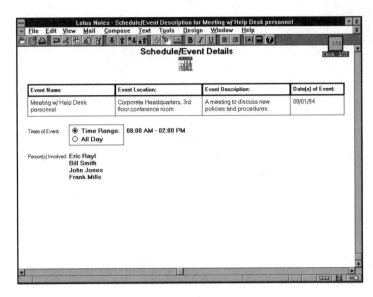

**FIGURE 7.21.**

*The results of having the display separator for the PersonsInvolved field set to Blank Line.*

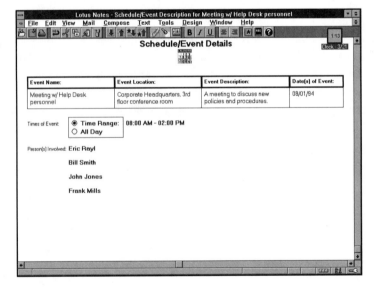

> **TIP**
>
> Select multivalue separators carefully to avoid producing unexpected results, such as having a person's name converted into multivalues because it contains a comma, as in company names such as "Alison, Rayl & Associates." Additionally, use the field's Help description to explain to users what multivalue separator is expected (for instance, "Type in the names of the resources required, separated by commas").

### Security... Button

Clicking the Security... button on the Field Definition window brings up the Design Field Security dialog box, shown in Figure 7.22, which has three options. The first two options, **S**ign this field during mail signing or when saved within a section and **E**nable encryption for this field, are discussed in Chapter 15, "Advanced Security Issues."

**FIGURE 7.22.**
*The Design Field*
*Security dialog box.*

The third option, **U**ser must have at least Editor access to update, is a useful feature that can be used in many simple Notes applications. Under normal circumstances, if a user is listed as an Author in the document's Access Control List, she can edit any document she has composed. In certain types of applications, this type of access might not be desirable. For example, suppose that an application is used to track an employee's ability to achieve self-defined goals and milestones. It might be useful to "lock" the field EstimatedCompletionDate from edits so that the user who composes the document can't go back and edit this field to reflect a slipping goal or deadline.

## Editing, Moving, and Deleting Fields

Editing a field's definition is as simple as double-clicking on the field. Alternatively, with the cursor on the field, you can select Field **D**efinition... on the **D**esign menu, or just press Enter or the Spacebar with the field highlighted.

> **TIP**
>
> If you have the field completely highlighted, that is, its name is in reverse-video, and you press Enter or the Spacebar, you will have overtyped the field, and it will have been replaced with a carriage return or a space. You can easily recover from this mistake by immediately selecting Undo Typing on the Edit menu.

Moving a field is generally accomplished by cutting and pasting. This technique can also be used to copy a field from one form to another, even in different databases.

Deleting a field is as simple as highlighting the field and pressing the Delete key (or selecting the Clear option on the Edit menu when a field is highlighted).

## Examining the Contents of Fields in a Notes Document

One of the most useful Notes application debugging tools is the Notes menu option Document Info..., which appears on the Design menu. Highlight a Notes document, and select the Document Info... menu option to get a listing of all the fields that appear in a particular Notes document, as well as other valuable information such as the field's data type and the actual contents of the field.

> **TIP**
>
> Hiding a document's fields or not having them available on a particular form should not be used as a security feature because any user who has Reader access to the document can use this menu option to see the contents of all the document's unencrypted fields.

# Inheritance

Although this option has been discussed briefly in the previous forms design and field formula sections, it is a very important Notes concept that requires some further elaboration and reemphasis. Basically, inheritance is the process by which the contents of a field in one document are transferred to a field on another Notes document.

A Notes document can inherit data from one and only one document. The way that Notes determines which document to inherit data from is based on what document is either highlighted (in a view) or open when a new document is composed.

One of the most important concepts of inheritance is that this transfer happens only one time, at compose time, and the contents of the field that inherits the data do not change in response to changes in the document that it inherited data from. The inheriting process generally leads itself to having response-type documents inheriting data from main documents, and response-to-responses inheriting data from response documents, but main documents can inherit data from other main documents also.

For data to be inherited into a field, two things must happen: The **I**nherit default field values option must be selected on the form's Design Form Attributes dialog box, and the formula for the field where data is to be inherited to must reference the name of the field on the document from which it is inheriting data.

For instance, in the Personnel/Event Tracking sample application, the Comment form has a (hidden) field called EventName that is used to compute the Comment form's window title. This field is computed when composed, and its formula is simply this:

```
EventName
```

This formula, in combination with the fact that the form attribute **I**nherit default field values is selected, causes the EventName field on the Comment form to inherit the contents of the EventName field on the document that is highlighted or open when the Comment form is composed. (If the highlighted document did not contain the EventName field, the EventName field on the Comment form would be blank.)

The important concept to understand is that if the contents of the EventName field change on the main document, this change is *not* reflected on the Comment form that inherited data from it. If this update is required, a Notes macro must be written that performs the update. Figure 7.23 illustrates the inheritance process.

Inheritance is a concept that eludes many beginning Notes application developers, and when they understand it, they feel extremely limited because the updates to documents don't "cascade" to the documents that previously inherited data from the document. But Notes 3.0 allows plenty of capability for handling this "synchronization" problem programmatically. The example Call Tracking Database that ships with Notes and that is usually found in the EXAMPLES subdirectory has an Organizational Profile form with a Synchronize button that illustrates this technique.

**FIGURE 7.23.**

*The process of a new document inheriting data from an existing document when it is composed.*

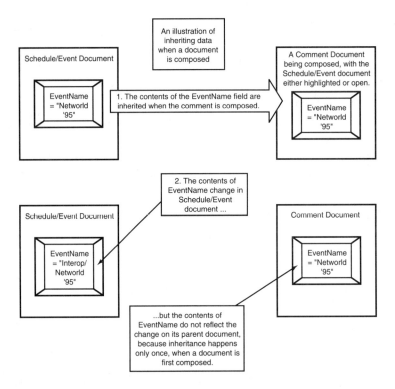

## Summary

Fields on a form are used to both enter data into documents and display data that is stored in a document. Several different fields, on the same or different forms, can be used to format and display the same underlying data in many different ways, as was explained with the Keywords field type.

Next, I'll show you how you can create and use Notes views to display the contents of fields not just from one document, as with a form, but from many documents at the same time.

# 8

## Views: Organizing Notes Documents

# Overview

Designing good Notes views depends a lot on how well the application's forms and workflow were thought out in the design process. If Notes forms and documents are designed to contain the right data, at the necessary point in the workflow, creating Notes views will be the easiest part of the design process.

In many applications, the Notes views are similar to reports and queries in traditional application development systems. Notes views have the power to consolidate information contained in Notes documents by performing mathematics such as totals and averages of numbers contained in Notes documents. Notes views can be categorized, and collapsed and expanded, so that a user can "drill down" by double-clicking the mouse to see as much detail as necessary. Additionally, because Notes views print exactly as they display on-screen, management reports targeting specific regions, products, or items can easily be produced by end users. Using views, combined with the view expand/collapse options on the Notes **View** menu, users can create custom reports and print or export views as they appear on-screen.

Good view design depends on understanding what data to display to help users use that application, and adequately exploiting the Notes response hierarchy when designing the forms.

In this section, the view design examples will be taken from the Personnel/Event Tracking sample application. You might want to have this database open so that you can try some of the examples and experiment with the views as you read this chapter.

# Creating and Editing Views

Designing and editing views is very easy to do, particularly if you have all the information you need in the all the right documents (more on this architectural issue in Chapter 12, "Notes Application Architectures"). Often, views can be created from existing views in a database simply by rearranging the columns, which makes view design rapid.

## The Design New View Dialog Box

To start designing a new view, select **Views...** on the Notes **Design** menu. This selection causes the Design Views dialog box to appear, which lists the names of any views that already exist in the database, as in Figure 8.1.

**FIGURE 8.1.**

*A database's Design
Views dialog box.*

Highlighting an existing view and clicking the **E**dit button opens an existing view in design mode, and the New **C**opy button makes a copy of an existing view and opens it in design mode. The **N**ew button opens a new view in design mode.

**TIP**

Many times, particularly when modifying Notes applications that you are not very familiar with or when creating a lot of similar views, you will be able to design a new view quicker by starting with an existing view. You can select the New **C**opy option and then move the columns around and adjust the view selection formula as necessary.

The **C**lear button deletes the view from the database. The view to be cleared cannot be the active view, and the deletion cannot be undone. When an existing view is highlighted and the **I**nfo... button is clicked, the Design Information window appears with information as to when the view was created, when it was last modified, the name of the person who last modified it, and, if the view is a design element of a template, the name of the design template (see Figure 8.2).

**FIGURE 8.2.**

*A view's Design
Information dialog box.*

**C**opy and **P**aste buttons are available on the Design Views window so that you can move a view's design between databases.

## Adding, Editing, and Deleting Columns

To add a new column to a view that is open in design mode, select **New Column...** from the **D**esign menu (you can also double-click on any undefined area of the view's top border). If you have an existing column highlighted when you select **New Column...**, the new column is inserted to the left of the existing column. Rearranging columns is accomplished by using the Cu**t**, **C**opy, and **P**aste commands on the **E**dit menu, and columns can be copied between different views in the same or a different database. Deleting columns is accomplished by using the C**l**ear command on the **E**dit menu.

---

**TIP**

After you make design changes to a view, the yellow question-mark (?) icon appears in the upper-left corner of the view, or question marks appear in the columns, as shown in Figure 8.3. Click the question-mark icon, select the Refre**s**h option on the **V**iew menu, or press F9 to refresh the view and see the results of your changes.

---

**FIGURE 8.3.**

*The ? icon in the upper-left corner of the view indicates that the view needs to be refreshed (clicking the icon refreshes the view).*

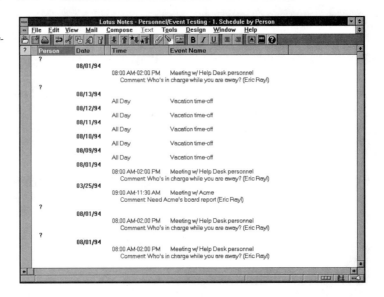

## The Design Column Definition Dialog Box

When New **C**olumn... is selected on the **D**esign menu, or when an existing column header or a blank area of the view header is double-clicked on, the Design Column Definition window opens (see Figure 8.4). The options available in this window are detailed in the following text.

**FIGURE 8.4.**

*The Design Column Definition dialog box.*

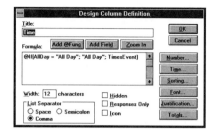

## Title

The **T**itle: box shows the static text that appears at the top of the column.

## Formula

Many times, a column's formula is simply the name of a field in a document. The formula can also be complex, with a lot of @If statements that cause different types of information to be displayed depending on the type of document or the form it was created with, or the column's contents will change based on the values of the fields within the documents.

For example, look at the formula for the Time column in either view in the Personnel/Schedule tracking sample database (see Figure 8.4). What this formula literally says is, "If the document's field called AllDay contains the string 'All Day', display 'All Day' in the column; otherwise, display the contents of the TimesEvent field."

## Width

The value given in the **W**idth: box is approximately the width in characters that a column is, but due to proportional fonts and the capability to change font sizes for a column, it is really only a reference or an index. The column width can also be set with the mouse by dragging the column's border to the desired new position.

## Hidden

Hidden columns are useful for forcing a desired sorting. For example, you might want to have a view in an event-tracking application that has a column listing the text of the event's month, as in January, February, March, and so on. But a column with these values would, when sorted, be listed alphabetically—not very natural. What you could do is put a hidden column with the formula @Month(DatesEvent) to the left of the text column. When sorted, this hidden column would cause the text columns to sort correctly.

## Responses Only

If the **R**esponses Only check box is selected on the Design Column Definition window, only data from Response (or Response-to-response) type documents appears in the column. A view can have only one of these types of columns (Notes enables you to select more than one, but data appears only in the leftmost column with this attribute). Additionally, for this option to have any effect, the No Response **H**ierarchy option cannot be selected.

---

### TIP

This option is a little tricky to understand at first. Some examples of how to use this option to easily create and manage views that use Notes response hierarchy are included in the section "The Keys to Good Views" later in this chapter.

---

## Icon

Notes can display one of five different icons in a column based on the results of the column's formula. The column's formula should return an integer between 1 and 5, and based on the value, one of five icons is displayed (see Figure 8.5).

**FIGURE 8.5.**

*Using an Icon column type. Notice the contents Icon column and the IconValue column in the background.*

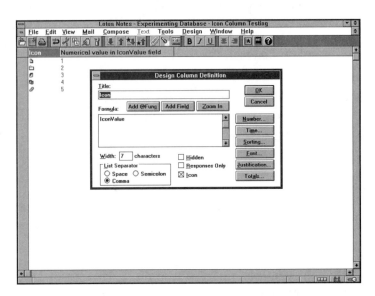

These icons can represent anything you choose. Lotus suggests using the following con-
notations:

1. Document
2. Folder
3. Person
4. Group
5. Attachment

## List Separator

If a column's formula returns a Notes multivalue list, the **List** Separator setting determines how the values will be separated when displayed in the column. Notice that there
is not a new-line separator option; if you want a separate row for each element of the
multivalue list, you sort and categorize the column using the **S**orting... button, discussed
shortly.

## Number... and Time... Buttons

Columns can format the way numerical and time/date data returned by column formulas is displayed. The Design Number Format and the Design Time Format dialog
boxes are the same as those for setting a field's format on a form.

The **N**umber... and **Ti**me... buttons are always active because Notes in general does not
know what data type a given column formula will return, but their settings have no effect
on data that is not of the correct data type.

## Sorting... Button

Clicking the **S**orting... button opens the Design Column Sort window (see Figure 8.6), which enables you to determine whether the column should be sorted and in which direction (ascending or descending).

**FIGURE 8.6.**

*The Design Column Sort dialog box.*

Additionally, the sorting dialog box enables you to **C**ategorize the column (you must first select to **S**ort the column in order to **C**ategorize it). This is the powerful Notes feature that enables you to create well-organized, uncluttered views that summarize data and enable users to drill-down to the details by double-clicking or pressing the Enter key when a category is highlighted in a view.

Categorized columns cause a "category" to be created for each unique value that is returned by the column's formula and cause all the corresponding documents to appear beneath the category label. Additionally, if a column formula returns a multivalue list of data, one category is created for each unique value in the list, which makes the same document appear in multiple categories within the view.

For example, in the Personnel/Event Tracking sample database, the Person column in the 1. Schedule by Person view is categorized (see Figure 8.7). Notice that the same Event document, Meeting w/ Help Desk personnel, appears in four categories, because the PersonsInvolved field for that document is a multivalue list containing four names. If the Person column were not categorized, the view would appear as in Figure 8.8 (the Person column was widened to display the complete contents of the PersonsInvolved field).

**FIGURE 8.7.**
*A view with the first column categorized.*

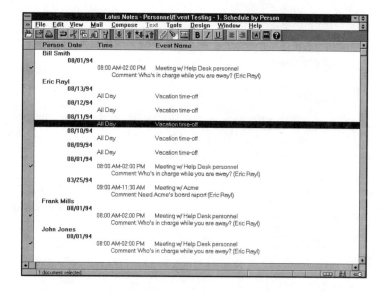

**FIGURE 8.8.**
*The same view as in Figure 8.7, but with the first column just sorted, not categorized.*

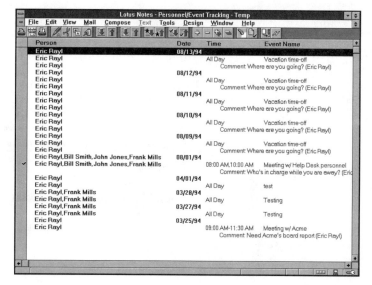

## Font... Button

Clicking the **F**ont... button opens the Font dialog box, where fonts, point sizes, and attributes such as bold, underline, and color can be selected for the column's data. Unfortunately, there is no way to format the column's title font.

## Justification... Button

Clicking this button enables you to change the default justification of a column from Left to either Centered or Right.

## Totals... Button

If a column contains numerical data, it can be mathematically manipulated using the Design Column Totals dialog box (see Figure 8.9), which is accessed by clicking the Totals... button on the Design Column Definition window.

**FIGURE 8.9.**

*The Design Column
Totals dialog box.*

Performing math at the view level is as easy as selecting the kind of math that you want to perform, Total, Averages or Percentages, from the Design Column Totals dialog box. Using this feature, views such as those in Figures 8.10 and 8.11 can be designed.

Figure 8.10 is a view from a crime-tracking system that computes percentages for the closed cases by how the criminal activity was discovered. Additionally, this view calculates gross and net loss totals for the period.

**FIGURE 8.10.**

*A view that calculates
totals and percentages.*

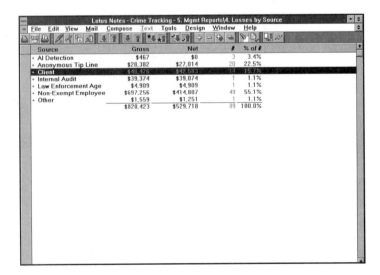

Figure 8.11 is a view from a company's telemarketing application that shows not only how totals are calculated but how they are "rolled up" to each higher category level, which enables the user to display or hide as much detail as desired by double-clicking on the categorized columns. For example, on 02/23/94, there were 329 catalog requests from potential customers, 99 of which were phone requests from retail ("no discount") customers, and Terri Patrick was responsible for processing 27 of those requests.

**FIGURE 8.11.**

*Another example of using column totals, along with categorized columns, in a view.*

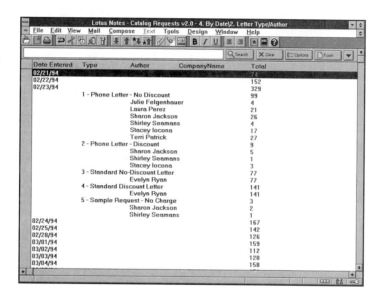

For more examples of using mathematics in views, see the several views in both the Inquiry Tracking and the Bug Tracking applications that use the Design Column Totals options.

## The Design Selection Formula Dialog Box

When a view is open in design mode, the **S**election Formula... option is available on the **D**esign menu. Selection formulas are special Notes formulas that determine what documents to display in a given view. The view's selection formula determines which documents will appear in a given view. Generally, a selection formula includes (or excludes) documents based on what form they were created with, and additionally can include documents that meet only certain criteria. For example, in the view from the investigation tracking database (see Figure 8.10), the selection criteria selected only closed-case documents that were closed within a given period.

When you create a view, the default selection formula is the function SELECT @All, which allows all documents in the database to appear in the view. In the simple Personnel/Event Scheduling sample application, both views use the selection formula SELECT @All.

To see how a selection formula works in the context of the Personnel/Event Tracking sample database, try creating a view that displays only the current month's events, along with their associated Comment forms. Before trying this example, you should compose an Appointment/Event document with an event date within the current month. Also compose a Comment document as a response to the current month's event.

Now make a new copy of the 2. Schedule by Date/Person view by opening the database and selecting **Views...** on the **D**esign menu and then selecting the view and clicking the New **C**opy button.

Now select **S**election Formula... from the **D**esign menu. Notice that the Design Selection Formula dialog box contains the formula SELECT @All. Change this formula to read

SELECT @Month(@Today) = @Month(DatesEvent)

as in Figure 8.12. Then click **OK** to save the formula. The view needs to be refreshed to reflect its new selection formula, as indicated by the yellow question-mark refresh indicator in the upper-left corner of the view. Either click on the question mark or select Refres**h** from the **V**iew menu. The view should now display only Schedule/Event documents that fit the selection formula and should look similar to Figure 8.13. Note that views with time-sensitive selection formulas—that is, that compare values to @Today and @Now—will always have the refresh question mark active because the time is constantly changing.

**FIGURE 8.12.**

*The design selection formula for a view.*

**FIGURE 8.13.**

*A view using the selection formula shown in Figure 8.12 (assuming that @Today returned a date in the month of March).*

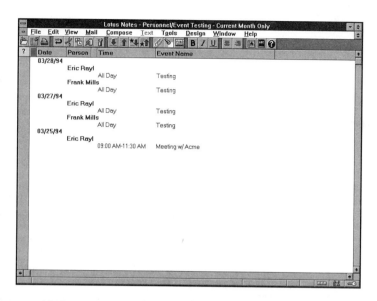

---

**TIP**

On view selection formulas, you never have to type the initial SELECT keyword because Notes automatically inserts it for you when you save the formula. In other words, you could just type

```
@Month(DatesEvent) = @Month(@Today)
```

in the preceding example.

---

The literal interpretation of this statement is to "display all documents in which the value of the month of the document's DatesEvent field is equal to the value of today's month.

Now, however, no Comment forms appear in this view. This is because the Comment form does not contain the field DatesEvent, and therefore its month will never be equal to the value of today's month.

To fix this omission, you need to modify the selection formula to this formula:

```
SELECT @Month(DatesEvent) = @Month(@Today) ¦ Form = "frmComment".
```

Notice that because the view uses a response hierarchy, the only Comment documents (responses) that will appear in the view are those with a corresponding Schedule/Event document. This key point is discussed further in the "Understanding Response Hierarchy in Views" section of this chapter.

## The Design View Attributes Dialog Box

When designing a view, you can access the Design View Attributes dialog box (see Figure 8.14) by selecting the View **A**ttributes... option on the **D**esign menu.

**FIGURE 8.14.**

*The Design View Attributes dialog box.*

This is where some of the key design characteristics of the view are selected, as outlined in the following text.

### Name

The view's name is what appears on the user's **V**iew menu when he is using the application. Many times, the name is also referenced in functions such as `@DbColumn` and `@DbLookup`, and in commands such as `@Command([OpenView])`. It is important that the name be descriptive to the user, sort correctly on the menu, yet be easy to reference in formulas.

My guidelines on naming a view are very similar to those for naming a form (or a macro):

■ It's a good habit to always use synonyms when naming views, even if you are not sure you will ever need to use the view for lookup purposes. Remember, the value to the far left of the | symbol in a view name is what appears on the menu, and the value to the far right of the | is what formulas should use to reference the view. For example, the name of the first view in the Personnel/ Event Tracking database is 1. Schedule by Person | vwLookupByPerson.

■ Using descriptive synonyms helps make your formulas much more understandable and "self-documenting." Don't be afraid of using long names rather than heavily abbreviated names.

■ Make good use of the capability to build "cascading" view menus using the \ symbol. The part of the view name to the right of the \ shows up as a submenu, as in Figure 8.15. Notes allows up to nine views on the menu before the **O**ther... option appears on the bottom of the **V**iew menu. When possible, arrange your views so that you never run into this situation because it can be confusing for users (for instance, look at the Other view dialog box for an investigation tracking system in Figure 8.16).

■ Begin view names and submenu names with numerals. This method enables you to enforce how the views are sorted on the menu, and provides easy-to-use accelerator keys for users.

**FIGURE 8.15.**

*A cascading View menu.*

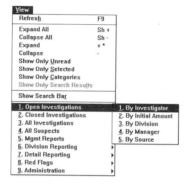

**FIGURE 8.16.**

*The Other view dialog box.*

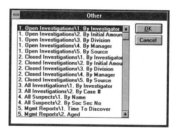

---

**TIP**

If you enclose a view's name in parentheses, such as (vwLookupByDate), you can hide it from appearing on the **V**iew menu. Note that this is not a security feature but is useful for hiding views that are used only for lookups and macros.

## Type

Most views are designed to be used by more than one person, and therefore their type is shared. Private views are not accessible by other users. Shared, private on first use views appear on the **V**iew menu for all users, but the first time a user accesses the view, it becomes private.

The biggest use for private views is for "power users" and database administrators to be able to create their own customized views that do not appear on the **V**iew menu.

> **TIP**
>
> It is important to remember that all users who have at least Reader-level access to a database can create their own private views. Therefore, using hidden views is not a security feature.

Shared, private on first use views are useful for creating views that have selection formulas based on a user's name (using the @UserName function). For example, you could create a view in the Personnel/Event Tracking database to track only the current user's schedule, a My Schedule view. You would want this view to be shared, private on first use so that one user's indexing information is not overwritten by the next user who accesses the view.

## Options

The **D**efault View option sets the view that the database defaults to the first time the database is opened. There can be only one Default View per database, and you should select a view that presents the broadest overall view to the new user.

The No Response **H**ierarchy option causes Notes to effectively treat all documents as main-type documents. Examples of how and when to use this option are explained in the "Understanding Response Hierarchy in Views" section later in this chapter.

## Categories... Button

Clicking this button on the Design View Attributes window causes the Categories window to appear (see Figure 8.17), with the choices Initially **E**xpanded and Initially Collapsed. Be aware that there are some inconsistencies with how these two options work, especially from the Windows to the Macintosh platform. With the Initially **C**ollapsed setting, sometimes Notes "remembers" exactly which categories a user had expanded and opens the view exactly as the user had it set, and sometimes it opens the view completely collapsed. My advice is don't get too excited about this feature, and just live with it.

**FIGURE 8.17.**
*The Categories dialog box.*

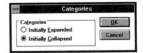

## Unread Marks... Button

Clicking this button on the Design View Attributes window causes the Unread Marks dialog box to appear (see Figure 8.18). Unread Marks are the little stars that appear next to documents that a particular user has not opened, and Notes tracks them on a per-user basis.

**FIGURE 8.18.**

*The Unread Marks
dialog box.*

If you select the **U**nread Documents Only option, views need to be fully expanded for a user to see the actual unread mark. That is, if the view is collapsed, the unread mark will not be visible. The option **C**ompute and Display at All Levels of View places unread marks next to collapsed categories, indicating that underneath that category is at least one unread document. Compare Figure 8.19, in which **U**nread Documents Only was selected, with Figure 8.20, in which **C**ompute and Display at All Levels of View was selected.

**FIGURE 8.19.**

*A view showing
documents marked
as unread.*

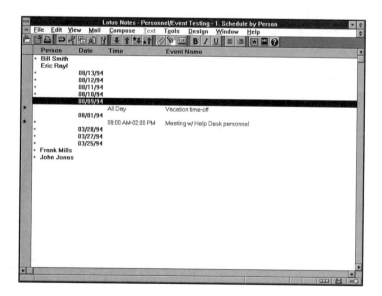

**FIGURE 8.20.**

*A view showing documents and collapsed categories as unread.*

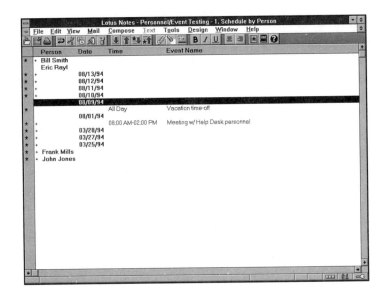

In many applications, unread marks are very helpful if users understand how to use them correctly. But some applications and views will not benefit from the use of unread marks, and the marks will only clutter up the screen.

## Colors... Button

Clicking this button on the Design View Attributes window causes the View Colors window to appear (see Figure 8.21). As with the color choices for forms, the color choices are not very exciting, but with some imagination, some interesting schemes can be created. Other than for documents that are unread, Notes does not enable developers to set the color of documents based on specified conditions.

**FIGURE 8.21.**

*The View Colors dialog box.*

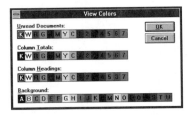

## Read Access... Button

The Read Access... button opens the Read Access Control List window, shown in Figure 8.22. If a user is not listed among the users, groups, or roles in the Only the following users: box, the view does not appear on the user's menu. This option is discussed in more detail in Chapter 15, "Advanced Security Issues."

**FIGURE 8.22.**
*The Read Access
Control List dialog box.*

## Index Options... Button

Clicking this button on the Design View Attributes window causes the Index Options window to appear (see Figure 8.23). In most instances, you will leave the indexing set at the defaults, **A**utomatic refresh frequency and **N**ever discard the index.

Only with databases and views that don't change very frequently should you consider changing this option, or in certain instances when server performance or disk space usage becomes an issue. For example, for infrequently used views in large databases, you might want to use the Discard Index After **e**ach use option, particularly when using Private Views, because the index is then stored locally.

**FIGURE 8.23.**
*The Index Options
dialog box for a view.*

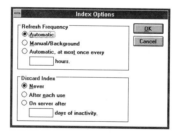

## Form Formula

Normally, when a user opens a document in a view, the form that the document is displayed with is determined according to the following rules:

■ The value in the document's Form field is used.

■ If the document has the form stored in it (and no Form field), the document is displayed with the form that is stored in the document.

■ The database's default form is used if the document does not have a form stored in it and does not have a Form field or if Notes can't find a form in the database with the name referenced by the Form field.

In certain applications, you might want to compose a document with one form and then have users view it with another form. One way to accomplish this is to use a view's form formula. The form formula overrides this form selection criteria and displays the document with the form that is specified by the formula. Form formulas *do not* override forms that have the form stored in them; you must set the document's Form variable in order to do that.

When writing form formulas, you need to remember that they must always be written using the @If function, as in this formula:

```
@If(@DbManager = @UserName; "frmManager"; "frmCaseAssignment")
```

This formula translates, "If the current user is listed as the database's manager, load the document using the frmManager form; otherwise, load the document with the frmCaseAssignment form."

> **TIP**
>
> When testing form formulas, you must first exit the view and then return to it for the form formula to take effect.

# The Keys to Good Views

Views are not hard to create, but if you understand the following three concepts, you'll be able to design good views quickly.

## Understanding Response Hierarchy in Views

I'm a strong believer that you must understand how Notes creates and uses a response hierarchy in order to create powerful Notes applications. Although you will on many occasions create views that need to have the No Response **H**ierarchy option selected on the Design View Attributes window, in most of your applications and views, you will depend on this response hierarchy.

A response hierarchy is created between two documents when either a Response or a Response to a response type of document is composed. The document that is highlighted (or open) when the document is composed becomes the "parent" document.

Views that capitalize on this response hierarchy, in conjunction with using a column with the **R**esponses Only attribute set, will make it easy for you to design and maintain Notes applications, particularly ones with many forms.

To get a better idea of how the response hierarchy works, you should experiment with the views in the Personnel Tracking/Scheduling sample application. Make a new copy of the view 1. Schedule by Person to play with. While in design mode, look at the definition for each of the columns.

The fourth column, the narrow one between the Date and Time columns, is the key (see Figure 8.24). Notice that it has **R**esponses Only selected in its definition. As mentioned earlier, a view can have only one **R**esponses Only column, but whatever data the column's formula determines to display will display directly under the document's parent document, without being limited by the width of the column. (In Figure 8.24, the Comment's Subject extends much wider than the one-character width of the column.)

**FIGURE 8.24.**

*The Responses Only column responsible for displaying the text from the Comment documents.*

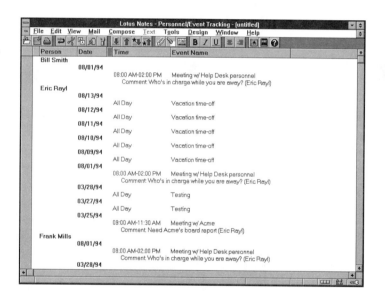

Now deselect the **R**esponses Only attribute of the fourth column, and refresh the view. Figure 8.25 shows the results (I've widened the fourth column so that you can understand what is happening). Notice that the indenting of the response document under the main Event document is now gone, and there is data in the fourth column now for the Event forms because they also contain a field called Subject. Notice also that data from the subject document is now appearing in the Event Name column because the Comment documents contain this field.

**FIGURE 8.25.**

*The same view as in Figure 8.24, but with the Responses Only attribute deselected for the highlighted column.*

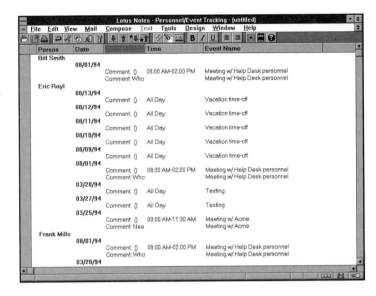

What many beginning Notes developers do when trying to create a view that looks like Figure 8.24 is try to simulate response hierarchy by using hard-to-maintain, complicated formulas in view columns. For instance, they might create a view that looks similar to Figure 8.26 by having formulas for the Time and EventName like those in Figure 8.27 and Figure 8.28.

**FIGURE 8.26.**

*A view in which the formula for the Time column is "simulating" a response hierarchy.*

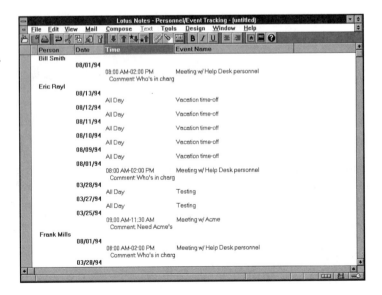

**FIGURE 8.27.**

*The formula for the Time column in Figure 8.26.*

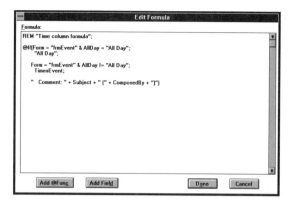

**FIGURE 8.28.**

*The formula for the Event Name column.*

Don't worry if the formulas don't make sense to you yet. Just understand that using this design approach causes formulas to get very complex as the number of forms for a database increases and that these formulas will need to be changed as new forms are added to the database (something that is very common with Notes applications). Also, notice that now the Comment text is being truncated at the width of the column, and you cannot change the font attributes of response documents independently of main documents.

Another advantage of using Notes response hierarchy is that response documents will not appear in views unless their parent documents also meet the criteria established in the view selection formula. In the section "The Design Selection Formula Dialog Box" earlier in this chapter, you saw how to easily create a view of only the current month's Events by changing the selection formula to this:

```
SELECT @Month(DatesEvent) = @Month(@Today) ¦ Form = "frmComment".
```

If you were not using response hierarchy in this view, you would have a mess because then you would need to inherit the DatesEvent field down to the Comment form so that you could filter out all comments that did not have the correct EventDate. And if the EventDate was changed in the parent document, this would not be reflected in the Comment document—Comment forms could start appearing in the view with no corresponding Event document.

There are some times when you need to bypass Notes response hierarchy, especially when you need views that contain only response documents. To see how this works, you should create a new view in the Personnel/Event Tracking database. Edit the default column's definition to have Subject as its title. Enter Subject into the **Formula:** box, and then click **OK**.

Next, enter the following formula as the view's selection formula:

```
SELECT Form = "frmComment"
```

Now click the **OK** button and then refresh the view. Notice that no documents appear. This is because the view is using a response hierarchy, and all the main documents were filtered out by the selection formula.

To allow the Comment forms to appear in the view, select the View **A**ttributes... option on the **D**esign menu, and check the No Response **H**ierarchy box. Then click **OK** and refresh the view. The column should now contain the contents of the Subject fields of all of your Comment documents.

Another situation in which you'll want to "turn off" the response hierarchy is when you need to perform a total of numbers contained in both main and response documents. Normally, the Total attribute for a column picks up data only from main documents.

A more real-world example of where No Response **H**ierarchy views are useful is the Suspect view in a Tracking application. Because there can be one or many suspects for a given case, there could be a suspect form that is a response to a main case document. Most of the views in the application would use a response hierarchy, but there should also be a view of only the suspect documents, sorted by last name, that would enable users to easily find out whether a suspect was involved in any other cases. This "suspect only" view would have to have the No Response **H**ierarchy attribute set.

There are certain applications that might have to be designed with total disregard for Notes response hierarchy. These are generally applications in which the response documents are likely to be moved from one parent document to another.

## Using Responses Only Columns

The **R**esponses Only attribute on the Design Column Definition window might seem restrictive at first, but in most instances, the benefits it gives a Notes application developer far outweigh its limitations.

Responses Only columns enable you as a developer to easily manage many different response documents in one application, and they always have Responses and Response to responses nested neatly under each other.

The main limitation of a Responses Only column is that data for response documents cannot be displayed in any column to the right of the Responses Only column. What this means is that you and your users might have to adapt to seeing data in columns to the *left* of the Responses Only column.

To see what I mean, look at Figure 8.29. This is a view in a complex audit management database that has more than 35 forms. In this figure, "Objectives" are main documents, and the numbered "Tests" (such as "#50: Petty Cash Shortages") are responses to the Objectives. Each Objective and Test document has a Status field (Not Ready For Approval, Ready For Approval, or Approved). To display the contents of the Status field in a neat column, I moved the column to the right of the Responses Only column. The users initially didn't like this approach because their paper-based status reports had this column on the right side of the paper, but after they used the application for a while, it was no problem. As I have said previously, designing Notes applications sometimes requires you to look at problems and solutions differently than you are used to.

**FIGURE 8.29.**

*A view that displays information from Response type documents in a column before the Responses Only column.*

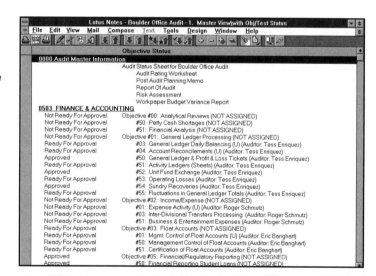

## The Importance of the Contents of the First Column

The contents of the first column of a view are very important. Many beginning users (and developers) do not realize that when you are in a view, you can just start typing and Notes moves the cursor to the first document (or category) whose first-column data matches the text you typed. This is a very efficient way to search for pertinent documents.

For example, at a major corporation that I have consulted for, a dummy Notes "Address Book" contained phone and address information for all of its 100,000-plus employees. A user that was in the view in which the first column contained the field LastName could just begin typing a person's last name, and Notes would move the cursor to the nearest record, usually in under five seconds. This method is much more efficient than trying to use the **F**ind... option on the **E**dit menu or using a Full Text Search query.

Your application should have a view for all of an application's most commonly needed information. This approach makes your users much happier in the long run.

Note that first columns in views that contain view statistical functions, such as @DocNumber and @IsExpandable, do not count as the "first column."

You might also want to consider how the **C**ategorize... option works on the Notes **T**ools menu. If you haven't tried this menu option, try it now. First, open your mail database, and change to the Categorized view. Now with a document highlighted, select the **C**ategorize... menu option on the **T**ools menu. The Categorize dialog box (see Figure 8.30) should appear, with a list of any categories that you have previously assigned mail to.

**FIGURE 8.30.**

*The Categorize dialog box.*

The **C**ategorize... menu option works in any application. The only restriction is that the user must be in a view in which the first column has this formula:

```
Categories
```

In practice, I use this feature only in discussion and document management-type applications in which the notion of a "category" is well-defined. In large applications, you might have 30 or 40 "categorized" views. There is usually no clear-cut reason to have one of the views (the one that has the Categories field first) use the **C**ategorize... menu option, whereas to "recategorize" a document in the other 29-plus views, the user has to take a different approach, such as editing a field or running a macro.

# Summary

Notes views are roughly equivalent to a query in traditional database systems. In a traditional DBMS, a pseudo-query such as

```
"Show me all of the bug reports where Status = Open, State = TBD,
  and AssignedTo = Unassigned"
```

could easily be handled by a collapsed Notes view, sorted and categorized first by Status, then by State, and finally by AssignedTo. To execute the preceding query, the user simply has to double-click on the word "Open" in the first column, then double-click on "TBD" in the now-expanded second column, and finally double-click on "Unassigned" in the third column to see all the bug reports that meet the given criteria.

Notes view design is actually one of the quicker parts of the application design process. If the database was designed correctly in the first place, with all the necessary fields available in the correct documents, it should be an easy process to design views that will be intuitive for users.

If you try to use the Notes response hierarchy as much as possible, combined with the Responses Only type of columns, you will have views that will be easy to maintain. Remember, Notes applications are (or should be) very dynamic. Users will always request new forms or views for one reason or another, and as a developer you don't want to have to change the column definitions in all of your views every time you add or change a form.

Next, I will show you how to write basic Notes formulas that not only will control what data appears in fields and columns but also can be used in views' selection formulas.

# 9

## Basic Formulas and @Functions

# Overview

The main building block of Notes formulas are @Functions and @Commands. This @ notation was borrowed from the macro language found in Lotus 1-2-3, but the functions and commands found in Notes enable an application developer to develop much more robust applications, mainly because of the rich Notes environment, with its forms, views, integrated mail engine, security, and so forth.

In this chapter, you'll learn how to get started writing Notes formulas. Notes formulas are the equivalent of "code" in other application development languages. Although the formulas might look crude and unrefined in comparison to modules in a structured programming language, Notes formulas can accomplish many powerful tasks, and they can be written very quickly.

The most commonly used @Functions will be described, along with examples of how and where to use these functions. The more complex @Functions, such as `@DbLookup`, `@DbColumn`, and `@MailSend`, as well as the @Commands, are covered later in Chapter 14, "Advanced Techniques."

At the end of this chapter, I'll also show you an important formula example that will help you further understand the differences between forms, fields, and the underlying document or "note." I stressed this very important concept in Chapter 6, "Forms: Creating Data-Entry and Display Windows," but I think that it can be better demonstrated with the use of field and form formulas.

After reading this chapter (and hopefully trying some of the examples), you should be ready for the next chapter, where you will learn how to write macros to control your Notes applications.

# Types of Formulas

In fthe Notes application development environment, formulas are used in eight basic areas:

■ Field formulas are used to calculate the value of a field within a form (or document) and to translate and validate the contents of fields.

■ View selection formulas are used to determine which documents to display in a view.

■ View column formulas are used to determine what data is displayed in a particular column in a view.

■ Form formulas are used in views to determine what form to use for entering and displaying data in documents.

■ Macros (including buttons) can add, change, or delete values in existing documents, or perform actions such as creating new documents.

■ Selective replication formulas determine which documents of a database should be replicated based on the criteria specified in the formula.

■ Window title formulas determine what should be displayed in a form's title bar.

■ Popup formulas determine what is displayed within a popup window when a user clicks on the popup.

# Writing Basic Formulas

No matter what type of Notes formula you are writing, the place where you type the formula, the "formula dialog box," has some common features and behavior that should be explained.

First, no matter what type of formula you are writing (computed field formula, view selection formula, macro, and so forth), the formula dialog box always has three buttons: Add @Fun**c**, Add Fiel**d**, and **Z**oom In, as in Figure 9.1 Some types of formula boxes, such as the Insert Button dialog box, have an Add Co**m**mand button also, as in Figure 9.2.

**FIGURE 9.1.**

*The Design Field
Formula dialog box.*

**FIGURE 9.2.**

*The Insert Button
dialog box, with its
additional Add
Command button.*

The Add @Fun**c** button causes the Paste Function listbox of the @Functions to display, along with a button that enables you to paste the @Function into the current formula dialog box (see Figure 9.3).

**FIGURE 9.3.**

*The Paste Function dialog box, which is accessed via the Add @Func button on any Notes formula dialog box.*

Although this feature is handy and helps avoid typos and spelling errors, the real benefit is that you can get online help on a given function just by highlighting it and pressing the F1 key.

---

**TIP**

I have found that with complex functions that require many arguments, I copy and paste the function right from the help description rather than from the Paste Function dialog box. This is because the formula that I paste in from the help window contains placeholders for each of the function's arguments, which I can just edit to suit my formula, whereas if you paste a function from the Paste Function window, you get only the function followed by open and close parentheses.

For example, if I need to use the @DbLookup function, I click the Add @Func button, highlight @DbLookup in the Paste Function window, and press F1 for help. Then I highlight the first line of the function's syntax (see Figure 9.4); for example:

```
@DbLookup("class":"NoCache";"database";"view";"key";"field"_or_column)
```

I use the keyboard copy command (Ctrl+C or Ctrl+Ins). Next, I press Esc twice to return to the formula window, then paste in the function with its syntax using the keyboard paste shortcut (Ctrl+V or Shift+Ins). This method helps me eliminate errors that are hard to debug when I omit one of a function's required parameters by mistake.

**FIGURE 9.4.**

*Using "copy and paste" to paste a function and its arguments into a Notes formula using the keyboard shortcuts.*

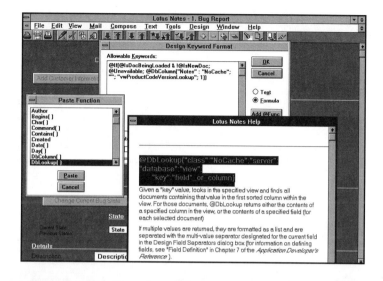

The Add Field button causes the Paste Field dialog box (Figure 9.5) to appear, which contains a list of all the field names you have used in your Notes application.

**FIGURE 9.5.**

*The Paste Field dialog box lists an application's field names and enables you to paste a name into a formula.*

**TIP**

One thing to remember is that the Paste Field window does not contain the names of fields you just defined on a form; you must save the form first before Notes updates its listing of fields in the application. Also, the Paste Field window *does* contain the names of fields you have used previously but deleted from all of your forms. To stop these old form names from appearing, you must make sure that no document contains the field (using the `@Unavailable` function in a macro—see the macro chapter), then compact the database using the Compact option on the **File|Database** menu.

Clicking the **Z**oom In button causes the formula window to expand in size, which is useful when you're writing lengthy, complex macros (compare Figure 9.6 with Figure 9.7).

**FIGURE 9.6.**

*Formulas in macros automatically wrap within the Edit Macro Formula window.*

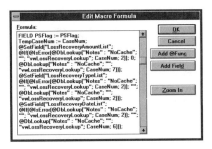

**FIGURE 9.7.**

*Clicking the Zoom In button causes the formula window to be expanded, making formulas easier to read and edit.*

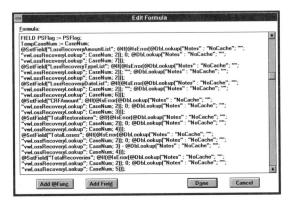

# Formula Syntax

The semicolon symbol plays an important role in Notes formulas. It is used not only to separate arguments within a Notes function, but also to separate functions and statements within a formula. For example, the formula

```
@SetField("ComposedBy"; "Eric Rayl);
@SetField("DateComposed"; @Today)
```

contains two @Functions, separated by a semicolon.

Functions and field names are not case sensitive, but I recommend that you use the "proper case" convention when specifying field, form, and view names in your formulas, which helps make the formulas more readable. Notes automatically converts functions in your formula to "proper case" and capitalizes keywords in an attempt to make formulas look more consistent and easy to read.

Manually formatting Notes functions so that they are easily readable is almost impossible, especially with complex formulas. When you're writing Notes functions, spacing and carriage returns do not matter because Notes strips out extra spaces (and adds spaces between field names, functions, and operators) as needed. Although this is a nice feature, it also is very unnerving because it is impossible to retain any "structure" in your formula. For example, the formula in Figure 9.8 is formatted and easily readable. But the first time the formula is saved, Notes does its thing and the formula becomes the rather unintelligible mess in Figure 9.9.

**FIGURE 9.8.**

*A manually formatted formula before it is saved for the first time.*

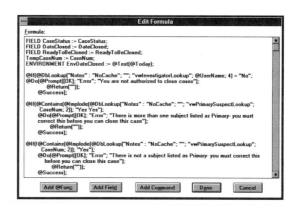

**FIGURE 9.9.**

*The same formula as in Figure 9.8, after it is saved.*

What can you do about this effect? Not much other than get used to it. In Chapter 14, "Advanced Techniques," I discuss one method of managing complex formulas, however.

Note that when using time-date values in a formula, you need to format the values in square brackets, as in

```
SELECT DatesEvent < [03/31/94]
```

or

```
@SetField("TimesEvent"; [08:00:00 AM] )
```

## Operators

Notes formulas use operators that will be very familiar to anyone who has programmed before. The following list shows the operators that can be used in Notes formulas:

| Operator | Description |
| --- | --- |
| + | Addition, concatenation (string) |
| *+ | Addition, permuted (lists) |
| <> | Not equal |
| != | Not equal |
| =! | Not equal |
| >< | Not equal |
| *<> | Not equal, permuted (lists) |
| < | Less than |
| *< | Less than, permuted (lists) |

| | |
|---|---|
| > | Greater than |
| >* | Greater than, permuted (lists) |
| <= | Less than or equal |
| *<= | Less than or equal, permuted (lists) |
| >= | Greater than or equal |
| *>= | Greater than or equal, permuted (lists) |
| ! | Logical NOT |
| & | Logical AND |
| ¦ | Logical OR |
| : | Concatenation (lists) |
| := | Assignment |
| - | Negative (unary) |
| + | Positive (unary) |
| * | Multiplication |
| ** | Multiplication, permuted (lists) |
| / | Division |
| */ | Division, permuted (lists) |

Many of these operators can be entered several different ways, and when the formula is saved, Notes converts the operator to a standard representation. For instance, <>, !=, and =! all mean "not equal," but Notes converts all of these references to != in formulas, helping to add a consistent look to formulas.

When writing statements that use the Boolean operators AND and OR, make certain your formula is complete. For example,

```
SELECT Form = "frm1" ¦ Form = "frm2" ¦ Form = "frm3"
```

is a complete Notes formula, whereas

```
SELECT Form = "frm1" ¦ "frm2" ¦ "frm3"
```

is not a complete formula.

Also, bear in mind that the NOT operator (!) can be used to negate Notes @Functions, as in this example:

```
!@Contains(ProblemDescription; "Windows")
```

This formula returns 1 if the field ProblemDescription does not contain the string "Windows".

# Keywords

In Notes formulas, there are several reserved words that perform special functions within a formula (Notes automatically capitalizes these words when you use them in a formula). When you use DEFAULT, ENVIRONMENT, or FIELD statements, they must be the first statements in a formula, and they are always used in conjunction with the assignment (:=) operator. The following list briefly describes how these keywords, as well as the SELECT and REM keywords, are used:

DEFAULT

Sets a default value for a field. If a document contains the named field, the field's value is used; if the document does not contain the field, the value assigned in the DEFAULT statement is used.

For example, look at the following window title formula:

```
DEFAULT Subject := "Response to " + OriginalSubject;
Subject
```

With this formula, the window's title will be the contents of the document's Subject field. If the Subject field does not exist in the document (probably because the user did not enter any text in the Subject field), then the Window Title will be the string "Response to" plus the contents of the OriginalSubject field. Note that this is equivalent to the following Notes formula:

```
@If(@IsAvailable(Subject);Subject;"Response to " + OriginalSubject)
```

ENVIRONMENT

Sets a Notes environment variable, which is actually a line in the user's local NOTES.INI file (the Preferences file for Mac users). The argument of the environment statement must be a text string or the statement will fail (but no error message will be generated). For example,

```
ENVIRONMENT LastUser := @UserName
```

could produce a line similar to the following line in my workstation's NOTES.INI file:

```
$LastUser=Eric Rayl
```

Later, the Notes function @Environment could be used to retrieve the value of the environment variable, as in

```
@If(@Environment("LastUser") = "Eric Rayl");@Success;
  @Failure("Error"))
```

which checks to see whether the value of the "LastUser" environment variable is equal to "Eric Rayl".

Environment variables are most often used for passing data between macros. The @SetEnvironment function performs the identical function, but it can be used anywhere in a Notes formula, not just in the beginning.

**FIELD**

Used to either change the contents of an existing field or create a new field within a document. It is always used with the assignment (:=) operator. For example,

```
FIELD DateClosed := @Today
```

sets the value of the DateClosed field to today's date (if the DateClosed field did not already exist, it would be created within the document).

**SELECT**

Used to identify which documents to process. The expression that follows the SELECT statement is performed on the documents that meet the SELECT statement's criteria. For example, the formula

```
SELECT Form = "frmComment";
@If(@Today - DateComposed / 86400 >= 5; @DeleteDocument; @Success)
```

processes all the documents that were created with the form "frmComment" and deletes the documents in which DateComposed is five days old or older.

The way that SELECT is used in Notes is a little confusing. View selection formulas always start with the keyword SELECT, but you don't need to worry about adding it because Notes adds it for you. Additionally, Notes automatically ends many macro formulas with this statement:

```
SELECT @All
```

Don't be too concerned with this in macros, because Notes adds the statement to the macro formula if it is needed.

**REM**

This keyword allows remarks to be added to your Notes formulas. Additionally, just REM by itself can be used to help format the formula to make it more readable. Any text following the REM must be in quotes, as in

```
REM "Check to see if user is Eric Rayl";
REM "If not, do not allow macro to run";
REM;
@If(@UserName != "Eric Rayl"; @Do(@Prompt([OK]; "Error"; "You
are not authorized to run this macro"); @Return(""));@Success);
```

# Commonly Used @Functions

This section is not intended to be a function reference—the *Notes Application Developer's Reference* and the online help database are excellent references. This section is intended to familiarize you quickly with the most commonly used functions and to start you thinking about how they can be used within your applications. I also use some other functions extensively, such as @DbLookup, @DbColumn, and @Prompt. But because these functions are more complex and trickier to debug, they are discussed in Chapter 14, "Advanced Techniques."

## @If

@If is probably the most used Notes @Function. It is the only Notes function that can be used for conditional control in a formula—there are no Case statements or looping in Notes formulas. Usually, @If is used in the format

```
@If(condition; thenaction ; elseaction)
```

as in this field input validation formula:

```
@If(PrimeType = ""; @Failure("You must select a primary type for this
  case before you can save it"); @Success)
```

When a user tries to save a document with the PrimeType field left blank, this formula does not allow the document to be saved and prompts the user with a reminder. If the PrimeType is not null (""), the document can be saved.

The @If function can support multiple conditions, up to 99, but it must also have one final action to perform if all the conditions fail. Here's the syntax for this:

```
@If(condition1 ; action1 ; condition2 ; action2 ; condition3; action3 ; elseaction)
```

For example:

```
@If(Priority = "High" ;
    @SetField("DateDue"; @Adjust(@Today; 0; 0; 1; 0; 0; 0));

    Priority = "Medium" ;
    @SetField("DateDue"; @Adjust(@Today; 0; 0; 5; 0; 0; 0));

  @Adjust(@Today; 0; 1; 0; 0; 0; 0))
```

This formula sets the value of the DateDue field according to the value of the Priority field; if the priority equals "High", DateDue is set to tomorrow; if the priority equals "Medium", DateDue is set to five days from today; otherwise DateDue is set to one month from today.

The idea to remember about the @If function is that no matter how many different conditions there are, Notes evaluates them one at a time until one of the conditions is equal to the number 1 (technically, any value greater than 0.0), which is the logical True in the Notes environment (False is represented by the number 0, of course).

This is worth mentioning because many Notes "Boolean" functions don't actually return values of True or False; they return the numbers 1 or 0, depending on the arguments used in the function.

## String Manipulation Functions

All the following string manipulation functions are fairly self-explanatory, but very useful. They operate on text strings (not on rich text fields, however), and they return a text string, except @Begins, @Ends, and @Contains, which return the number 1 if a substring is contained at the beginning, at the end, or anywhere in the string, respectively.

```
@Left, @LeftBack
@Right, @RightBack
@Middle
@Length
@LowerCase
@ProperCase
@UpperCase
@Repeat
@Trim
@Begins, @Ends, @Contains
```

### TIP

Use the @Trim function judiciously in your field translation formulas, particularly on fields that you might want to use in comparisons. If a user types extra spaces before, after, or in the middle of a field, your comparisons could fail. For example, the strings

```
Eric··Rayl
```

```
·Eric·Rayl
```

```
Eric Rayl·
```

are not equal to

```
Eric·Rayl
```

## Time-Date

All the time-date functions return a particular component of a Time-Date argument, except for @Today, @Now, and @Adjust.

```
@Date
@Day
@Second
@Minute
@Hour
@Month
@Year
@Weekday
@Today, @Now
@Adjust
```

@Today returns just the date portion of the current date, whereas @Now returns the current time and date.

@Adjust is a very useful formula that changes its date argument by the parameters specified. It has the following format:

```
@Adjust(time-date value; years; months; days; hours; minutes; seconds)
```

For instance, the formula

```
@Adjust(@Today; 0; 1; 0; 0; 0; 0)
```

returns a date one month *later* than today's date, whereas

```
@Adjust(@Now; 0; 0; 0; -8; 0; 0;)
```

returns a time that is eight hours *before* the current time.

## Conversion

```
@Text
@TextToTime
@TextToNumber
```

You will use these functions heavily in your formulas to convert the contents of fields between text, numbers, and time-dates. For example, you will commonly need the @Text function in formulas similar to the following view column formula:

```
Subject + " (composed on: " + @Text(DateComposed) + ")"
```

> **TIP**
>
> Many of the "runtime" errors in Notes formulas will be caused by type mismatches. Always double-check your formulas to ensure that you are not mixing data types and that the @Functions you are using have arguments with the appropriate data type for the function. Additionally, use the Document Info... dialog box to double-check the data types of fields contained within a document.

## @UserName and @Name

@UserName returns the current user's name as contained in the active ID. This function is very useful in ComposedBy-type fields, and in macros to verify that a person should be allowed to run the macro.

@Name is for manipulating distinguished names. If you are developing applications for an organization that is using hierarchical names (such as CN=John Smith/OU=Tools/ OU=Audit/O=Acme Bank/C=US), you need to become familiar with this function to avoid unwieldy and awkward-looking user names.

## @Success and @Failure

@Success and @Failure are frequently used in a field's input validation formula to verify that some condition exists before a form can be saved. @Success is used without any arguments and always returns the value 1, but @Failure is used with a text string and prompts the user with a dialog box that includes that text string.

Here is an example of this type of usage in a field's input validation formula:

```
@If(Subject= ""; @Failure("You must enter a subject for this document before you can
   save it"); @Success)
```

This would cause the prompt in Figure 9.10 to appear.

**FIGURE 9.10.**
*The prompt created*
*when @Failure is used*
*in an input validation*
*formula that fails.*

## @Do

This function is used for stringing together multiple statements, generally in the action part of an @If statement, as in

```
@If(Priority = "High" ;
   @Do(@SetField("AssignedDeveloper"; "John Smith");
       @SetField("AssignedQA"; "Mary Jones"));

   @Do(@SetField("AssignedDeveloper"; "Bob Douglas");
       @SetField("AssignedQA"; "Beth Everett")))
```

## @DeleteField, @Unavailable, and @IsUnavailable

Both @Unavailable and @DeleteField delete a field from a document. Don't confuse @Unavailable with the function @IsUnavailable, which checks to see whether a document contains a given field. The formula

```
FIELD ComposedBy := @Unavailable
```

would delete the field ComposedBy, and its contents, from the document (the field would no longer show up when the document was highlighted and the Document Info... option was selected on the Notes Design menu). An equivalent formula to the preceding one is this:

```
FIELD ComposedBy := @DeleteField
```

@IsUnavailable could be used in a view selection formula, such as

```
SELECT @IsUnavailable(Form)
```

to display only documents that do not contain a Form field.

## View Statistics

View statistics functions are mainly in view column formulas, but they can also be used in window title formulas and field formulas. These are the view statistics functions:

```
@DocChildren
@DocDescendents
@DocNumber
@DocParentNumber
@DocLevel
@DocSiblings
@Responses
@IsExpandable
```

They are valid only in views with a response hierarchy (otherwise they always return 0), and they are most useful in collapsed views for displaying the number of response documents a given document has (DocChildren are direct responses to the document, whereas DocDescendents are all the responses and response to responses that a given document has).

These functions are a little tricky to understand in that they are "phantom" values; they don't exist anywhere other than in the view, and they cannot be used in math computations and such. Additionally, they are dependent on the view's selection formula—they don't return the *absolute* number of responses a document has, but only the number of responses that appear in the current view.

For instance, you can have a computed field on a form that has as its formula @DocDescendents, and when a document created with that form is open, the field displays the correct number of responses to the document in the current view. But the value will never be saved in the document; its value will always be "". You should experiment with these functions in a populated discussion-type database to see how they behave, and try adding computed fields to the forms in a discussion database to get a better understanding of why I say they return "phantom" values.

`@IsExpandable` behaves differently than the other functions listed here. It can be used in column formulas to identify when a document has other documents collapsed beneath it.

For instance, in the Personnel/Event Tracking sample database, the first column in the view 2. Schedule by Date/Person has the formula

```
@IsExpandable("+"; "")
```

which produces the results shown in Figure 9.11, depending on whether a document (or category) is fully expanded.

**FIGURE 9.11.**

*A partially collapsed view that uses* `@IsExpandable` *to indicate which documents have collapsed response documents.*

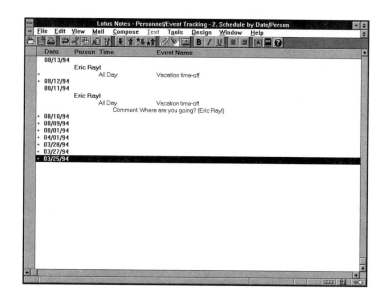

## *@Set and @SetField*

`@Set` is used to create a temporary field or variable that exists only for the duration of the formula. The two formulas

```
@Set("TempCaseNum"; CaseNum)
```

and

```
TempCaseNum := CaseNum
```

are equivalent, but the `@Set` statement does not need to be at the top of the formula and can be embedded in an `@If` statement, whereas the assignment statement with the `:=` has to be one of the first statements in the formula.

### TIP

For the @Set to work, you must have initialized the temporary variable at the beginning of the formula. For example, the formula

```
@Set("temp"; ComposedBy);
temp + " (author)"
```

would always return the string " (author)", no matter what the ComposedBy field contained. However,

```
temp := temp;
@Set("temp"; ComposedBy);
temp + " (author)"
```

would behave as expected, with its results equal to the value in the ComposedBy field concatenated with the static text " (author)".

## @SetEnvironment and @Environment

These are very useful functions for setting and returning the values of Notes environment variables, which are text strings stored in a user's local NOTES.INI file (Notes Preferences for Macintosh users).

The key to using these two functions is that they can only operate on text strings, and @SetEnvironment will not return an error message if its argument is not text; it just won't set the environment variable. Make sure that you use the @Text function on the @SetEnvironment function's argument if you are trying to store a date or number. Then use the @TextToTime or @TextToNumber function with @Environment to convert the text string back to proper format when you need to read the environment variable.

For example, use

```
@SetEnvironment("LastNumberUsed"; @Text(CallNumber))
```

to convert a numerical value (LastNumberUsed) into a text value that can be stored in a Notes environment variable, and

```
NextCallNumber := @TextToNumber(@Environment("CallNumber")) + 1
```

to assign an environment variable's contents to a numerical field (NextCallNumber).

## @Return

@Return is used to stop the execution of the formula immediately. I use @Return extensively to control macro execution, as in the following example from a button's formula:

```
@If(@IsNewDoc; @Do(@Prompt([OK]; "Error"; "This Main Case document has
not been saved yet- please save it before setting up an
investigator"); @Return("")); @Success);
@Command([Compose]; ""; "frmInvestigatorSummary")
@Command([Compose]; ""; "frmInvestigatorDetail")
```

This causes the formula to stop execution if the current document has not been saved (@IsNewDoc = 1).

# Documents Versus Forms—Modifying Fields with Formulas

One of the hardest concepts for people new to Notes is understanding the relationship between fields, forms, and documents. This concept is very hard to describe, but in this section I'll show you an example that might help you start to understand this relationship better, which will help you design more robust Notes applications.

Contained on the sample disk is a file called FORMUBAS.NSF, which is a Notes database titled Basic Formula Example. This simple database has two forms that should help you understand the Notes environment better. Additionally, this database illustrates how to create a view form formula to display a document with a different form depending on certain conditions.

There are only two forms in this database, the Trouble Ticket Entry Form, and the Trouble Ticket Resolution Form (see Figure 9.12 and Figure 9.13).

**FIGURE 9.12.**

*The Trouble Ticket Entry Form.*

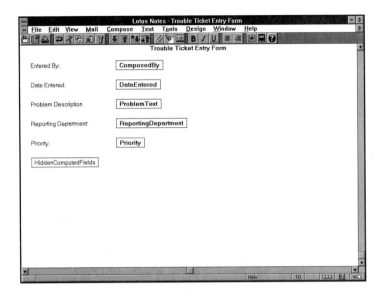

**FIGURE 9.13.**

*The Trouble Ticket Resolution Form.*

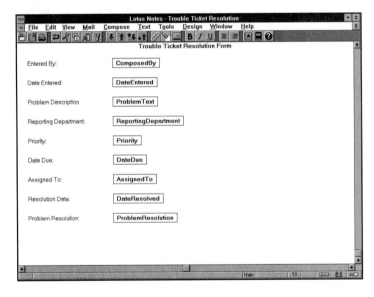

First notice the field HiddenComputedFields on the Trouble Ticket Entry Form, and look at the formula for this computed field:

```
FIELD AssignedTo := AssignedTo;
FIELD DateDue := DateDue;
@SetField("AssignedTo";
   @If(ReportingDepartment = "Development";
       "Eric Rayl";

       ReportingDepartment = "Marketing";
        "Maria Enriquez";

        "David Alison"));

@SetField("DateDue";
   @If(Priority = "High";
       @Adjust(DateEntered; 0; 0; 1; 0; 0; 0);

       Priority = "Medium";
       @Adjust(DateEntered; 0; 0; 3; 0; 0; 0);

       @Adjust(DateEntered; 0; 1; 0; 0; 0; 0)))

@SetField("HiddenComputedFields"; @Unavailable)
```

What this formula does is actually create two additional fields in the document, the fields AssignedTo and DateDue. It is important for you to understand that even though those field names do not exist physically on the form, they are being created by a formula within the HiddenComputedFields field on that form.

To see how this works, compose a new Trouble Ticket Entry document, save it, and look at the Design Document Info dialog box (as in Figure 9.14).

**FIGURE 9.14.**

*Design Document Info dialog box, where the contents of a document's fields can be examined.*

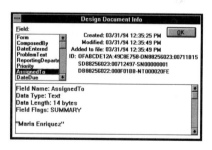

You will see that the document actually does contain the fields AssignedTo and DateDue. Additionally, note that there is not a field called HiddenComputedFields within the document (it was deleted with the @Unavailable statement in the formula).

Now open a Trouble Ticket document that already exists. Notice that the document is now being displayed with the Trouble Ticket Resolution Form. This is because of the view's form formula. Switch to Edit mode, and notice that some of the fields, such as

ProblemText, are "locked" because the field is now defined as computed when composed, rather than editable.

To better understand how form formulas work, open the view Trouble Tickets by Dept/Priority in design mode, and look at the form formula (by selecting the Form Formula option on the **D**esign menu). This is the formula:

```
@If(@IsNewDoc; "frmTroubleEntry"; "frmTroubleResolve")
```

It translates literally, "If a new document is being composed, display the form named "frmTroubleEntry"; otherwise, display documents in this view with the form "frmTroubleResolve".

In a real-world application, the use of the hidden field HiddenComputedFields on the Trouble Ticket Entry Form would not be a very good design. The Trouble Ticket Entry Form should have two hidden, computed fields, one called AssignedTo and one called DateDue, each with an appropriate formula. This would make the application much easier to understand for other developers and make it more "self-documenting."

Hopefully this example helped you better understand the relationship between fields, forms, and documents in a Notes database.

## Summary

Writing Notes formulas can be a fast and easy process when you get an understanding of what @Functions are available. The most important thing to remember about Notes formulas is to make sure that the formulas use data types correctly and that the arguments of @Functions are of the proper data type. Notes catches spelling errors in @Functions and does not enable you to save formulas with improper syntax, but it cannot catch data type errors until the formula actually executes, which can cause you much grief.

Next, I will show you how to use formulas to write macros that not only will help your users but that will help you maintain your Notes application.

# 10

## Macros

# Overview

In Lotus Notes, macros are similar to functions and procedures in traditional application development systems.

Many basic Notes applications require hardly any macro programming. Applications such as modified discussion databases and the Personnel/Event Tracking sample database can be used quite productively without any macros. But as an application developer, you might need to use macros even in simple databases. Macros are especially useful in making mass changes to the documents in a database after a design change has been made to the application (when a new field was added to a form, for instance).

There are several types of macros, and the use of each will be described in this chapter:

- Filter macros
- Execute-once macros
- Background macros
- Mail-in/paste-in macros
- Button macros
- Search macros
- SmartIcon macros

# Filter Macros

The most commonly used macro type in Notes applications is what Lotus calls a filter macro. The term *filter* can be misleading, and it is really a carryover from the Notes 2.x days when there were no macros, just filters. This type of macro is generally used to add, edit, or delete the contents of fields in one or more Notes documents. As an application developer, you'll use filter macros extensively when making changes to and maintaining your databases.

## Creating a Filter Macro

For example, suppose that you have a contact management database that includes a field called ContactName on the Contact Information form (see the data in the second column of the view shown in Figure 10.1). This field contains the complete name for the individual, including the title, as in "Mr. John Smith" or "Dr. Anne Phelps."

**FIGURE 10.1.**

*A view in a contact database showing the contents of the ContactName field (second column).*

After the application has been in use, it is determined that you want to create a mail-merge form that will be used to print the letters in conjunction with the form override feature. The problem is that you need to be able to have a merged-in salutation, such as "Dear Mr. Smith" or "Dear Dr. Phelps."

You can easily create the mail-merge form and add a field called Salutation in the correct location, as in Figure 10.2, but how do you get the correct data in the Salutation field without having to manually edit each document and add the data?

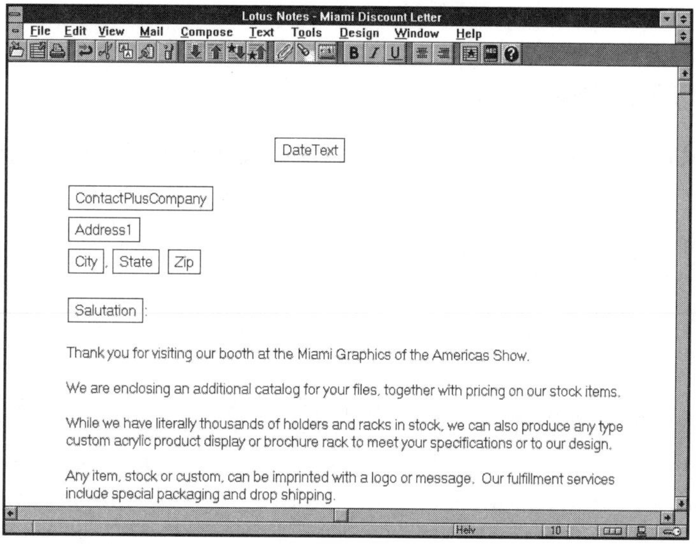

**FIGURE 10.2.**

*A mail-merge form with a Salutation field.*

The answer is to create a filter macro that will do 95 percent of the work for you. What the macro will do is create a field in each document called Salutation, then compute the contents of the field using the logic of taking the first word and the last word of the ContactName and concatenating them with a space between them. This technique should work for the data in 95 percent of the ContactName fields, but you should double-check your data after you run the macro.

To create the new filter macro, you select the **M**acros... option on the Notes **D**esign menu, which opens the Design Macros dialog box (see Figure 10.3).

**FIGURE 10.3.**

*The Design Macros dialog box.*

Notice that the Design Macros window has the same basic options as the Design Forms and Design Views windows. For instance, a list of the macros that currently exist in the database is displayed in the **M**acros box, and there are buttons on the right side of the window labeled **E**dit, **D**one, **N**ew, New **C**opy, **C**lear, and **I**nfo.... These buttons behave with macros as they do when you're designing forms and views. That is, they enable you to edit a selected macro, create a new macro (or a copy of an existing one), clear (delete) macros, and exit out of the Design Macros window (**D**one). The **I**nfo... button opens the Design Information window, which has information about when the macro was created and its size, but additionally it is where the macro's design information is viewed or changed (see Figure 10.4).

**FIGURE 10.4.**

*The Design Informa- tion dialog box for a macro.*

Notice also that you can copy and paste macros between databases using the **C**opy and **P**aste buttons at the bottom of the Design Macros window.

In this case, you would click the **N**ew button to create the new filter macro that is needed. This would open the Design New Macro window, complete with the default values shown in Figure 10.5.

**FIGURE 10.5.**

*The Design New Macro dialog box, with its default values.*

The macro's name behaves very similarly to how a name of a form or a view behaves. Whatever you type here appears on the **R**un Macros menu in the database (unless, of course, you deselect the **I**nclude in 'Tools Run Macros' menu check box below the macro's name—see Figure 10.5). Additionally, you can (and probably should) use synonyms for macros' names by using the vertical bar (|) symbol. Only the text to the left of the bar will appear on the menu, whereas the actual form name will be the text to the right of the vertical bar. The synonyms are most helpful when you are writing complex macros that call other macros (see the advanced section of the book).

Again, macro names, like form and view names, can create a cascading menu by the use of the backslash (\) in the macro's name. And just as you can with form and view names, you can cascade the menu only one level. For example, the two macro names

```
1. Admin\1. Go To Master Case Info¦macroFindCaseMaster
1. Admin\2. Mgmt Reporting Selection¦macroMgmtSelect
```

would produce the cascading **R**un Macro menu shown in Figure 10.6.

**FIGURE 10.6.**

*A cascading Tools **R**un Macro menu.*

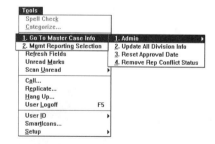

---

**TIP**

Be aware of how the display in the **I**nclude in 'Tools Run Macros' menu check box works, because it behaves differently from the similar options for form and views. Deselecting the check box causes Notes to *internally* put parentheses around the macro's name, but these parentheses do not appear in the macro name box in the Design New Macro or Edit Existing Macro dialog box (the macro's name does appear with parentheses around it in the initial Design Macro window, however).

This point will become very important as you start writing advanced macros that call other macros, because when one macro calls another macro, you must be sure to reference the macro's name with parentheses around it.

A macro's run options essentially determine what type of a macro this will be—the run option called Run via menu command is the run option for filter-type macros. The other run options are used for other types of macros. They will be discussed briefly later in this chapter. Several of the macro types, such as Execute Once and Background macros, are discussed in more detail in Chapter 14, "Advanced Techniques."

Filter macros can perform one of three types of operations. The default, Update existing document when run, is the most commonly used, although the other two options, Select document when run and Create new document when run, are useful in special circumstances and for debugging a macro before you actually update the real documents.

The options in the **Run** macro on: box enable you to tailor what documents will be processed by the filter macro. Five selections are available:

1. Run on all documents in database.
2. Run on documents not yet processed by macro.
3. Run on documents not yet marked read by you.
4. Run on all documents in view.
5. Run on selected documents in view.

Options 1, 4, and 5 are the most frequently used selections. Options 2 and 3 are used primarily in advanced macros, particularly in workflow-type applications.

**TIP**

It's often a good idea to select the default value, Run on selected documents in view, even if you intend for your macro to process many documents. This choice enables you to test the macro on one document before you run it against all the documents in the database, for example.

All the default values in the Design New Macro window are correct for a filter macro to create the Salutation field on the frmContactInfo form, but you need to type a name for the macro—for example, Create Salutation Field. There's no need to worry about fancy names or synonyms here because the macro needs to be run only once, and then it should be deleted. Additionally, if this macro were to be a permanent macro in the database, you could explain what the macro does in the Comment: box in the Design New Macro window.

Now you need to click the **Formula...** button to open the Edit Macro Formula window, where you enter the actual formula for the macro. To create the Salutation field, you would enter the following formula:

```
FIELD Salutation := "Dear " + @Left(Contact; " ") + " " +
  @RightBack(Contact; " ")
```

After you type this formula into the box, click the **OK** button to save the formula and return to the Design New Macro window. If you now click the **Formula...** button again to review the formula, you'll notice that Notes has added the statement SELECT @All to the end of your formula (see Figure 10.7).

**FIGURE 10.7.**

*The formula for the Create Salutation Field macro.*

All filter macros will include a SELECT statement in the macro's formula. Many times, this SELECT statement will just be SELECT @All, because the actual selection of the documents to be processed will be controlled by the setting Run macro on. (That is, if the Run macro on setting was set to Run on selected documents in view, and you have SELECT @All in your macro's formula, the macro will process only the selected documents, not all the documents in the database.)

---

**TIP**

When writing filter macros, especially in large databases, I have found that macros are faster if a *view* is used to control what documents are processed by a macro, instead of using SELECT statements in macros. In the preceding Salutation field example, an alternative way to design the macro would be to set the macro to Run on all documents in database, and then to change the SELECT statement to

```
SELECT Form = "frmContactInfo"
```

This would have the same result as selecting Run on all documents in view, using a SELECT @All statement, and running the macro from a view that contained only Contact forms, but it could be substantially slower.

For testing purposes, you should leave the macro set to Run on selected documents in view, in case there is a problem or a bug in the macro. To best see the results of your macro, you could create a private view that is a copy of the view by company name, but add a column to display the contents of the Salutation field.

Now run the macro by selecting it from the **T**ools **R**un Macros menu, and notice the contents of the Salutation column (see Figure 10.8). The selected document should now have a Salutation field. Then you can go back and edit the macro, changing its settings to Run on all documents in view, and create the Salutation field for all the Contact documents.

**FIGURE 10.8.**

*The view after running the Create Salutation Field macro.*

After you run the macro, you should browse through your private view to verify that all the names were handled correctly. For example, names with a suffix such as "Frank Jones, Jr." and "David Smith III" would not be handled correctly by this macro as it stands.

---

**TIP**

Although the Notes Help database states, "Filter macros cannot use the @Command function to perform commands," Notes does not produce an error message when you use the @Command in a filter formula, but your macro will most likely behave incorrectly. This is due to the iterative way that Notes runs a filter macro and the fact that it saves up all @Commands and processes them at the end of the macro. For instance, a filter macro with the formula

```
FIELD Printed := Printed;
@SetField("Printed"; "Yes");
@Command([FilePrint]); SELECT @All
```

would work when only one document is selected, but it would produce unpredictable results if multiple documents were selected. I strongly advise against using @Commands in filter macros.

---

Filter macros are the main method in Notes for adding, editing, and deleting fields and their contents without using a form. Filter macros can process one or many documents, and you can control what documents the filter macro will process by a combination of the Run macro on setting and the SELECT statement within the macro's formula.

# Execute-Once Macros

There are two main uses for Execute-Once macros:

■ Processing multiple documents with a macro that contains one or more @Commands, (that is, printing multiple documents, as in the preceding Tip)

■ Serving as a "main" macro that calls multiple other macros

Execute-Once macros are further explained, along with examples, in Chapter 14, "Advanced Techniques."

# Background Macros

Background macros are generally macros that run automatically on a server, although they can run on either a Windows or an OS/2 client, either automatically or manually. These macros can be used to provide powerful database features, such as automatically migrating documents from one database to another based on certain criteria, or rerouting "stalled" documents in a workflow system. These types of macros and their usage are evaluated in detail in Chapter 14.

# Mail-In/Paste-In Macros

This type of macro is run every time a document is mailed into or pasted into a database. These types of macros are used heavily in forms routing applications in which documents move from database to database (usually by Notes mail from one user's mailbox to another user's mailbox).

Applications can also be designed that allow for users to cut and paste documents at the view level, such as in the Bug Tracking sample database included with this book. Additionally, mail-in macros are used extensively in the real-world workflow application in Chapter 18, "The Travel Authorization Request Workflow System."

# Button Macros

Button macros are created during form design. To create a button macro, you must have a form open in design mode. With the cursor located on the form where the button is desired, select the Notes menu option **Edit Insert Button**, which opens the Insert Button dialog box (see Figure 10.9).

**FIGURE 10.9.**
*The Insert Button dialog box.*

# Creating a Button Macro

For example, suppose that you wanted to add a button to the Appointment/Event form in the sample Personnel/Event Tracking database. This button would enable users to simply click it to set the DatesEvent field automatically. For instance, the form could have a button with the text "Tomorrow" and a button with the text "All Next Week." The Insert Button dialog box for the Tomorrow button would look like that shown in Figure 10.10.

**FIGURE 10.10.**

*The Insert Button dialog box for a Tomorrow button on the Appointment/Event form.*

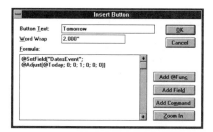

---

**TIP**

You might be tempted to use the following syntax for the Tomorrow button:

```
FIELD DatesEvent := @Adjust(@Today; 0; 0; 1; 0; 0; 0))
```

If you tried to save the button macro with this formula, you would receive an error message like the one in Figure 10.11. To work around this problem, you could add the statement @Success to the end of the formula, as in

```
FIELD DatesEvent := @Adjust(@Today; 0; 0; 1; 0; 0; 0));
   @Success
```

You would essentially be adding a "null" Main expression to the formula, which would allow Notes to save it.

**FIGURE 10.11.**

*An error message generated when a button's formula does not have a main expression.*

> ### TIP
>
> While you are still in design mode on the form, you should format the button's paragraph to be hidden when reading and printing (using the **H**ide When check boxes on the Format Paragraph dialog box. This is not only for aesthetics but because a button macro cannot be executed unless a user has the form in edit mode.

When you are composing a new Appointment/Event document, the form now should look similar to Figure 10.12. If a user clicks the Tomorrow button, tomorrow's date should be inserted into the Date(s) of Event field.

**FIGURE 10.12.**

*Composing an Appointment/Event document—note the new button.*

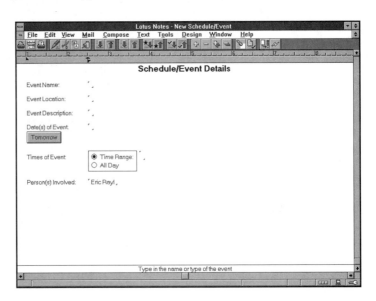

In a similar fashion, an All Next Week button could be added to the form, which would compute the dates of the following week and put all five values in the DatesEvent field. The following formula, although a little intimidating at first, performs the necessary computations and sets the DatesEvent field accordingly:

```
TodaysDay := @Weekday(@Today);
@If(TodaysDay = 1;
  @SetField("DatesEvent";
    @Adjust(@Today; 0; 0; 1; 0; 0; 0) :
    @Adjust(@Today; 0; 0; 2; 0; 0; 0) :
    @Adjust(@Today; 0; 0; 3; 0; 0; 0) :
    @Adjust(@Today; 0; 0; 4; 0; 0; 0) :
    @Adjust(@Today; 0; 0; 5; 0; 0; 0));

  TodaysDay = 2;
  @SetField("DatesEvent";
    @Adjust(@Today; 0; 0; 7; 0; 0; 0)  :
    @Adjust(@Today; 0; 0; 8; 0; 0; 0)  :
    @Adjust(@Today; 0; 0; 9; 0; 0; 0)  :
    @Adjust(@Today; 0; 0; 10; 0; 0; 0) :
    @Adjust(@Today; 0; 0; 11; 0; 0; 0));

  TodaysDay = 3;
  @SetField("DatesEvent";
    @Adjust(@Today; 0; 0; 6; 0; 0; 0)  :
    @Adjust(@Today; 0; 0; 7; 0; 0; 0)  :
    @Adjust(@Today; 0; 0; 8; 0; 0; 0)  :
    @Adjust(@Today; 0; 0; 9; 0; 0; 0)  :
    @Adjust(@Today; 0; 0; 10; 0; 0; 0));

  TodaysDay = 4;
  @SetField("DatesEvent";
    @Adjust(@Today; 0; 0; 5; 0; 0; 0) :
    @Adjust(@Today; 0; 0; 6; 0; 0; 0) :
    @Adjust(@Today; 0; 0; 7; 0; 0; 0) :
    @Adjust(@Today; 0; 0; 8; 0; 0; 0) :
    @Adjust(@Today; 0; 0; 9; 0; 0; 0));

  TodaysDay = 5;
  @SetField("DatesEvent";
    @Adjust(@Today; 0; 0; 4; 0; 0; 0) :
    @Adjust(@Today; 0; 0; 5; 0; 0; 0) :
    @Adjust(@Today; 0; 0; 6; 0; 0; 0) :
    @Adjust(@Today; 0; 0; 7; 0; 0; 0) :
    @Adjust(@Today; 0; 0; 8; 0; 0; 0));

  TodaysDay = 6;
  @SetField("DatesEvent";
    @Adjust(@Today; 0; 0; 3; 0; 0; 0) :
    @Adjust(@Today; 0; 0; 4; 0; 0; 0) :
    @Adjust(@Today; 0; 0; 5; 0; 0; 0) :
    @Adjust(@Today; 0; 0; 6; 0; 0; 0) :
    @Adjust(@Today; 0; 0; 7; 0; 0; 0));

  TodaysDay = 7;
  @SetField("DatesEvent";
    @Adjust(@Today; 0; 0; 2; 0; 0; 0) :
    @Adjust(@Today; 0; 0; 3; 0; 0; 0) :
    @Adjust(@Today; 0; 0; 4; 0; 0; 0) :
    @Adjust(@Today; 0; 0; 5; 0; 0; 0) :
    @Adjust(@Today; 0; 0; 6; 0; 0; 0));

@Success)
```

> **TIP**
>
> Button macros are very useful on forms for providing functionality to users, but I suggest that you use them only to provide functionality that is not easily accessible via Notes menu options. Using this method tends to make your users understand how to access the basic Notes functions from the Notes menus, which in the long run decreases your training time and costs as users become more familiar with the general Notes environment.
>
> For example, I see too many forms with buttons for such functions as Save or Mail. These kinds of button macros cause problems in the long run because many users are lost when new forms or applications are added that don't include the exact button combination they are used to.

# Search Macros

Search macros are used with a database's full text index, and therefore the database must be full text indexed to use these types of macros. Basically, they are used to edit fields in selected documents just like filter macros—it's just that the full text search engine is used to select the documents that meet a certain criteria instead of using the SELECT statement in a filter macro. This method makes search macros much faster in large databases. For more information, see Chapter 16, "Inquiry Tracking System."

# SmartIcon Macros

Because the SmartIcon palette does not vary from database to database, and because SmartIcon macros can be individually modified user by user, you must carefully consider how SmartIcon macros are used. SmartIcon macros are very similar to button macros in that an individual SmartIcon can have a formula associated with it, but the difference is that the macro is not tied to any particular database—it is local to the user.

> **TIP**
>
> I personally recommend teaching users how to modify their icon palettes as part of Notes basic training. Then, within each application you develop, if you have useful macros that appear on the **Tools Run** Macros menu, your users can be coached into how to add a particular macro to their personal SmartIcon palettes.

I feel that the customizable SmartIcon palette is part of what makes a Personal Computer "personal," and I think your users will be much happier with your application, and the Notes environment in general, if you help them understand how to use and create SmartIcons.

To create a SmartIcon macro, select the SmartIcons... option on the Notes Tools menu. This selection opens the SmartIcons window, shown in Figure 10.13.

**FIGURE 10.13.**

*The SmartIcons window, which enables users to customize their SmartIcon palettes.*

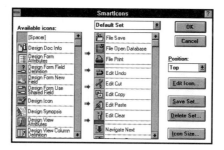

To create a SmartIcon macro, you first click the Edit Icon... button (it does not matter what icon you have selected when you do this). This action causes the Edit SmartIcons dialog box to open (Figure 10.14), which lists all the editable SmartIcons.

**FIGURE 10.14.**

*The Edit SmartIcons window.*

In this example, I'll show you how you would create a SmartIcon macro to run one of the macros in the software bug tracking sample database. That database already has a macro with the name 1. Go to Main Bug Report doc | macroGoToARDoc. Briefly, this macro allows a user to quickly maneuver from a customer report document to the bug report document in the main view, regardless of what view the user is currently in (the actual workings of the macro and its real usefulness are explained in Part IV, "Real-World Examples"). To simplify the application for the users, I will create a SmartIcon they can click on, instead of having them use the menu options Tools Run Macros and then select the appropriate macro.

First, select the icon you want to assign the formula/macro to (unfortunately, there is no way to edit or add to the available icon choices). After the icon is selected, change its description to describe what the button will do—for example, "Go To Main Bug Report." Now click the **Formula...** button, which opens the SmartIcons Formula window (see Figure 10.15), and type this Notes formula:

```
@Command([ToolsRunMacro]; "macroGoToARDoc")
```

**FIGURE 10.15.**

*The formula for the Go To Main Bug Report SmartIcon.*

Now click the **OK** button on the SmartIcons Formula window, then the **D**one button on the Edit SmartIcons window. At this point, you are back to the SmartIcons window, and you have a new available icon, but you still need to add the icon to your current icon set. This is done by clicking the Go To Main Bug Report icon in the Available icons: listbox, then dragging it and dropping it where you want it on your current icon palette. If you want to reposition it on your palette, you can just drag-and-drop it within the palette to move it. To remove it completely, just drag it outside of the palette and drop it, which removes it from the palette. Now you close the SmartIcons dialog box by clicking the **OK** button, and the new SmartIcon is added to your icon palette. Just be aware that this example icon is specific to the bug tracking application and that it will produce an error message if it is clicked when another database is open.

# Summary

Using Notes R3 macro capabilities, you can develop complex but user-friendly applications. Although the macro language is not as robust or flexible as some development environments, such as Visual Basic or PowerBuilder, it is powerful enough to do just about anything you need to do, if you are creative.

Filter macros are the "bread and butter" of Notes applications. Although many basic applications might not require any macros, as an application developer you'll always use filter macros to maintain and update the data as the application changes during its lifetime.

Button macros enable you to create user-friendly forms by automating certain activities and giving users visual cues on how to perform certain actions.

Mail-in/paste-in macros are very useful not only in workflow applications, but for creating custom "filters" on users' mail databases. Many electronic mail applications tout their capability to intelligently have mail agents and filters, but properly designed Notes macros can be used to create much more robust mail systems that offer much more control over the mail system.

Notes background macros, although complex, are useful for building automated workflow systems and for helping manage large systems of databases by automatically moving or purging documents based on certain criteria.

Many complex macros use a main execute-once type of macro to be the "main program" that calls many other macros. Additionally, execute-once macros can be used to write quick little routines to help simplify an application.

With a little imagination and experimentation, you can use macros to help you create your robust Notes environment.

# 11

## Two Techniques for Rapid Notes Applications Development

To rapidly prototype and deploy production Notes applications, many times I'll use one of two techniques that I've found to be very effective. One of the techniques involves prototyping an application's architecture using a Notes database created from the standard Notes discussion template. The other technique uses a computed field called Subject on all documents that is used to help manage view design and keep view response snappy.

# Prototyping Using the Notes Discussion Database Template

Many of the more complex Notes applications you will develop will have some sort of response hierarchy that will be used to create relationships between documents and data. The Notes discussion database has a perfect design to enable you to start prototyping your application's forms and views. Experimenting with different types of forms, and placing fields on different forms to see what the effects are, can easily be accomplished by starting with a database based on the standard discussion template (DISCUSS.NTF).

To demonstrate how to use the discussion template to help you visualize and prototype an application, I'll show you how this technique can be used to create a basic prototype for a project management application within an MIS department. The system will track the status of projects, and each project will have various tasks assigned to it. Additionally, users will be enabled to compose comments that are related to individual tasks, to the overall project, or to another comment.

First, create a new database using the Notes **File|New** Database... menu option. Then select the Discussion Design Template, supplying appropriate server, file, and database names, and then click the **N**ew button (see Figure 11.1).

**FIGURE 11.1.**

*Creating a new database from the standard Discussion template in preparation for developing a quick prototype.*

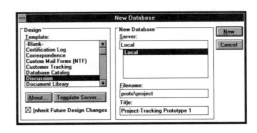

The standard discussion database has three forms: a Main Topic (main document), a Response form, and a Response to a response form. This makes it an ideal starting point because there is one of each type of Notes documents.

For this project tracking prototype, I suggest that you use a Main Topic document to simulate a Project document, a Response document to simulate a Task document, and a Response to a response document to simulate a Comment. Before you begin, you should disable the prototype database's design template using the **File|Database|Information** menu option, clicking the **Design** Template... button, and disabling the **I**nherit Design from Template check box (see Figure 11.2). This action ensures that the database will not have its design accidentally refreshed by a Notes server, negating all of your work.

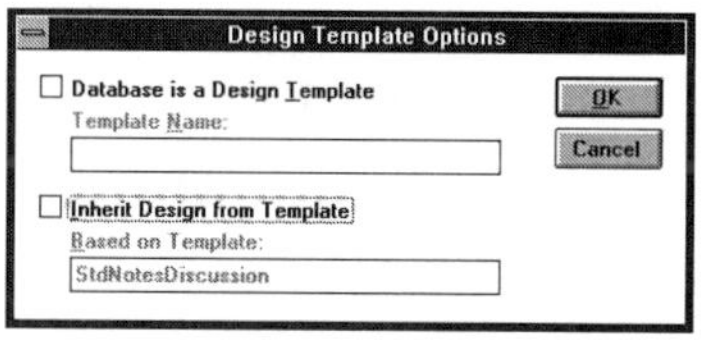

**FIGURE 11.2.**

*Disabling the prototype database's design template.*

To get a better feel for how the application will look and feel, I suggest hiding the three standard discussion forms by using the **Design|Attributes** option on each form and deselecting the Include in **C**ompose Menu check box.

Now, create a Project form by selecting **Design|Forms...** from the Notes menu, selecting the Main Topic form, and clicking the New **C**opy button. For now, leave all the fields just as they appear on the form. The items of the form's design that you should change are its Form **A**ttributes. Name the form 1. Project | frmProject, and make certain to check the Include in **C**ompose Menu check box. Then exit and save the Form Attributes dialog box, and exit and save the form. You now should have only one form appearing on the database's **C**ompose menu: 1. Project.

Next, create a Tasks form by creating a new copy of the Response form and editing its form attributes. Name this form 2. Response | frmResponse, and make sure that its Include in **C**ompose Menu check box is selected. Again, leave the fields on the form alone for now, save the form, and exit design mode.

The third and final form you need to create is the Comment form. Make a new copy of the database's Response to Response form, and this time name it 3. Comment | frmComment. As before, make sure that the form will appear on the **C**ompose menu. Then save the form as-is, and exit design mode.

In a Notes prototype, the more data you have in the application, the better it is to look at the underlying architecture and design of the database. You now should compose some sample documents to get an idea of how the data can be viewed.

First, change to the view By Category. Now, begin by composing a Project document and entering the following information in the Subject and Categories fields:

Subject:    Ensure that accurate backup logs are being maintained

Category:  Backup Procedures & Techniques

Leave the body of the project document empty, and save the form.

Next, compose four more project documents, with Subjects and Categories similar to these:

Subject:    Upgrade SF3 tape backup to 2GB DAT

Category:  Backup Procedures & Techniques

Subject:    Implement an Expense Report workflow system

Category:  Application Development & Maintenance

Subject:    Upgrade servers to Notes v3.1.5

Category:  Network Upgrades/Maintenance

Subject:    Setup OpenView network management station

Category:  Network Upgrades/Maintenance

After these documents are composed, the view By Category should look similar to Figure 11.3.

**FIGURE 11.3.**

*Five Project documents with data entered into the Subject and Category fields simulating Projects and Project Areas.*

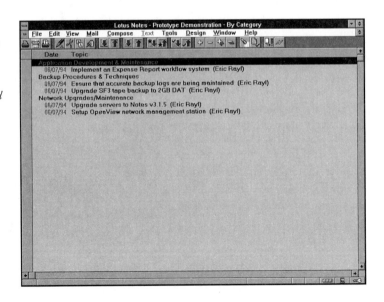

Now you need to add some tasks to these projects to help your prototype better represent how the application's "master project view" could look with this choice of application architecture. Start by composing a few Task documents with the "Upgrade servers to Notes v3.1.5" project document checked. For these documents, you only need to enter data in the Task form's (current) Reply field. Try composing Tasks with the following three replies:

"Upgrade Colorado servers"

"Upgrade Cupertino servers"

"Upgrade Hong Kong server"

Try composing a couple of Task documents for the Project "Ensure that accurate backup logs are being maintained." Enter data in the reply field similar to this:

"Audit Hong Kong's backup log"

"Audit Colorado's backup log"

Then compose a couple of tasks for the project "Upgrade SF3 tape backup to 2GB DAT" with the reply field containing information such as this:

"Evaluate current 2GB price/performance, and order"

"Install new backup drive"

Your By Category view should now look similar to Figure 11.4. Are you starting to see how a project management system could take shape?

**FIGURE 11.4.**

*The Project Management prototype after a few Tasks have been composed.*

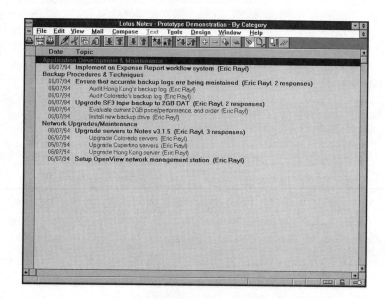

If you add a few Comment documents to this database, you'll get an even better idea of how one of the main views of the prototype will look. Figure 11.5 shows the database in Figure 11.4, but with a few comments. It's important to remember at these early stages of prototyping that the views still need much work—it's hard to imagine how a lot of comments about a given project can be informative when they are all authored by "Eric Rayl." But bear with me; prototypes need some data to work with, even if it's not completely realistic. (Besides, for a presentation, you could run macros and change the contents of fields as necessary to make a good presentation.) Notice how some of the comments in Figure 11.5, such as "Are we sure that the LA servers are backed up regularly?" blend in with the tasks, and notice how the view is becoming confusing. I will soon address how to clean up this main view.

**FIGURE 11.5.**

*Comment documents as Response documents in the Project Tracking prototype.*

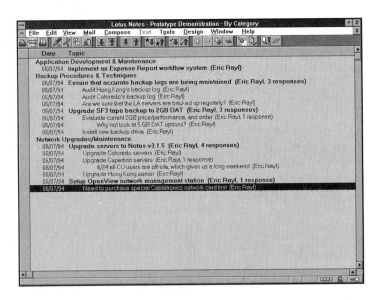

Next, relevant fields need to be added to each of the forms. The most basic fields that could be added to the forms include these:

> Project Form: DateProjectDue, ProjectAssignedTo, ProjectStatus
>
> Task Form: DateTaskDue, TaskAssignedTo, TaskStatus

Don't worry about the form aesthetics at this point; just add the fields anywhere on the forms. Make the status fields standard keywords. For now, don't bother to define the allowed keywords, just check the **Allow values not in this list** check box.

After these fields have been entered, go back through the documents that you've already created, and enter realistic data in these new fields (as I've said, half the trouble of creating a prototype is populating it with realistic data).

Assuming that you have entered data into the new fields in the Project and Task documents, you should be able to easily create a Projects by Status view in the prototype database. This view will be like the By Category view except that the second column, the Categories column, will have the formula ProjectStatus instead. Make a new copy of the By Category view, and then change the formula for the second column from Categories to ProjectStatus. Additionally, while designing the new view, delete the Date column—this @Created column is not relevant in this application.

Now save the view, and name it 1. Projects\2. By Status. After you change the contents of the ProjectStatus field in your sample Project documents, your new view should look similar to Figure 11.6.

**FIGURE 11.6.**

*An example of the prototype's view of Projects\By Status.*

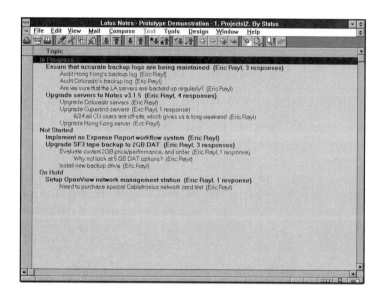

Additionally, other views (such as Projects by Assigned To and Projects by Due Date) can easily be created by modifying the second column of the standard view All by Category.

Using the standard discussion database template as a starting point for your prototype design should, if nothing else, give you the application developer a way for deciding how to architect your application. But it might also help you speed up application development because many of the prototypes you develop using this process will be able to be used as-is, without modification, after they are approved by the users.

# Using a Subject Field to Drive Views

The technique of using a computed Subject field on all forms to drive what appears in views is very similar to the previous approach of using the standard discussion database template.

When you're developing Notes applications that will use many different types of forms, it's often advisable to use a hidden Subject field to help manage the way that the document will appear in views. This technique has the additional benefit of making view performance faster because most of the computation is done in the form, when the form is saved or refreshed.

For example, a criminal investigation tracking system that I designed had more than 40 different forms in it. Most of the forms were either Response or Response-to-response types of forms. It therefore made sense to have hidden Subject fields on the forms, and then use very simple views that had responses-only columns with the formula of Subject to display the documents (similar to how the discussion database template uses a Responses only column in the All by Category view).

This same technique is very useful anywhere that you might need to have many different types of Response documents associated with a main document. For example, in sales-management types of applications, the architecture might be such that there is one main document per company, then many related Response-type documents associated with the main doc—documents for contact information, for incoming and outgoing correspondences, for action items, and so forth. If all of these forms have a hidden, computed Subject that computes what needs to be displayed in most views, the database's views will be easy to design and manage, because many of the views will require only a responses-only column with the formula Subject to display myriad forms.

What you want to avoid is an application that uses many forms and then needs very complex formulas in every column in a view. Not only are these types of systems hard to maintain, but they also can cause performance problems because the views' columns have to do a lot of computations to figure out what to display in each column for each document displayed within the view.

# Summary

Although Notes application development is already very rapid when compared with traditional development systems, using the two techniques outlined in this chapter should help you to design prototypes faster and to manage large Notes applications that contain many forms and views.

Using the Discussion database template to prototype Notes applications makes sense in many instances, because most applications are a combination of main documents, responses, and response to responses. This template contains one of each of these types of documents, along with a suitable view (the By Category view) for envisioning a "master view" in your completed application.

Using the hidden, computed Subject field technique for driving your views will help you make the design and management of your application's views easier, and you will have the added benefit of having "snappier" views because the view's columns will have to perform fewer computations.

When using a combination of these techniques, you should be able to prototype many Notes applications in a period of a couple of days. Just be sure to remind your users that you have only developed a prototype; otherwise, they might become too enthusiastic about when the system will be ready for production.

# III

## Architecting, Developing, and Deploying Complex Notes Applications

LOTUS

NOTES

# 12

## Notes Application
## Architectures

# Overview

The development and management of Notes applications is significantly different than for traditional application development systems. One of the biggest differences is in how fast a Notes application can be designed and brought to a usable state. Additionally, production Notes systems can be changed much more easily than other types of applications because the application is part of the database, and the changes made to the application can be distributed via replication.

Although Notes applications can be designed very quickly, making the initial architectural decisions and managing to "roll out" of the application can take longer than people might expect. Deciding on the underlying architecture of the application is very critical because it affects the reporting, security, and performance attributes of the application.

Additionally, new Notes systems must be monitored very closely as they are put into production because even thoroughly tested systems can encounter problems when they are used in a production environment. Watching the system closely enables you to make corrections to the system before the problems become severe.

In this section of the book, I'll help you understand how to select an application architecture, and then I'll explain the development and deployment process, mainly from the management point of view. In the last three chapters of Part III, I'll illustrate some useful formulas as well as some advanced design and security techniques.

# Application Architectures

In their simplest form, Notes applications might consist of only one or two types of forms, and several views of the documents within the database. Such is the case for document library and discussion-type applications, as well as the sample Personnel/Event Tracking database.

Notes applications can, however, be very complex, containing dozens of forms, views, and macros. Designing the views is easy if the application is designed correctly. This task is usually the last step in designing an application. Designing an application's core macros is influenced the most by form design, because the core macros are many times used for moving data between documents, or for moving documents between databases. Deciding what forms are needed and what fields belong on what forms is the trickiest part—the wrong choice might keep the necessary reports from being generated later.

# Key Factors in Determining Architecture

Three key factors help determine the necessary application architecture:

*Security Requirements:* Who will need editor access, and to what types of forms? Who will need read-only access, and to what types of forms? Will certain users or groups be blocked from accessing certain data? Is the data isolated to all the fields on one type of document or to just data in one field on a document? For instance, in a sales management application, can each sales representative see information about other reps' accounts? Can they edit other reps' documents? At an architectural level, it's easiest to limit access to a database simply by using a database's ACL, and you might be breaking up an application into several separate databases for security reasons.

*Reporting Requirements:* What information needs to be extracted from the data in the application's documents? Pay close attention to any numerical or statistical information that might need to be reported, because this factor can strongly affect the overall design of the application.

*Projections of Database Size:* How many documents do you anticipate will be added to the database on a daily/weekly/monthly basis, and how large will these documents be?

After analyzing these three factors, you also need to study the current business process, if it exists, to design a system that makes best use of the current workflow.

# Analyzing the Current Workflow/Processes

In any business process, there are steps or events that occur, sometimes simultaneously and other times in a set sequence. At any given point in the process, you should be able to identify who is responsible for creating, editing, reading, and perhaps deleting information. The main goal of this analysis is to help design a Notes application that eliminates the possibility of replication conflicts and that does not contain redundant or nonessential data.

The key areas to focus on are what happens (or should happen) when

- New projects/problems/cases are composed
- Tasks get assigned, reassigned, or completed
- Projects/problems/cases get completed/closed
- The status or state of an account/project/case changes

As you analyze the current process, try to envision mapping it to a series of Notes main documents, response documents, and response-to-response documents. Also start thinking about what fields should appear on what forms at any given point in the process.

A couple of real-world examples should help you get a better idea of how the real-world workflow can influence the application's design.

The sample software bug tracking system was designed with the idea that at any given time, one individual (or group of individuals) was responsible for editing the information on the main bug report document, and determining who was responsible was a function of the State field on the document (see Figure 12.1). When a bug is reported, an individual in the technical support document composes a new bug report and creates a new company information document. The state of the bug initially is TBD (To Be Determined), which means that now the bug is the responsibility of the Quality Assurance department. After an individual in QA analyzes the bug report, he or she changes the state of the bug to one of several options (Confirmed, Duplicate, No Issue, Unable To Confirm). At this point, if the bug's state is Confirmed, an individual in Development is assigned responsibility for fixing the bug, and it is out of QA's hands until a bug-fix is submitted back to QA to verify that the fix works. The whole idea of this workflow is that at any given time, only one person should be editing the master bug document, thus eliminating the possibility of replication conflicts.

I once designed a Crime Tracking database that was designed to meet the following business process: A call about a suspected crime is taken at a master location, where a data entry clerk composes a new main case document, with the initial case information, and an investigator is assigned to the case. All subsequently gathered information (suspect data and actual criminal activity information) becomes response documents to the main case document—the investigator never edits the main case document because doing so could cause replication conflicts. As the case continues, various other response documents are created for reporting information to external agencies. Then, when the case closes, all the necessary information from these response documents is "rolled up" into the main case document, and the unnecessary response documents are deleted to save space. Additionally, all the fields on the closed case document are "locked" to prevent editing.

**FIGURE 12.1.**

*How the responsibility for a bug report shifts between departments depending on its state.*

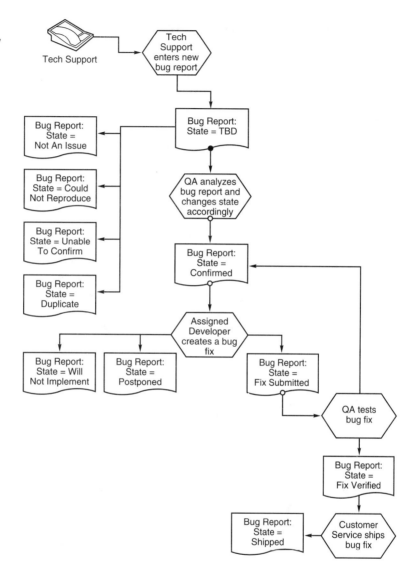

# Selecting a System Architecture

Based on your analysis of the security and reporting requirements, the current business workflow, and your projected document size or volume, you should be ready to start selecting a Notes application design that best meets these requirements.

The first task is to decide how many actual databases will be required for your system. From experience, I have formed several basic guidelines that I try to adhere to:

- *Minimize database size:* In most applications, you'll want to keep the true database size under 100M. The *true* database size refers to the size of the document data without considering the indexes, or the size of the database that results when you create a new replica or new copy of a database, before anyone uses it (the database size grows as users access the various views because new indexes are being created and updated). For most types of documents, without imbedded objects, I estimate approximately 3K per document when figuring a database's true size. If your database contains only one document type and contains no complex view selection formulas (as in the case of many document libraries and lookup databases), the size of the database can be substantially large without causing any performance problems.

- *Keep your remote users in mind when designing the system:* Their disk space for local databases is limited. This might mean that you have to design the system so that selective replication can be used, and you must be careful when you perform lookups into large databases. If you are going to use large lookup-type databases, design the system so that the forms that use these lookups are composed when a user is attached to a server. For instance, suppose that you want to design an expense-report routing system that would automatically default some information for a user, such as his phone number, department name, and profit center. It would probably not be a good idea to look up this information from the master Notes Name & Address because remote users do not generally have a replica of this on their local hard drive. (I'll show you a more elegant solution to this problem in Chapter 18, "The Travel Authorization Request Workflow System.") In some instances, you might have to design your systems and workflow so that forms which perform lookups from large master lookup databases are composed only by server-based users.

- *Design for purging or archiving old or noncritical documents:* To keep the database size down, and to help keep it "uncluttered" for users, design your system with some criteria and mechanism for purging or archiving old documents. For example, in a software bug tracking application, bugs related to previous versions of a product could be archived to a separate archive database. Or in a project management system, completed projects older than, say, 90 days could be moved to an archive database.

> **TIP**
>
> Many large-scale Notes applications actually consist of several Notes databases. This design allows maximum flexibility from a design and security standpoint and helps keep the individual databases from becoming slow and unmanageable.

If you feel that the volume of documents will be sufficiently high, or if there are security concerns, you might want to divide your system into several databases. Although this might seem a little strange or cumbersome at first, it really is not that much more work to scan several properly designed Notes databases for information that relates to you, rather than trying to maneuver through one huge database that tries to do everything for every user. Following are some examples of how I have successfully divided an application into multiple databases:

- By breaking a sales management database into smaller databases by region or product line and then "rolling" them up into one master database.
- By creating a separate bug tracking database for each line of software products instead of putting all bugs in one database.
- By creating an individual audit database for each of a company's audits.
- By setting the Access Control List individually for each audit.

This last example deserves a little more explanation, to give you an idea of how a very large system can be architected in Notes.

An audit department in a large corporation performed more than 1500 audits per year. It needed not only a method of cataloging the various audited items (divisions, functions, and so forth), but also a system for scheduling audits, taking into account previous audit history. The desired security was such that auditors should be allowed to see only the audits they were assigned to, and the assignment of audits could vary from day to day due to illness and reassignments. Standard objectives and tests were required for certain types of audits, but the system needed the capability to save some of the custom objectives and tests for use in future audits.

The architecture that was chosen included one central audit management and scheduling database, an audit database template, and audit library databases (see Figure 12.2).

Although this system might seem complex, it was fully operational after less than one year of development. Additionally, it is part of a much larger Notes application within the corporation that consolidates all the corporation's important security information from not only audits but all of its security systems as well, as shown in Figure 12.3.

**FIGURE 12.2.**

*An audit application
that consists of many
databases.*

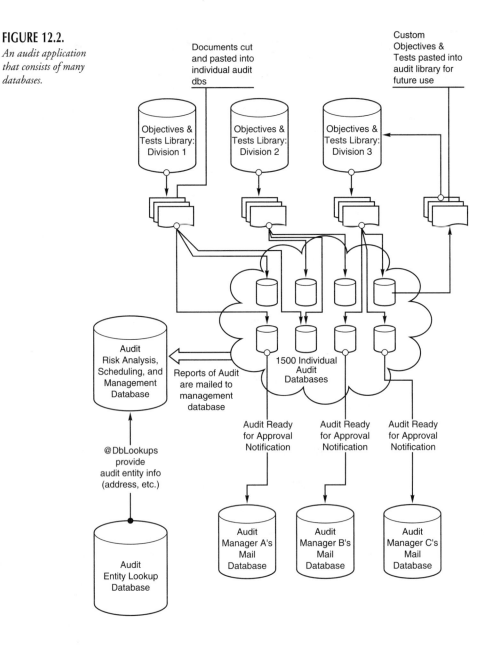

**FIGURE 12.3.**

*The audit system as a component in a Notes system that consolidates all important security and audit information into one reporting database.*

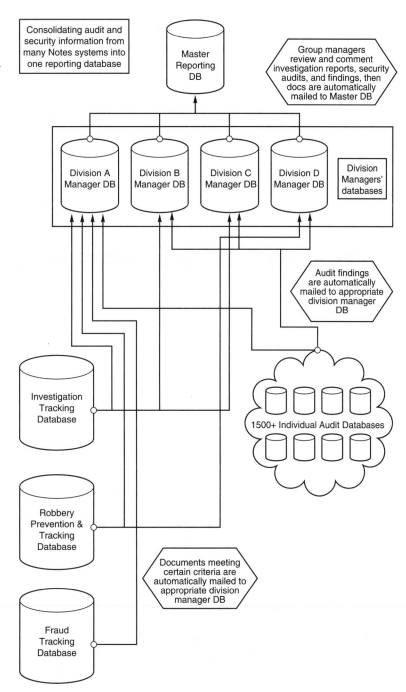

One other idea you might want to consider is using selective replication as a security feature. I know, the *Notes Application Developer's Reference* states that selective replication is not a security feature, but as long as the selective replication is server-to-server, and your servers are secure, selective replication might help you solve some tricky security problems.

For example, suppose that you are designing a sales management application, and sales reps in one territory should not be able to see details about activity in other territories. Additionally, groups of individuals/sales managers need access to data from all regions. There are several ways to accomplish this task, but one way is to set up selective replicas of the master database, as depicted in Figure 12.4. The selective databases contain only the documents pertinent to the given region, and the access control lists of the selective replicas are set to allow only salesmen from the appropriate region to access the database. Additionally, the ACL of the database on the Main server does not list servers East and West as a Manager, so their ACLs do not replicate back to the Main server.

The point of these examples is that when deciding on an application's basic database structure, don't be afraid to break the database into smaller, more manageable pieces. In Notes, it's relatively easy to consolidate important information in multiple databases into one main database for reporting purposes, whether it is by moving documents from database to database using Notes mail engine and the @MailSend command or by using selective replication.

## Deciding What Forms Will Be Necessary

Deciding how many types of forms will be required in a given application depends largely on the results of your current business process evaluation. It also resembles relational database design in that you need to consider entity relationships to a certain degree—there can be one-to-many relationships (a given main document can have many response documents), and using advanced formulas, you can create unique one-to-one relationships (by limiting the number of response documents a given document can have). If you can envision the business process in terms of one-to-many and one-to-one relationships and then envision this process as a combination of main documents and response documents, you'll have much of the design work done. Here are some examples to get you thinking (but remember, depending on your particular circumstances, these designs might not be appropriate):

- In a software bug tracking application, a bug (main document) might have been reported by many companies (response document).
- In a sales management system, a company (main document) might have many sites (responses), and multiple contacts per site (response-to-responses), and action items might be associated with each contact (response-to-responses).

**FIGURE 12.4.**

*Selective replication, when used between databases on servers, can be used to enhance security.*

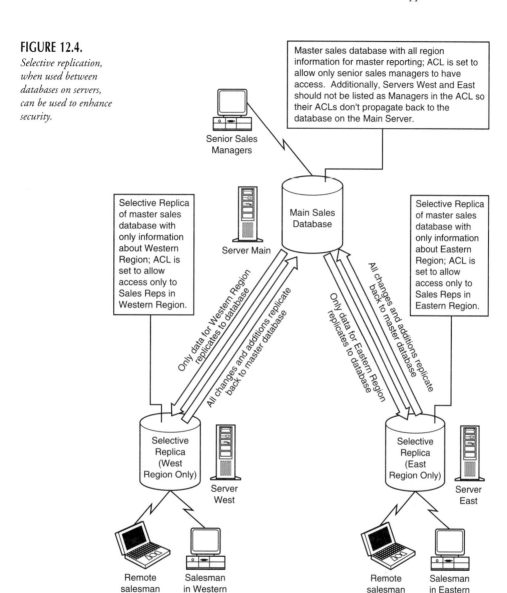

Master sales database with all region information for master reporting; ACL is set to allow only senior sales managers to have access. Additionally, Servers West and East should not be listed as Managers in the ACL so their ACLs don't propagate back to the database on the Main Server.

Senior Sales Managers

Selective Replica of master sales database with only information about Western Region; ACL is set to allow access only to Sales Reps in Western Region.

Server Main

Main Sales Database

Selective Replica of master sales database with only information about Eastern Region; ACL is set to allow access only to Sales Reps in Eastern Region.

Only data for Western Region replicates to database

All changes and additions replicate back to master database

Only data for Eastern Region replicates to database

All changes and additions replicate back to master database

Selective Replica (West Region Only)

Server West

Selective Replica (East Region Only)

Server East

Remote salesman in Western Region

Salesman in Western Region

Remote salesman in Eastern Region

Salesman in Eastern Region

- A project management system might consist of many projects (main documents), with associated tasks (responses) and related comments (response-to-responses).

- An audit database might consist of audit master status sheets (main documents), along with associated objectives (responses) and tests (response to responses).

> **TIP**
>
> When you are deciding what forms you need, it's also a good time to decide whether your application will enable users to cut and paste response documents from one document to another.

In a Notes application, response documents can be selected and then cut and pasted to be responses to another document. To do so, you would select the appropriate documents, select **Cut** on the **E**dit menu, highlight the new document that they should be responses to, and then select **P**aste from the **E**dit menu, effectively "pruning and grafting" response hierarchies. The only problem is that most response documents inherit information when they are composed, and because inheritance happens only once, at compose time, their fields are not updated to reflect the new parent document.

In some instances, however, the capability to move or copy documents is very useful—perhaps in a sales application when you want to move a contact document and all of its related documents from one company site to another. If you want this capability, you'll probably have to write a Paste-in macro that automatically updates the fields. Otherwise, you should still think about writing a Paste-in macro that warns users if they cut and paste documents.

> **TIP**
>
> When a Notes document is open, in either read or edit mode, if you click on the Notes **V**iew menu, you'll notice that all the form names appear on the **V**iew menu, with a check mark next to the active form (see Figure 12.5). Although this sometimes is a useful tool, I strongly discourage you from using it as a way for users to edit and create documents because it can lead to users' trying the same technique in other Notes applications.
>
> A user can select a different form from the menu, which causes the document to be displayed with the selected form. If the document is saved, the document's Form variable is changed accordingly. In all but a few instances, I strongly recommend that you do not use this capability in your database design,

especially in databases with response-type forms, and that in training, you emphasize to your users not to use this capability. The main reason is that users will inevitably take this action in other databases, which can cause disastrous results, especially when main docs are turned into response docs and the document and all of its responses disappear in views with response hierarchy.

**FIGURE 12.5.**

*When a document is open, the* **View** *menu lists the database's forms, with a check mark next to the active form.*

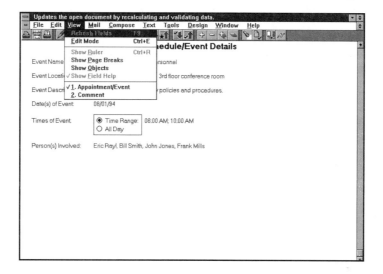

Don't get too consumed with the system's current paper-based forms that are either manually created or printed from a spreadsheet or a word processing program. Many times in Notes, one paper-based form might need to be split into two or more Notes forms to avoid replication conflicts and performance problems. Later, the information in the multiple Notes documents can be merged into one document, or form override can be used for printing.

A department within a large corporation wanted to use Notes for an expense-report routing system. The corporation's accounting department was not using Notes, so the final output from the Notes system would be a piece of paper that looked identical to the corporation's standard expense form. We managed to design a form that, when printed, looked almost identical to the corporation's expense form (see Figure 12.6). But the problem was that, due to the calculations involved, the form was excruciatingly slow to load and recalculate. We spoke with the users, and we found that they generally entered only one item type per line on the paper-based form. Additionally, they found the paper form confusing. That's when I decided to design a new, easy-to-use form for data entry (see Figure 12.7). Then we would use the Notes form override feature when printing, and print using the standard corporate expense report form. Although it took quite a bit of work to get all the formulas and logic correct, the users liked the faster-responding worksheet, and most of the computing was done at print time.

## When to Use Mail Enabling and Forms Routing

Even if your organization is not using the Notes electronic mail system, you can mail-enable your Notes applications as long as you are running a gateway program between Notes mail and your corporate mail system (of course, you lose Notes-specific items such as doc links, encryption, electronic signatures, and potentially the formatting if the Notes gateway is not set up to handle the form you are mailing). Mail-enabled applications are a big buzzword in the industry now, but I don't consider the capability to select a **S**end menu option within my spreadsheet program to be a great mail-enabled application. Besides, in my experience, at least half of the "point-to-point" mail messages sent to groups of users are better handled by an appropriate Notes discussion-style database. This method is much more organized and efficient, and people aren't "left out of the loop" when users reply to a memo.

Well-designed Notes applications, combined with well-educated users, should not need overly mail-enabled applications (in fact, mail usage should drop dramatically within workgroups that are using Notes). Notes users should be encouraged to look in important databases frequently, and should be trained how to use views and unread marks to find new information that pertains to them. Overdue reminders and notices of events in a database that a particular user might not look at frequently are my suggested uses of mail-enabled applications.

For instance, the software developer responsible for fixing bugs for specific products should not get a new piece of mail every time a bug is confirmed on a product he is responsible for. I think that a much better solution is to train the user to look in the database regularly, probably in a view categorized by an AssignedTo column, and see whether there are any new bugs he needs to work on. Additionally, while he is in the database, it might be a good idea for him to look at the other bugs of interest that have not yet been assigned to him. He might know an immediate answer to a problem, and by posting a quick comment, he could save another individual days of work. After all, Notes is about communications and leveraging on the information or experts available within your company. Now if a bug was assigned to a developer and he had not resolved it within a certain period, an automatic mail message sent to his manager might be a good use of mail-enabling.

**FIGURE 12.6.**

*A Notes expense form designed to look like a paper-based corporate form.*

| Date | Description of expense | Auto Miles Driven | Auto Expense | Other Transp. | Meals | Lodging | Entertain-ment | Other Expense | TOTAL |
|---|---|---|---|---|---|---|---|---|---|
| 12/06/93 | LAX - Orlando | | | 360 | | | | | $360.00 |
| 12/06/93 | Taxi | | | 12 | | | | | $12.00 |
| 12/06/93 | Dinner | | | | 24 | | | | $24.00 |
| 12/10/93 | Hotel- Dolphin | | | | | 725 | | | $725.00 |
| 12/10/93 | Taxi | | | 15 | | | | | $15.00 |
| 12/10/93 | Parking -LAX | | 60 | | | | | | $60.00 |
| | | | | | | | | | $0.00 |
| | | | | | | | | | $0.00 |
| | | | | | | | | | $0.00 |
| | | | | | | | | | $0.00 |
| | | | | | | | | | $0.00 |
| | | | | | | | | | $0.00 |
| | | | | | | | | | $0.00 |
| | | | | | | | | | $0.00 |
| | | | | | | | | | $0.00 |
| | | | | | | | | | $0.00 |
| | | | | | | | | | $0.00 |
| | | | | | | | | | $0.00 |
| | | | | | | | | | $0.00 |
| | | | | | | | | | $0.00 |
| | | | | | | | | | $0.00 |
| | | | | | | | | | $0.00 |
| | **TOTAL EACH COLUMN** | 0 | $60.00 | $387.00 | $24.00 | $725.00 | $0.00 | $0.00 | $1,196.00 |
| | | | (A) | (B) | (C) | (D) | (E) | (F) | (G) |

**FIGURE 12.7.**

*The expense report worksheet data entry form.*

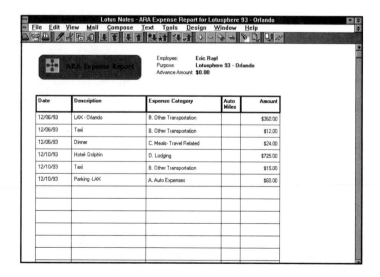

Forms-routing applications, however, are a different breed. One of the main reasons these applications are so useful is because of the security of the user's mail database, and they are "point-to-point" applications that model how the real world works. For instance, I want to take my paper-based purchase requisition to my boss for him to sign, and then have it dropped off at the appropriate purchasing clerk. I don't want to post my requisition for, say, a new 100 MHz Pentium with a 21" Trinitron monitor on a bulletin board and have everyone read it while I wait for my boss to sign it and then for the purchasing department to order it. In Notes, I can design a system that models this paper-based workflow.

> **TIP**
>
> If you are going to design a forms-routing workflow application, be sure to have policies and procedures in place *before* you try to design the Notes system.

The policies and procedures that govern a Notes workflow should adequately address all issues a paper-based system would face, and you should be able to draw it on paper. You would not believe the number of times I have tried to design a workflow system for a company that supposedly has policies and procedures in place, and halfway through development I hear comments like these:

- "But *certain* secretaries need to be able to create and/or approve purchase requisitions for their bosses."
- "Sometimes I'll call the travel desk and ask them to make airline/hotel/car reservations *before* my request gets approved because I want to make sure I get a reservation—how can I ensure that they don't duplicate the reservations?"
- "Sometimes I'll leave a purchase request on my boss's desk for him to sign; then when I find out he's not going to be in today, I'll go into his office and retrieve the requisition and take it to someone else for approval—how can I do that in Notes?"

The point is, Notes forms-routing applications can be some of the neatest and most useful applications, and they can be flexible. But policy and procedure issues can make them very complex to develop. Try to get your users to sign off on a fairly strict workflow before you start development.

## Mathematical and Statistical Computation Considerations

Notes, for a document-oriented database, can perform some fairly powerful mathematical computations, especially with a little creativity. The main concern you should have is knowing what kind of numbers and summations your application will have to provide before you select an architecture. For example, in Figure 12.8, not only totals are calculated, but percentages as well, and the user can double-click on the categories to "drill down" to see more detail about where the numbers are coming from.

**FIGURE 12.8.**

*A Notes view showing some of its mathematical capabilities.*

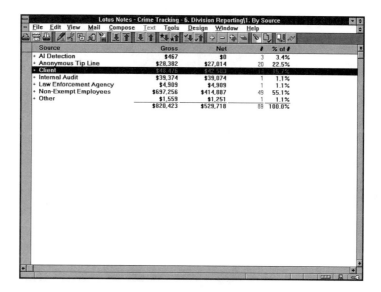

---

**TIP**

The main concern you have when designing your application is that the totals that appear in views are not available for use in any Notes form.

---

A real-world example will help you understand this information a little better. When I was first designing a Crime Tracking application, I considered having multiple Loss and Recovery documents for each case (many cases at the bank involve more than one actual loss per case, and these losses can be recovered over a period, which is the same for recoveries). With this type of design, a user could always see the gross and net loss amounts from a view. But the problem was that the investigators needed a way to get the net dollar amount into certain forms when they composed them, such as the Investigation Report (there were several more complex reporting issues as well). We could return the list of numbers to a computed field on the investigation report, but we could not perform any mathematics on the values that @DbLookup returned. A rather crude way would be to have the investigators write down the totals that appear in the view, and then compose an Investigation Report.

Finally, we opted for a design that used a single Loss/Recovery form with a field that contained the current net loss (see Figure 12.9). In that way, that single loss value was in one field and could easily be looked up by any form that needed the net loss value.

**FIGURE 12.9.**

*The Loss/Recovery document in a crime tracking application. Note that the form includes the current net loss.*

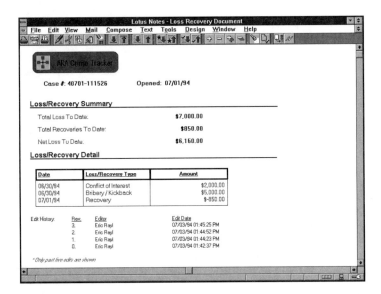

As you can see, with the proper design, Notes can perform many useful mathematical computations.

# Summary

When designing Notes applications, you first need to analyze three key factors: security requirements, reporting requirements, and projected document volume. Then you should talk with users about their current business processes and examine the current forms they use or documents they generate. With these factors in mind, you should be able to make a first pass at designing a system that will meet the requirements while keeping security tight and performance high. Remember that many times, complex Notes applications are best broken down into multiple databases. In the next chapter, I show you how to actually start developing a complex application and provide some suggestions on how to manage the development/deployment process.

# 13

## Managing the Development and Deployment of Notes Applications

# Introduction

Lotus Notes is one of the few true network applications, much different from "network aware" applications that support sharing files on a network file server or mainframe applications that are accessed via 3270 emulation. As such, the development, implementation, and management of Lotus Notes applications are very different from what organizations are used to, and if they are not prepared, they will surely have problems.

Notes applications do not fit the traditional life cycle of application development. I think the best Notes applications are continuously evolving and improving applications. Traditional applications are usually rolled out in versions or phases; in many instances, this is counterproductive with Notes applications. Granted, major architectural changes need adequate planning and testing, but Notes applications should be allowed to change through many small, incremental changes without the need for a lot of fanfare.

Notes embodies the concept of "personal computers" to its fullest. Users have a lot of freedom over how they configure their own version of Notes, and this freedom can cause trouble because of the myriad options available. Many features in Notes cannot be "hidden" from the user, such as the numerous setup options, which makes training and support very important for companies using Notes. As mentioned before, this is a double-edged sword. If users are trained well in Notes and a well-trained support organization is in place for the users, then over time, training and support should decrease within organizations that use Notes extensively.

Don't let my comments scare you. Users not familiar with Notes probably are shaking their heads as they read this, wondering whether Notes is right for their organization. The answer is most definitely yes, if your organization needs an application development platform that can change rapidly to meet changing business needs and that can easily embrace new technologies, such as phone- and video-enabled applications.

# The Notes Development Process

Notes applications are generally developed much more quickly than traditional applications. One of the longest phases of the Notes development process can be generating a functional specification for the application. In this initial phase, there are decidedly two kinds of organizations: One type of company is either already using Notes or has decided to use Notes for a specific project based on its feature set (multiplatform, distributed databases with remote access, and so forth), and the other type of organization is still trying to determine what the *perfect* set of development tools will be for a given application. In my experience, the former type of organization, which has decided to use Notes for a given project (never mind that only 95 percent of the requirements can be met), will have its new application up and running while the latter type of organization is still deliberating what tool to use. In today's rapidly changing business environment, this added speed can give companies a competitive advantage.

## The Importance of Prototyping

It is important to allow plenty of time in the development process for prototyping. In the Notes environment, this time is used in a rather nonlinear fashion, however. What I mean is that Notes prototypes can be developed very quickly, even when compared with systems such as Visual Basic, but many times these systems might have to be completely scrapped and the application started from scratch due to an architectural problem. Don't be afraid to overhaul your prototypes from the ground up. The time spent on finding an architecture that will address all of your security and reporting requirements is well worth it.

The good news is that with Notes, when a prototype is tested and approved by the users, it's basically the completed product. Maybe you'll still need to build the help system or pretty up the forms and views, but much of the hard work is done.

During the prototyping process, I've found it useful to get as many users involved as possible. First, these initial users will fast become your application's power users and will be able to help some of their cohorts when it comes to supporting the application. Second, your prototype needs as much varied sample data as possible to validate the prototype. A Notes database is not very exciting without some data, and preferably it should have lots of data. An application developer can spend a lot of time just entering sample data into the prototype so that it can be demonstrated, but if you can get some users to help you enter some real-world data into your prototype, both the developer and the users will benefit from the process.

## Notes Application Development Management

Many companies will be tempted to manage the development of Notes applications using methods that were well proven for managing the development of mainframe applications. Although traditional application development and change management techniques can be used for developing Notes applications, they tend to be counterproductive. Notes applications can be developed very rapidly, and the best applications tend to evolve as they are used.

The good news, however, is that you already have one of the best tools available for managing projects—Lotus Notes. Notes databases can and should be used throughout the development process, from brainstorming and developing the specification through online documentation and change-management databases. This technique helps improve communications and the flow of information between the developers, the managers, and the users.

## Group Notes Development Projects

Group Notes development projects need to be managed much differently than in traditional languages in which developers can be assigned different routines or functions to write. In large systems in which multiple databases are used, it makes sense to assign different developers each to a different database (or type of database) within the application. In my experience, it is counterproductive to have two or more people working on the same Notes database. Sure, you can do it, but there is no easy way to divide a database between two or more developers.

The best use for group development in Notes is in brainstorming on what architecture to use for a specific application. Having two or more Notes developers meet and work together in this way can be very productive and can lead to a much better application in the long run. But after the development starts, having one developer work on each individual database makes the most sense.

## Managing the Development Process

It should come as no surprise to you that I find Notes to be one of the best tools for managing software development projects, whether the project is a Notes application or even commercial software. If nothing else, a Notes database can be used as a "container" for all of your project management Gantt charts and related documents, but it can be much more.

A modified discussion-style database works quite well during all phases of the development process, from deciding on the architecture all the way through change management. Encourage all members of the development team, including your pilot users, to use the database for their comments and feedback, rather than using E-mail and phone messages, to ensure that no one is left out of the loop.

Careful use of the subject and category fields in the discussion database are all that is needed to make the discussion template usable as-is, but you might want to add a field on the main topic form to indicate whether an issue is open or closed, and then create corresponding views to filter out resolved issues.

## Documenting Notes Systems

Unfortunately, documenting Notes databases is not very easy, and truthfully, the time you spend meticulously documenting every aspect of your database might be counterproductive. I think that a well-designed Notes database is almost self-documenting. The easiest way to document a Notes database is to use very descriptive field, form, view, and macro names whenever possible. Additionally, hidden text can be used on forms to document the purpose of fields and buttons.

Beginning with Notes 3.0, Lotus provided a way to print the *synopsis* of a database. To create a synopsis for a database, select the S**y**nopsis... option on the Notes **D**esign menu, which brings up the Design Synopsis dialog box (see Figure 13.1).

**FIGURE 13.1.**

*Using the Design Synopsis dialog box, you can select which elements of the database's design to include in the synopsis.*

When you click the **O**K button on the Design Synopsis dialog box, Notes produces a window with output detailing the design elements you have selected. Figure 13.2 shows a screen of output about the fields in the Personnel/Event Tracking sample database.

**FIGURE 13.2.**

*The field information generated by the S**y**nopsis... option.*

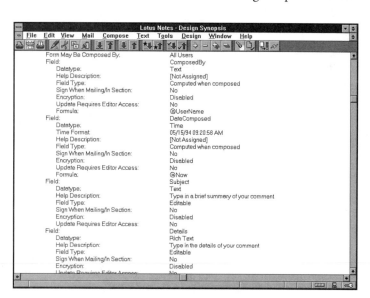

At this point, you can print the synopsis by selecting **P**rint... on the **F**ile menu, or you can save it to a text file by selecting **E**xport... on the **F**ile menu.

The addition of the synopsis is a step in the right direction, but Lotus still has a long way to go. The problem is that in complex databases, the synopsis quickly gets unmanageable. The synopsis for an audit application template I designed was more than 500 pages long. It's easy to print this information, give it to a client, and say, "Here's your documentation," but it really is next to worthless.

What is needed is some way to organize the output from the synopsis. What better way than to use a Notes database, we thought. So an associate (the technical editor of this book, Saeed Naderi) wrote a "quick and dirty" XBase program to parse the text file generated by the synopsis into data that could be imported into Notes. The goal of this project was to build a data dictionary of all the fields used within the client's Notes applications, so all we were concerned with importing was the field information from the synopsis. That way, we could create views that listed field names by application and by which form they were used on.

The overall strategy of this "data dictionary" was to import all the field definitions for all the applications as they were under development, then have project management review the field names and definitions, ensuring that they followed the corporate conventions and were consistent across all applications. At this point, I'm sure this sounds like exactly what some of you have been looking for, but again, I think it was merely an exercise in work for work's sake. Six months after its inception, with countless hours spent on it, the data dictionary died a quiet death, and no one complained. There was only a marginal return for having to pore over thousands and thousands of field names and definitions, and applications were held back from being in production during this process. Lotus might eventually come up with a more elegant way of allowing the synopsis data to be stored in a central Notes database and automatically updated nightly, similar to the way the database catalog works, but until then, I cannot recommend relying on the synopsis for any meaningful data.

One interesting use of a Notes data dictionary is in the new Customer Service sample application that ships with Notes v3.1.5. In this application, there is a separate data dictionary database whose main purpose is to serve as a central location where keyword lists can be looked up. Although I think that this type of data dictionary is most useful for building generic applications that can be easily distributed, you should definitely take a look at this example application.

Documenting large Notes systems, or forms-routing systems, is best done using standard tools such as flowcharting and word processing programs. Each critical step within an application or a workflow can then be described and illustrated, complete with formulas if applicable. Using these tools, the complete relationship between all the databases and the data that flows between the databases can be documented.

## Suggested Standards and Conventions

Creating extensive Notes application standards and conventions is another task that, if taken to extremes, can be counterproductive. The most important convention, as far as I'm concerned, is that a Notes application should behave like a Notes application. In other words, when you want to create a new document, you select it from the **C**ompose menu; when you want to edit a document, you switch to edit mode (or use Ctrl+E); and all form changes required within an application are handled either by a view's form formula or by macros, not by users selecting a different form from the view menu. If this basic convention is followed, users should have little trouble learning new Notes applications as they are introduced.

I've found several other minor conventions useful for both application developers and users. Starting all date-type field names with "Date," as in DateCreated, DateStarted, and DateDue, can help developers and power users who create private views. The reason is that many Notes formulas will involve date fields, and it's easier to search for these field names when pasting in a field name or when using the **D**esign|Document **I**nfo... menu option.

Another minor convention I've found useful is to consistently use the field help text to identify keyword-type fields. For instance, all keyword help text might start with the phrase "Press <Enter> and select...," which gives users a visual cue that the field contains a keyword list.

In views, I usually stick to the convention of making the font for a categorized column bold, and actual documents normal font. Then users will know that if they double-click on a bold label, the column will expand, whereas double-clicking on a column in normal font opens the document. I also try to stick to the convention of using the "+" symbol, in conjunction with the @IsExpandable function, in the first column to indicate that a column is expandable (see Figure 13.3). Another variation on this concept that I like is to use the icon type of column, and depict categories with the "folder" icon and documents with the "document" icon, as shown in Figure 13.4.

**FIGURE 13.3.**

*My preferred view convention for providing visual cues as to categories and collapsed documents.*

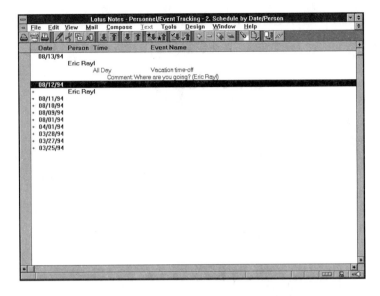

**FIGURE 13.4.**

*An alternative method of identifying categories in a view using an icon type of column.*

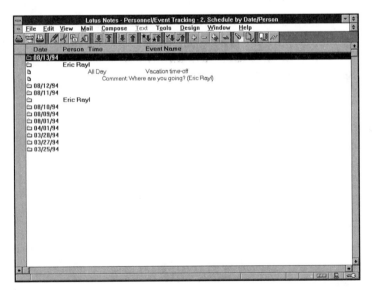

Of course, when designing an application, you must be conscious of what types of computers will be running the application. Cross-platform applications will look and print best when the Lotus cross-platform fonts (Tms Rmn and Helv) are used exclusively. Monochrome laptops can display color forms, views, and fonts in an unreadable fashion, and applications should be tested on monochrome computers if they will be used on that type of computer.

# Deploying Notes Applications

When your application is ready to go into production, you need to be concerned with a few issues: data conversion, training, and support.

Data conversion is one of the hardest processes because Notes import facilities are very limited, and it is hard to import data into Notes applications that use any sort of a response hierarchy. Unless the database you are trying to populate is a "flat file" type of lookup or document reference database, you will probably save time and money by hiring some temporary clerical help to rekey the data. In databases that will use a response hierarchy, importing data is next to impossible because response-type documents can be imported only one document at a time manually. I strongly urge you to resign yourself to the fact that for many complex applications, you'll have to manually enter the data or import archive data into a simplified Notes database that does not have complex response hierarchies.

Training issues for Notes applications are much different than for traditional applications. Even if you think your users will be using only one Notes application (and perhaps Notes mail), I think that you should still train users on Notes fundamentals before embarking on the application-specific details. Every company I have worked with has, after a short period, ended up with numerous Notes applications. If the users are not fully aware of how to use Notes, it becomes tedious just trying to get users to add a new database to their Notes workspace.

Training materials should be electronically based if at all possible. I suggest creating a computer-based training program for your users using various Notes databases. Lotus has a very good computer-based training program for end users that you can purchase and modify to suit your needs. I've seen companies spend tens of thousands of dollars developing printed training materials for their Notes applications, and these materials were out of date within months because of the dynamic nature of Notes applications. If the documentation was available in electronic form, it could easily be updated. Another obvious suggestion I've seen ignored is that your trainers should be very well versed in Lotus Notes. Nothing discourages users more than trainers who repeatedly can't answer questions or solve problems.

The support requirements for Notes applications, and Notes in general, vary widely with the experience level and background of the individuals within an organization. At one software company where I have worked, Notes was rolled out with hardly any impact on MIS due to the very experienced network staff that had no problems integrating Notes onto the WAN and keeping it running, combined with the rather high competence of the users. At another organization that consisted largely of Mainframe and Localtalk networking professionals, there were many crises. This turmoil was primarily due to the fact that no one on the team was very familiar with LANs/WANs, protocols, and PCs in general. As I have mentioned, Notes is a true network application, and as such, Notes applications need a solid network infrastructure. Problems with applications not working properly can many times be traced to a network software that is configured improperly. I do not recommend embarking on a Notes project without having at least one seasoned network veteran who can troubleshoot various network problems.

# Modifying Production Systems

When using traditional application development systems, applications are usually changed in phases or versions, with all the new features and enhancement request saved up and integrated into an application's next version. Retaining this "version" philosophy when developing Notes applications can cause you to lose some of the benefits the Notes environment has to offer. Traditional systems rely on executable programs, and in a distributed environment, it is time-consuming to simultaneously upgrade the executable program on several hundred users' computers. Additionally, the application must generally be shut down while maintenance, such as adding or changing field and table definitions, is performed on the application's data.

Notes is much different, primarily because the application *is* the database. As the application changes, the Notes replication engine takes care of distributing the changes to all the users. Many changes to Notes applications can be made right in the production database, and the database can be replicated as necessary. Changes such as adding forms, views, and macros or modifying field keyword lists can safely be made to databases while users are working in the database.

Other changes, particularly running macros that "massage" data, such as deleting fields from documents or changing computed-when-composed fields, must be made more carefully. Here the danger is not that the application or database will crash, but that in the distributed environment, some documents might not be processed by the macro. After running a macro that significantly changes documents in a database, it is best to create a private view that contains a column displaying the field that was changed. Then this view should be monitored for a week or two to look for documents that might not have been processed by the macro due to the distributed nature of Notes databases.

Of course, major architectural changes to a Notes database need to be carefully planned and monitored, but minor changes to production systems should be allowed because they will help improve the usability of the application, and users will perceive your support organization as much more responsive.

# When Things Go Wrong...

As any user of personal computers and local area networks (LANs) can attest, Murphy's Law comes into play more frequently than we would like. Notes is a very complex environment, and from time to time, there will be problems. Because of the complexity of Notes, occasionally something will happen that will probably never be fully explained. The important idea here is to focus on how to get your application running again, and then secondarily to try to find out what caused the problem and how to prevent it from happening again.

Many problems are attributable to "pilot error"—users not using Notes or the application correctly. Remote users seem to have the most problems because replicating can be a little confusing if the users are not trained properly. You will not believe how many times users have told me that replication is not working correctly because they did not send or receive all the information they expected to, when the real culprit is either a noisy phone line or call-waiting disconnecting the phone call.

The most common "real" problem that I've seen with Notes applications is some sort of database corruption. The most severe type of database corruption is the kind that will replicate to other databases, causing all replicas to eventually become corrupted. Many types of corruption will not replicate to other databases and will remain isolated.

Because Notes databases are generally distributed over several computers, and perhaps even remote users' computers, it is easy to fix most corruption problems if they are caught in time. Many times, the easiest solution is to just delete the corrupted database and make a new replica from a good version of the database. But other times, you might have to try some other tricks to restore your database to working condition.

Database corruption generally does not involve actual data corruption but view (or index) corruption. This type of corruption usually manifests itself as categories behaving funny, not collapsing or expanding properly. Occasionally, users get an error message indicating that the view is corrupted and cannot be opened. Notes provides an executable, $FIXUP.EXE, that resides in the Notes program directory. The executable file can be loaded at the server console to fix minor database corruption. From the server console, type

```
LOAD FIXUP databasename
```

in which *databasename* is the path and filename of the database relative to the Notes data directory—for instance,

```
LOAD FIXUP SALES\PROJTRAK
```

To be honest, I've had little success fixing corruption with the FIXUP program. My most successful remedies have always been making a new replica of the database, or as an extreme measure, making a new copy of the database. Making a new replica seems to fix many problems, and I use this method not only on servers but on users' local copies of databases that get corrupted and don't replicate properly. Of course, you can always restore from tape in the event of a major catastrophe. (You do have a solid backup strategy, don't you?)

# Summary

There is much talk about using Notes to reengineer business processes, but MIS organizations implementing Lotus Notes must consider reengineering their processes also. Organizations that choose Notes as an application development platform should leverage on its capability to develop (and change) distributed applications rapidly. Companies that try to map traditional project management and application development techniques to the Notes environment will not reap nearly as many benefits or as much return on investment as is possible with Notes applications.

Notes application support definitely is demanding, but companies that already have extensive LAN/WAN expertise will not be as affected as organizations that are used to mainframe systems and applications. Additionally, companies that buy into the "Notes environment" approach versus developing a single Notes application stand a much better chance of getting a high return on investment and gaining a competitive edge by using Notes as an application development platform.

# 14

## Advanced Techniques

# Overview

This chapter is intended to give you some ideas on advanced techniques that you might be able to use in your applications. Some of the more complex Notes @Functions and capabilities are discussed here, but remember that the Notes online help is a great reference that provides the exact syntax of any @Function or @Command. Syntax will not be extensively covered here unless it is necessary to understand the tip or technique.

Many of the sections in this chapter build on functions or features described in a previous section in this chapter. If something is confusing, try looking back a section or so to see whether more explanation is provided there.

# Using *@DbLookup* and *@DbColumn*

In Notes 3.0, Lotus added two new functions, @DbLookup and @DbColumn. These functions are two of the most useful Notes functions because they enable developers to look up data from fields in other documents, in the same or a different Notes database. @DbColumn can also be used to build dynamic keyword lists. Additionally, these functions have hooks that, when used with the Lotus DataLens product, allow Windows-based computers to look up data from non-Notes databases.

The syntax for @DbLookup is as follows:

```
@DbLookup("class":"NoCache";"server":"database";"view";"key";"field"_or_column)
```

When using @DbLookup, make sure that the first column of the view you are "looking up into" is sorted, or the lookup will fail with the error message shown in Figure 14.1. Also, lookups are faster if you look up a specific value in the column (by using the column number as an argument) instead of specifying a field name, which causes Notes to search the document for the specified field.

**FIGURE 14.1.**

*The runtime error message generated when an @DbLookup fails to find a key value.*

Many times you'll have a case in which @DbLookup fails to find a matching key value in the view and database that are specified. This error brings up the cryptic runtime error message Entry not found in index (see Figure 14.1), and it might prevent a document from being available to be composed or opened. You can trap this error using the @IsError function, as in the following example:

```
@If(@IsError(@DbLookup("Notes" : "NoCache"; "";
   "vwLossRecoveryLookup"; CaseNum; 3));
 @Prompt([OK]; "Error"; "You must compose a Loss/Recovery
   document before composing a CRF");
 @DbLookup("Notes" : "NoCache"; "";
   "vwLossRecoveryLookup"; CaseNum; 3))
```

Be very careful when entering the arguments for these functions. The errors that incorrect syntax produces might not be caught by Notes when the formula is saved, and these errors can be cryptic and hard to debug. For that reason, I suggest that you don't add too many DbLookups or DbColumns at one time to a formula before testing it.

I recommend that when deciding what views to use for "looking up into," you design specific hidden lookup views (and use "lookup" in the view name to remind you that it is used in lookups) instead of using visible views. It's all too easy to change the design of a view to meet a user's request and forget which @DbLookup and @DbColumn formulas you also need to change.

# Using @MailSend

@MailSend is a very powerful function that can be used in formulas to either mail the current document or to mail a custom message. In its simplest form, the syntax is

```
@MailSend
```

which causes the current document to be mailed. Of course, the document must have the correct fields for the document to be mailed without an error. At a minimum, the document must have a SendTo field, but other mail-related fields include CopyTo, BlindCopyTo, DeliveryPriority, DeliveryReport, and ReturnReceipt.

With the syntax

```
@MailSend("sendto";"copyto";"blindcopyto";"subject";
  "remark";"bodyfield1":"bodyfieldn";[flag1]:[flagn])
```

a custom mail message can be composed using variables and even features such as a doc link in the mail message back to the document where the formula was run. This feature is handy to use. For example, in an audit system that I designed in which there were more than 1500 individual audit databases, when a Report of Audit in one of the 1500 audit databases was completed and ready to be approved by the audit manager, the auditor would click a button on the audit report, and a mail message was automatically sent to the audit manager, complete with a doc link back to the form that needed approval. The button macro used a formula similar to this:

```
TempSubject := AuditDivision + ";" + AuditRegion + ";" + AuditManager + ";" +
  AICName + ";" + AuditID + ";" + "Report of Audit Ready For Your Approval:  ";
@MailSend("Audit Manager"; ""; ""; TempSubject; ""; ""; [IncludeDoclink])
```

The message would arrive in the audit manager's mail database, with the subject of the memo that a certain audit report was ready for approval, and the body of the memo was simply a Notes doc link right to the appropriate audit report.

> **TIP**
>
> You cannot electronically "sign" documents that are mailed using the @MailSend function. If you need to sign the document as it is mailed, you must use @Command([MailSend]) instead.

# Using *@Prompt*

@Prompt can be used to generate several types of dialog boxes with various user input options. @Prompts are most often used in macros to get a user's input. There are seven types of prompts that can be displayed. This is the generic @Prompt syntax:

```
@Prompt([type]; "Title"; "prompt"; "default"; "choices")
```

Figures 14.2 through 14.8 illustrate the seven various types of @Prompts available.

## *[Ok]*

The most basic type of @Prompt, the [Ok] type, is generally used to temporarily halt macro processing and supply some information to the user.

> **TIP**
>
> Many times, I'll use an `[Ok]` type of `@Prompt` to help me debug my macros. Simply place an `@Prompt` in your macro that will display the contents of temporary variables or the results of computations.

**FIGURE 14.2.**
*`@Prompt` using `[Ok]` as the type.*

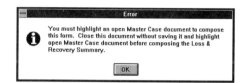

# [YesNo]

This `@Prompt` presents a dialog box with a **Y**es button and a **N**o button, as in Figure 14.3. The function returns TRUE (1) if the user selects **Y**es, and FALSE (0) if the user selects **N**o, making it useful as an argument in an `@If` statement.

**FIGURE 14.3.**
*`@Prompt` using `[YesNo]` as the type.*

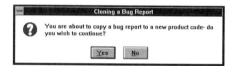

# [OkCancelEdit]

The `@Prompt` usage

```
@Prompt([OkCancelEdit]; "Select Cases For Reporting"; "Type in the beginning
  date for the reporting period in the box below:"; "")
```

creates the dialog box shown in Figure 14.4. The nice feature about any prompt with a Cancel button is that at any time within a macro, if a user clicks a prompt's Cancel button, the macro execution terminates.

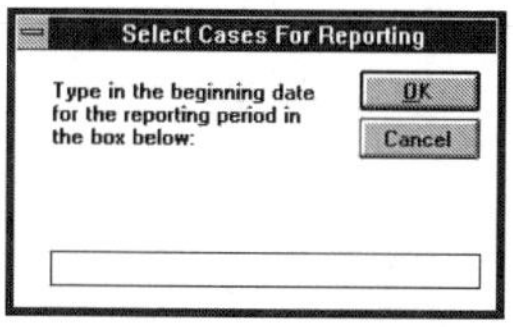


**FIGURE 14.4.**
*`@Prompt` using `[OkCancelEdit]` as the type.*

## [OkCancelList]

The prompt syntax

```
@Prompt([OkCancelList]; "New Loss/Recovery"; "Select the type of loss/recovery
  from the list below"; ""; LossRecoveryKeywords);
```

produces the dialog box shown in Figure 14.5.

**FIGURE 14.5.**

*@Prompt using*
*[OkCancelList] as*
*the type.*

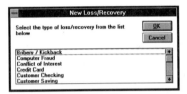

---

**TIP**

The "choices" argument, `LossRecoveryKeywords`, in the preceding usage of `@Prompt` is actually a hidden multivalue field on the form that is computed when composed. This technique is used to make the formula more readable because there are 25 keywords in the list.

---

## [OkCancelCombo]

The following formula is an example of a more complex `@Prompt` usage:

```
@Prompt([OKCANCELCOMBO]; "Cloning a Bug Report"; "Select the appropriate
  version of " + TempProductCode + ":"; @Subset(@DbLookup("Notes" : "NoCache";
  ""; "vwProductCodeVersionLookup"; TempProductCode; 2); -1); @DbLookup("Notes" :
  "NoCache"; ""; "vwProductCodeVersionLookup"; TempProductCode; 2))
```

This formula produces the prompt shown in Figure 14.6. This `@Prompt` illustrates several techniques:

- ■ Using a formula for the prompt message
- ■ Using `@Subset` to get the last value in a list returned by `@DbLookup` and using the value as the prompt's default value
- ■ Using `@DbLookup` to return a list of values that match a particular key

**FIGURE 14.6.**

*An example of the*
*[OkCancelCombo]*
*type of @Prompt.*

## [OkCancelEditCombo]

Using @Prompt with the [OkCancelEditCombo] type produces a prompt like that shown in Figure 14.6, except that the user can enter a new value in the list.

## [OkCancelListMult]

The formula

```
@Prompt([OkCancelListMult]; "Select one or more Topics"; "Assign this bug
   to one or more of the topics listed below:";
   ""; @DbColumn("Notes" : "NoCache"; ""; "vwAllARTopicsLookup"; 1))
```

illustrates not only the usage of the [OkCancelListMult] type of @Prompt but also the use of @DbColumn in a prompt to return a list of all items in a specific view's column. The preceding formula produces the dialog box shown in Figure 14.7.

**FIGURE 14.7.**

*An example of the*
*[OkCancelListMult]*
*type of @Prompt.*

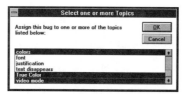

**TIP**

Be careful with the syntax for @Prompt because many types of syntax errors will not generate errors when the formula is saved but will generate a runtime error, as in Figure 14.8.

**FIGURE 14.8.**

*A runtime error message generated by the improper syntax*
`@Prompt([OK];`
`"You must compose a Loss/Recovery document before composing a CRF").`

# Using @Commands

The @Commands feature was added in Notes 3.0 to enable you to create many more automated applications than were possible previous to release 3. Essentially, @Commands give you as the developer access to any command that a user could run from the Notes menu. For example, @Commands can be used to copy and paste documents, to open documents or views, or to close windows.

In their simplest usage, @Commands are used in button macros to help a user perform a basic Notes function. For example, a Send button might be added to a form, and the following formula might be assigned to the button:

```
@Command([MailSend]);
@Command([FileSave]);
@Command([FileCloseWindow])
```

When the Send button is clicked, the user is prompted with the Mail Send dialog box, shown in Figure 14.9. If the user clicks the **S**end button in the Mail Send box, the document is mailed and then saved, and the document is closed.

**FIGURE 14.9.**

*The Mail Send dialog box that appears when* `@Command([MailSend])` *is used.*

There is one major limitation that you must remember when using @Commands—no matter where @Commands appear in a formula, they will execute last, after any @Functions. You can work around this limitation by chaining together macros, calling one macro that performs some @Functions while in another macro.

# Ensuring That Response Docs Inherit the Correct Information

In many Notes applications, you'll want to ensure that a user has the proper type of document highlighted when composing a document, to ensure that the proper information is inherited into the new document and that the response hierarchy is correct. You can't really stop users from composing a document when an incorrect document is highlighted, but you can warn them immediately that they have made a mistake, and then not allow them to save the document.

To take this action, you need two hidden fields at the top of the form, as in Figure 14.10. (I put the fields at the top so that their formulas execute first, and a warning is generated immediately if something is amiss.)

**FIGURE 14.10.**

*The two fields that warn users if they have the wrong document highlighted when composing a new Loss/Recovery form.*

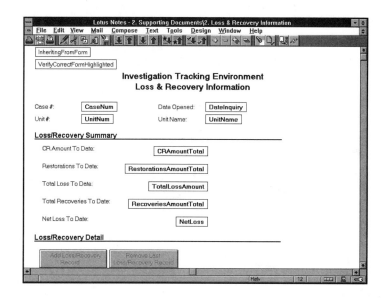

The field InheritingFromForm is a hidden, editable field. You might wonder why an editable field is hidden, but I use the Input Validation Formula feature of an editable field to stop the form from being saved if an error has occurred. The field has a Default Value Formula of Form, which means that it inherits the highlighted document's Form variable as its default value. You therefore immediately know what type of form was highlighted when the document was composed. Additionally, the field's Input Validation Formula is

```
@If(InheritingFromForm != "frmMain";
  @Failure("You must recompose this document
    with an Open Master Case document highlighted in order to save it");
  @Success)
```

This formula is activated when the document is saved and InheritingFromForm has not inherited the proper value from the parent document's Form variable. Because of the @Failure function, the new document cannot be saved.

The second field that is used, VerifyCorrectFormHighlighted, is used to give the user an immediate warning that he has the wrong document highlighted and will not be able to save the form. This field is computed when composed so that its formula will be activated immediately. This is the formula for VerifyCorrectFormHighlighted:

```
@If(InheritingFromForm = "frmMain";
  @Return("");
  @Prompt([OK]; "Error"; "You must highlight an open Master Case document
    to compose this form.  Close this document without saving it and
    highlight an open Master Case document before composing the Loss
    & Recovery Summary."));
```

This formula looks at the value of InheritingFromForm. If it's the correct form name, it executes @Return(""), and the formula stops executing. Otherwise, an Ok-style prompt is displayed with instructions to the user.

You probably wonder why the document cannot just be automatically closed after the user has been warned about the error. This is because @Command([FileCloseWindow]) would be needed, and @Commands can't be used in field formulas.

# Multivalue Fields: Notes Pseudo-Arrays

The Notes field option Allow Multi-Values, found on the Field Definition dialog box, is a very useful feature when you fully understand its implications. Essentially, it enables you to create one-dimensional arrays without having to specify the number of elements or the size of the elements.

Many times, multivalue fields are simply used so that documents can appear multiple times in a view, under different categories. For example, the Personnel/Event Tracking database includes the multivalue field on the Schedule/Event form called PersonsInvolved. This field allows a single event document to appear multiple times in a view that has a categorized PersonsInvolved column (see Figure 14.11 and Figure 14.12).

**FIGURE 14.11.**

*An event document with four names in the multivalue PersonsInvolved field.*

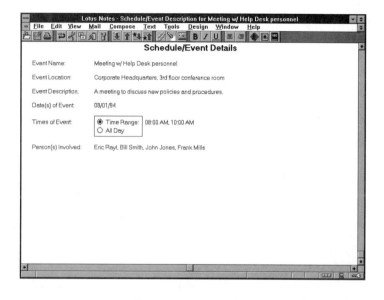

**FIGURE 14.12.**

*In a view categorized by the PersonsInvolved field, the same document appears four times.*

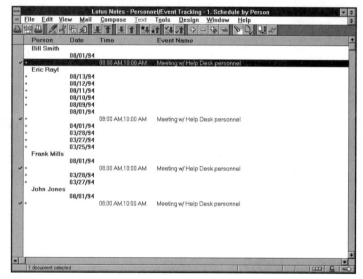

More complex uses of multivalued fields involve using them to build histories of the previous states of fields, to create edit histories, and to create tables in forms. These examples are discussed in upcoming sections.

## Manipulating Multivalued Fields

Notes includes several functions that are useful in manipulating lists or multivalued fields. I use the following functions the most:

`@Elements(list)`

> @Elements returns the number of text, number, or time-date values contained in the *list*.

`@Member(value;stringlist)`

> @Member returns a number indicating the position of the *value* within the *stringlist*; it returns 0 if the *value* is not contained in the list.

```
@IsMember(string;stringlist)
@IsMember(stringlist1;stringlist2)
@IsNotMember(string;stringlist)
@IsNotMember(stringlist1;stringlist2)
```

> @IsMember is a Boolean function that returns TRUE (1) if the *string* is an element of the *stringlist*; otherwise, it returns FALSE (0). When the first argument of @IsMember is also a *stringlist*, it returns TRUE only if all elements of *stringlist1* are contained in *stringlist2*. @IsNotMember returns TRUE if *string* is not an element of *stringlist*, or TRUE if all the elements of *stringlist1* are not contained in *stringlist2*.

`@Subset(list;number)`

> @Subset is very useful in manipulating lists, especially for getting the first or last member of a list. @Subset parses the *list* from left to right and returns *number* values. If a negative *number* is used, the *list* is searched from right to left. For example, @Subset(NameList;5) returns the first five elements of the NameList, and @Subset(NameList - 4) returns the last four elements of the NameList.

```
@Implode(textlist)
@Implode(textlist; separator)
```

> @Implode is used to convert a text list into one string. Without the *separator* argument, the values in *textlist* are concatenated with one space between them; otherwise, the character that appears in the *separator* argument is placed between the elements of the list. I commonly use @Char(9) (the tab character) and @NewLine as separators to produce table-like effects in fields.

The upcoming sections on adding edit histories, simulating multirow tables, and simulating column-oriented tables all use multivalued fields and the preceding functions extensively.

> **TIP**
>
> You can't easily find what element is the maximum or minimum of a multivalue numerical field, but you can try to build the list so that the maximum value occurs either first or last. Build the list using a @DbLookup into a view that has a column sorted by the numerical data, and then the first value in the list will either be the maximum or the minimum, depending on how the column is sorted.

# Adding Edit Histories to Documents

One of the more useful features I generally incorporate into all forms in an application is an edit history. The edit history shows the last five editors of the document, the edit number, and the date and time of the edit. Even though you might not initially think you need the edit history, you will not believe how many times it can help you. Many times I have wished that a form in a given application had this feature.

I can't take any credit for the upcoming example; it has shipped as part of the Lotus Notes Formula Catalog database for as long as I can remember. In addition to being useful, this example does illustrate a good use of multivalue fields and their associated functions. A long time ago, when compiling the formula catalog database, someone at Lotus made the arbitrary decision to show information on only the last five edits. I have found no reason to change this feature, but you could easily show any number of past editors that you desired using the technique outlined here.

If you want to add an edit history to a form in your application, you should never have to manually enter the fields into your form. You can just cut and paste them from a form in one of the sample databases (most of my applications use this feature). Figure 14.13 shows a form in design mode with the relevant fields that I will describe next.

**FIGURE 14.13.**

*A form in design mode showing the fields necessary for tracking a document's edit history.*

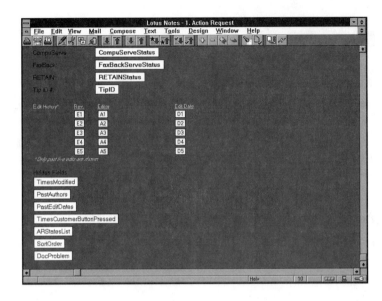

There are three primary, hidden fields that drive a form's edit history. These are the three fields and their corresponding attributes:

TimesModified: Number, Computed
Formula:

```
@If(@IsNewDoc; 0; TimesModified + @IsDocBeingSaved)
```

PastAuthors: Text, Computed, Allow Multi-Values
Formula:

```
@If(@IsDocBeingSaved;
  @If(TimesModified <= 0;
      @UserName;
      PastAuthors : @UserName);
    PastAuthors)
```

PastEditDates: Text, Computed, Allow Multi-Values
Formula:

```
@If(@IsDocBeingSaved;
  @If(TimesModified <= 0;
      @Text(@Now);
      PastEditDates : @Text(@Now));
    PastEditDates)
```

The TimesModified field is used to count the number of times a document has been saved. When a document is first composed (@IsNewDoc = TRUE), the field is initialized to zero, and every time the document is saved, 1 is added to the current value of TimesModified.

The PastAuthors and PastEditDates are multivalued text lists that each contain TimesModified number of elements. The first time the document is saved, the values are initialized to `@UserName` and `@Text(@Now)`, respectively. Then each additional time the documents are saved, one more entry is added to the end of the list by the statements `PastAuthors : @UserName` and `PastEditDates : @Text(@Now)`, respectively.

All the fields used to display the edit history information (A1, E1, D1, A2, E2, and so on) are computed for display type fields—there is no reason to save the information in individual fields within the form. Fields E1, A1, and D1 display the most recent edit information. The formula for E1, which computes the last edit number, is as shown here:

```
DEFAULT PastAuthors := 0;
DEFAULT TimesModified := 0;
X := @Elements(PastAuthors) - 0;
Y := X - TimesModified;
@If(@IsNewDoc; " "; Y >= 0; @Text(X - 1) + "."; " ")
```

This is the formula for A1:

```
@If(@IsNewDoc;
  " ";
  @Subset(@Subset(PastAuthors; -1); 1))
```

And this is the formula for D1:

```
@If(@IsNewDoc;
  " ";
  @If(TimesModified >= 0;
    @Subset(@Subset(PastEditDates; -1); 1);
    " "))
```

Although some of the computations performed in the preceding formulas may seem unnecessary, they are performed to establish a pattern as to how to pick the *n*th edit from the lists and to number it correctly.

Looking at the formulas for E2, A2, and D2, you will begin to see a pattern.

E2:

```
DEFAULT PastAuthors := 0;
X := @Elements(PastAuthors) - 1;
@If(@IsNewDoc;
  " ";
  X - 1 >= 0;
  @Text(X - 1) + ".";
  " ")
```

A2:

```
@If(@IsNewDoc;
  " ";
  @If(TimesModified >= 1;
    @Subset(@Subset(PastAuthors; -2); 1);
    " "))
```

D2:

```
@If(@IsNewDoc;
   " ";
  @If(TimesModified >= 1;
     @Subset(@Subset(PastEditDates; -2); 1);
      " "))
```

The formulas for E*n*, A*n*, and D*n* would be as shown next.

E*n*:

```
DEFAULT PastAuthors := 0;
X := @Elements(PastAuthors) - (n - 1);
@If(@IsNewDoc;
   " ";
   X - 1 >= 0;
   @Text(X - 1) + ".";
   " ")
```

A*n*:

```
@If(@IsNewDoc;
   " ";
  @If(TimesModified >= (n - 1);
     @Subset(@Subset(PastAuthors; -n); 1);
      " "))
```

D*n*:

```
@If(@IsNewDoc;
   " ";
  @If(TimesModified >= (n - 1);
     @Subset(@Subset(PastEditDates; -n); 1);
      " "))
```

# Reverse Inheriting

Reverse inheriting is a term I use to describe the process of updating (or creating) fields on a main document from the contents of fields in response documents. Reverse inheritance has to be forced to happen; that is, a macro must be run to perform the updates to the main case document. This macro can be one that is run either "on demand" when a specific event occurs, such as when a button is clicked, or by a background macro that runs automatically on the server.

To fully understand how reverse inheriting can be useful in your applications, you should try this quick example. Suppose that you wanted a simple project management database, and you were going to architect it such that each project was a main document and each task was a response to a project document. To quickly get this application started, you create a new database from the discussion template (but remember to turn off the design template feature on your database using the

**File|Database|Information|Design** Template menu option, and then uncheck the **Inherit** Design from Template option).

First design the Response form, and add a keyword field called Status below the subject field. Make the keyword options for this field Not Started, In Progress, and Complete. Your form should look similar to the one in Figure 14.14.

**FIGURE 14.14.**

*The Response form with the new Status keyword field.*

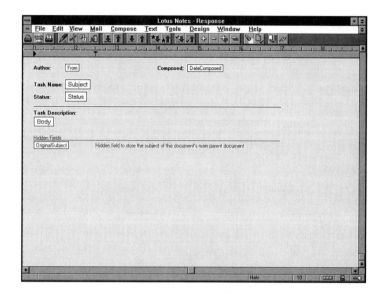

Now create a new view that will be used for lookups of the tasks and their associated status. Design a new view, and define the views attributes as in Figure 14.15, with the name vwTaskLookup, and click the No Response **H**ierarchy button.

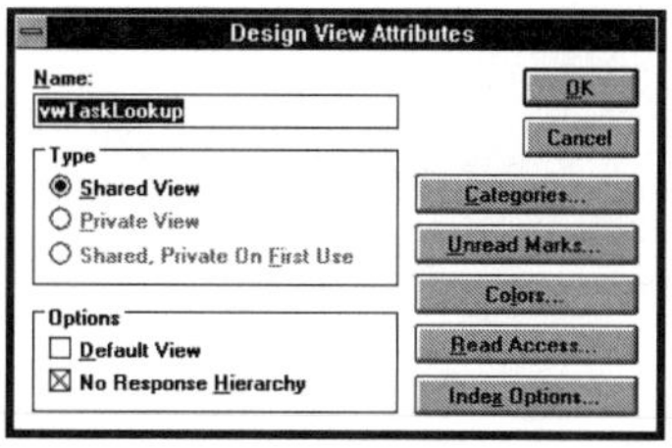

**FIGURE 14.15.**

*The Design View Attributes dialog box for the view that will be used for looking up task information.*

Next, you need to define the columns in the view. The first column's definition should be the field OriginalSubject. Make sure that this column is sorted. The second column's definition should be the formula

```
Subject + @Char(9) + Status
```

@Char(9) inserts a tab between the two fields, which will be used to format the display of the information on the main document. This view is now complete, so save it.

Now you need to add a field to the main project document that will be used for displaying its associated tasks. Enter design mode on the Main Topic form, and add a field called Tasks below the Body field. Set the field to be Computed for display, check the Allow Multi-Values check box, and the set the multivalue display separator to be a new line by clicking the **S**eparators... button and making the appropriate choice. Next, enter the following formula for the field:

```
@If(@IsError(@DbLookup("Notes" : "NoCache"; ""; "vwTaskLookup"; Subject; 2));
  "No Tasks";
  @DbLookup("Notes" : "NoCache"; ""; "vwTaskLookup"; Subject; 2))
```

Then save the field definition.

Next, you should add a little static text to the form to better envision how reverse inheriting can be used in your application. As in Figure 14.16, add the static text Task to the form, press Tab, and type the static text Status. Next, format the static text and the field lines of the form to have a tab stop at 4", as in Figure 14.16. Now exit design mode, saving the form's new design.

**FIGURE 14.16.**

*The modified Main Topic document—note the tab stop setting for the selected area.*

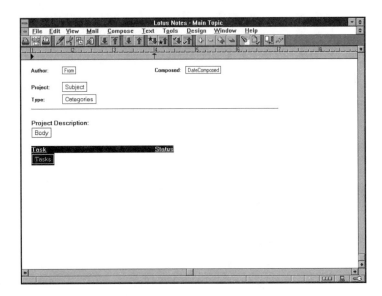

Now you need to compose a few sample documents to see how reverse inheriting works. First, compose a master project document (a Main Topic). Fill in the fields as shown in Figure 14.17. Next, compose a couple of tasks (Responses) for the upgrade project, filling in the fields similar to the task in Figure 14.18. Your database's view By Category should look similar to Figure 14.19.

**FIGURE 14.17.**

*A Main Topic document with sample data to simulate a main project-type document.*

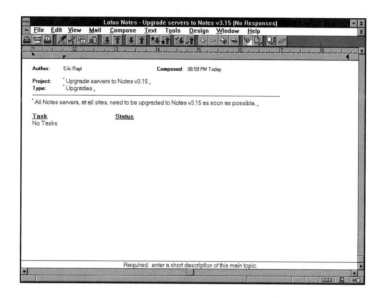

**FIGURE 14.18.**

*A Response document with sample data to simulate a task-type document.*

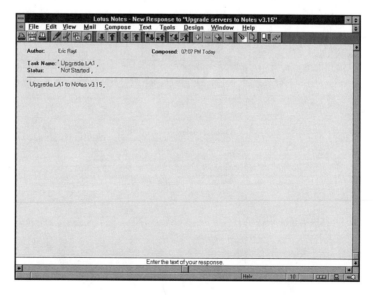

**FIGURE 14.19.**

*The view By Category with some sample data.*

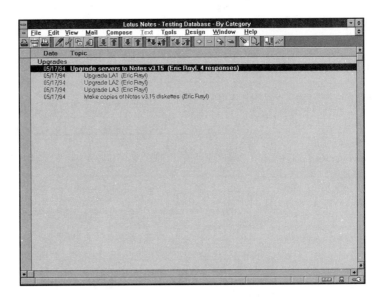

Now open the Main Project document, and notice the contents of the Tasks field—it should look similar to what's shown in Figure 14.20. Because this field is computed for display, its contents are completely dynamic and reflect the current status of the tasks. This type of field would be ideal for producing a concise printed report of the current status of the projects. If you had needed to use the information contained in the Tasks field for any sort of computations or in any formulas, you would have wanted to a use a computed field instead, the drawback being that you would have to manually refresh the fields on the main document to update the Tasks field.

**FIGURE 14.20.**

*The main project document with data being reverse inherited into the Tasks field.*

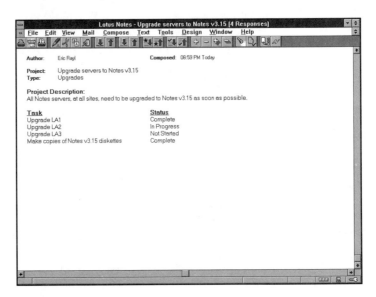

TIP

The one limitation with reverse inheriting is that no mathematical computations can be performed. For instance, if each task document in the preceding example had an HoursWorked field, the total hours worked per project could not be "rolled up" into the main document—this information would still have to be computed in a view.

# Using @*MailSend* and Macros to Move Data Between Databases

One of my favorite uses of the @MailSend function is to automatically move data between databases. Besides simply mailing a document from one database to another with @MailSend, I use the subject argument in the @MailSend statement to contain a multivalued list, basically an array of data. By my convention, the first element of the list always contains a field that distinguishes how the following data should be handled. Then I compose a mail-in database document for the target database in the main Notes Name and Address Book (see Figure 14.21).

**FIGURE 14.21.**

*A mail-in database document in the Notes Name and Address Book database.*

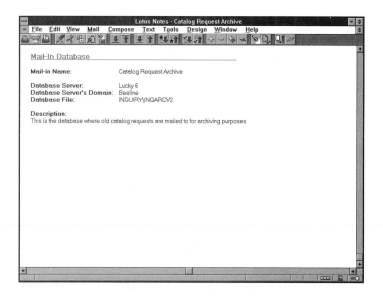

Next, in the target database, I write a mail-in macro that parses the Subject field of mailed-in documents. The macro gets the first element of the Subject, and based on its contents, sets fields in the document equal to the contents of other elements of the Subject list.

Now I'll show you an example of how I've used this technique.

In a company's consolidation and reporting system outlined in Figure 14.22, key fields in certain documents within each audit and tracking database are forwarded to division manager databases using the @MailSend technique. For example, when an investigation is closed in the crime and investigation tracking database, the Control Code and Risk information contained within the case's Investigator Summary document (see Figure 14.23) is mailed to the appropriate management database, and the document becomes an Objective document (see Figure 14.24).

**FIGURE 14.22.**

*@MailSend is used in a system that consolidates all of a bank's security and audits into one reporting database.*

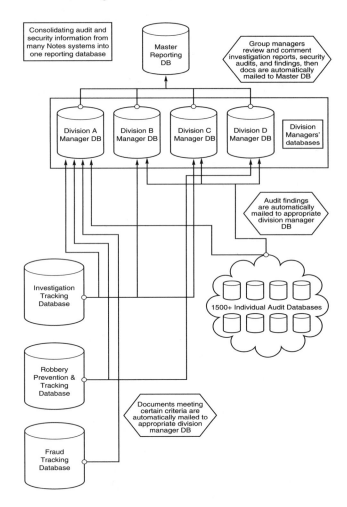

**FIGURE 14.23.**

*The Investigator Summary form with the control code information in the investigation tracking database.*

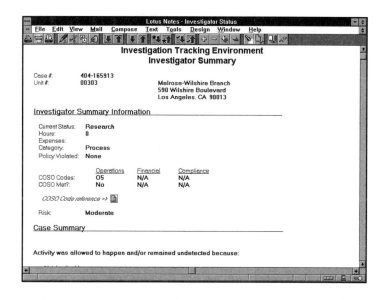

**FIGURE 14.24.**

*The control code information that has been mailed to the Security Division Management database and has become an Objective document.*

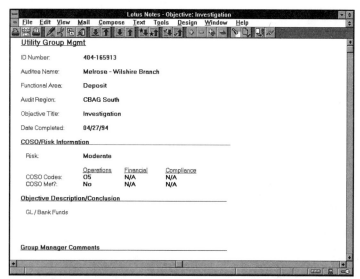

Figure 14.25 shows how fields become elements of the Subject field and then are mailed into the target database, where the mail-in macro parses the list into its Objective form's fields.

**FIGURE 14.25.**

*Data is transferred between databases in the multivalued Subject field of a mailed document.*

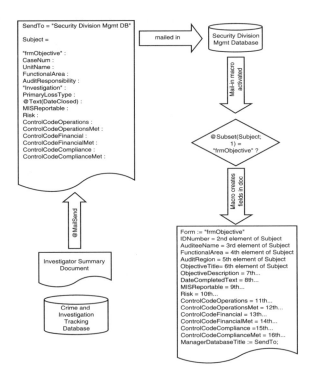

The macro that runs in the investigation tracking database when a case closes is as follows:

```
MailSubject := MailSubject;
@Do(@Set("MailSubject"; "frmObjective" : CaseNum : UnitName : FunctionalArea :
  AuditResponsibility : "Investigation" : PrimaryLossType : @Text(DateClosed) :
  MISReportable : Risk : ControlCodeOperations : ControlCodeOperationsMet :
  ControlCodeFinancial : ControlCodeFinancialMet : ControlCodeCompliance :
  ControlCodeComplianceMet);
@MailSend("Security Division Mgmt DB "; ""; ""; MailSubject; ""; ""));
```

The macro essentially builds a list of data in a temporary variable called `MailSubject` and uses this temporary variable as the subject argument of the `@MailSend` function.

> **TIP**
>
> When using `@MailSend`, ensure that all the values are text; otherwise, the `@MailSend` will be processed, but the Subject field will be blank. For example, in the preceding formula, if the field `DateClosed` were not converted to text using `@Text`, the entire Subject field would be blank in the mailed document.

Then, in the Security Division Management database, I use a mail-in macro, part of which is as shown here:

```
FIELD Form := Form;
FIELD ManagerDatabaseTitle := ManagerDatabaseTitle;
FIELD IDNumber := IDNumber;
FIELD AuditeeName := AuditeeName;
FIELD FunctionalArea := FunctionalArea;
FIELD AuditRegion := AuditRegion;
FIELD ObjectiveTitle := ObjectiveTitle;
FIELD ObjectiveDescription := ObjectiveDescription;
FIELD DateCompletedText := DateCompletedText;
FIELD MISReportable := MISReportable;
FIELD Risk := Risk;
FIELD ControlCodeOperations := ControlCodeOperations;
FIELD ControlCodeOperationsMet := ControlCodeOperationsMet;
FIELD ControlCodeFinancial := ControlCodeFinancial;
FIELD ControlCodeFinancialMet := ControlCodeFinancialMet;
FIELD ControlCodeCompliance := ControlCodeCompliance;
FIELD ControlCodeComplianceMet := ControlCodeComplianceMet;

@If(@Subset(Subject; 1) = "frmObjective";
  @Do(@SetField("Form"; "frmObjective");
    @SetField("IDNumber"; @Subset(@Subset(Subject; 2); -1));
    @SetField("AuditeeName"; @Subset(@Subset(Subject; 3); -1));
    @SetField("FunctionalArea"; @Subset(@Subset(Subject; 4); -1));
    @SetField("AuditRegion"; @Subset(@Subset(Subject; 5); -1));
    @SetField("ObjectiveTitle"; @Subset(@Subset(Subject; 6); -1));
    @SetField("ObjectiveDescription"; @Subset(@Subset(Subject; 7); -1));
    @SetField("DateCompletedText"; @Subset(@Subset(Subject; 8); -1));
    @SetField("MISReportable"; @Subset(@Subset(Subject; 9); -1));
    @SetField("Risk"; @Subset(@Subset(Subject; 10); -1));
    @SetField("ControlCodeOperations"; @Subset(@Subset(Subject; 11); -1));
    @SetField("ControlCodeOperationsMet"; @Subset(@Subset(Subject; 12); -1));
    @SetField("ControlCodeFinancial"; @Subset(@Subset(Subject; 13); -1));
    @SetField("ControlCodeFinancialMet"; @Subset(@Subset(Subject; 14); -1));
    @SetField("ControlCodeCompliance"; @Subset(@Subset(Subject; 15); -1));
    @SetField("ControlCodeComplianceMet"; @Subset(@Subset(Subject; 16); -1));
    @SetField("ManagerDatabaseTitle";
@If(@Contains(SendTo; "@"); @Trim(@LeftBack(SendTo; "@")); SendTo)));

@Subset(Subject; 1) = next type of mail-in doc to check for;
  @Do(parse next subject list)

@Success);
SELECT @All
```

This formula is the part of the mail-in macro that checks to see whether the first element of the Subject list is equal to frmObjective, and if it is, it sets the documents fields accordingly. The database's actual mail-in macro is much longer because it also checks for other kinds of documents being mailed in to the database.

# Advanced Keyword Fields

There are two types of Keyword field formats: Text and Formula. This option is selected from the Design Keyword Format dialog box, which can be accessed by clicking the **F**ormat... button when setting the Field Definition for Keyword field. When a formula is entered into the Allowable **K**eywords: box and the **F**ormula radio button is selected, as in Figure 14.26, the results of the formula are used to build the keyword list for the field. Generally, the formula contains an @DbColumn function. In this manner, dynamic keyword lists can be built that are based on the contents of a column in a view.

**FIGURE 14.26.**

*A formula that uses the contents of the first column of the view vwAllARTopicsLookup to create the keyword list for a field.*

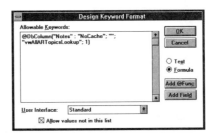

### TIP

When keyword list formulas using @DbColumn return an extremely large number of entries, forms can become slow to load, even in read mode, because Notes has to perform the lookup to see whether a keyword synonym is being used. Most the time, you will not use synonyms in conjunction with keyword list formulas, so you can speed up form loading by using @IsDocBeingLoaded in keyword list formulas as shown here:

```
@If(@IsDocBeingLoaded & !@IsNewDoc;
    @Unavailable;
        @DbColumn("Notes" : "NoCache"; ""; "vwAllARTopicsLookup"; 1))
```

When supporting subcategories in your applications, you must be careful when using formulas for the keyword lists. For example, look at a database created with the standard Notes discussion template. Users can create subcategories simply by using the backslash (\) character when entering data in the Categories field. Look at Figure 14.27. Notice that the @Commands category has two subcategories, FileCloseWindow and ToolsRunMacro. When you compose a new Main Topic document and press Enter in the Categories field, you bring up a keyword list that is inaccurate and confusing (see Figure 14.28).

**FIGURE 14.27.**

*A categorized view in a discussion database with subcategorized documents.*

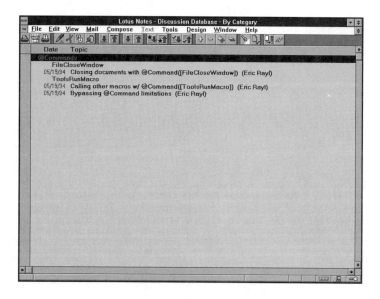

**FIGURE 14.28.**

*The keyword list for the Categories field when the view used by @DbLookup has subcategories.*

If you anticipate using subcategories in your view, you should create a hidden view that is used for the argument of the @DbColumn in the keyword list formula. The first column in the hidden view should contain the field to be looked up, but it should not be categorized. This view, when used with @Unique as in the keyword formula

```
@If(@IsDocBeingLoaded;
  @Unavailable;
  @Unique(@DbColumn(""; ""; "(CategoryView2)"; 1)))
```

would produce a keyword list as in Figure 14.29.

**FIGURE 14.29.**

*The keyword list for the Categories field with the view used by @DbLookup.*

# Using Popups in Form Design

Popups can be used in any rich text field during edit mode, but inserting popups in forms at design time can be a very effective way of providing help to users. For example, look at the popup on the Bug Report form in the sample software bug tracking database (see Figure 14.30).

**FIGURE 14.30.**

*A popup for the static text Priority: on the Bug Report form.*

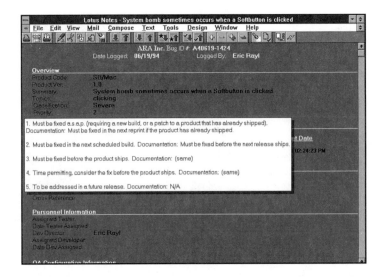

Notice the faint boxes around the Classification: and the Priority: static text on the form. The box indicates that there is an embedded popup that can be activated by clicking on the box and holding down the mouse button.

Adding a popup to a form at design time is simple. Just highlight the text where you want the popup located, and then select **Edit|Insert|P**opup from the Notes menu (fields and buttons cannot be included in the highlighted text). This action opens the Insert PopUp dialog box, shown in Figure 14.31, where you can type the text to appear in the popup. Notice that popups can also be formulas.

**FIGURE 14.31.**

*The Insert PopUp dialog box.*

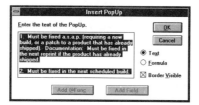

# Execute-Once Macros

Execute-once macros are very similar to button macros, with the primary difference being that execute-once macros can be run only from a view, and button macros can be run only when a document is open. Execute-once macros, like button macros, are used when you do not want a macro to iterate through a series of documents.

I use execute-once macros as a kind of "master macro" that calls other macros (using the command @Command([ToolsRunMacro])). For instance, in the crime tracking application I designed, I used the following execute-once macro to select documents for management reports:

```
DatePeriodStart := DatePeriodStart;
DatePeriodEnd := DatePeriodEnd;
@SetEnvironment("DatePeriodStart";
@Prompt([OKCANCELEDIT]; "Select Cases For Reporting"; "Type in the beginning
  date for the reporting period in the box below:"; ""));
@SetEnvironment("DatePeriodEnd";
@Prompt([OKCANCELEDIT]; "Select Cases For Reporting"; "Type in the ending date
  for the reporting period in the box below:"; ""));
@Command([OpenView]; "(vwMgmtReportingSelectNew)");
@Command([ToolsRunMacro]; "(NewSetReportingField)");
@Command([FileCloseWindow]);
SELECT @All
```

This execute-once macro prompts the user for a starting date and an ending date for the reporting period and stores the dates as environment variables. It then calls another macro (NewSetReportingField) that selects cases for inclusion in the management reports based on whether the case's close date is in the reporting period.

## TIP

Remember, in Notes version 3.1.5, the preceding macro could potentially create many replication conflicts due to the difference in the way macros operate on documents in this latest version of Notes.

Another simple use of an execute-once macro is described in the upcoming section "Navigating Between Response-Only Views and Master Views."

# Background Macros

Background macros are some of the most powerful types of macros because they can be used to perform actions automatically based on certain criteria. When you create a background macro, you need to specify where the macro will be run. Generally, this will be a server, but for testing purposes, you might want to specify your workstation (see Figure 14.32).

**FIGURE 14.32.**

*The Design New Macro dialog box that appears when the run option "Run periodically in the background" is selected.*

Background macros can be set to run automatically hourly, daily, weekly, or never. Additionally, you can force a background macro to run by selecting the Run **B**ackground Macros option on the Notes **T**ools menu. (On a Notes server console, you can also type "load chronos hourly," "load chronos daily," and so forth to force the server to run all background macros of a specific type.)

One limitation of background macros is that you cannot use @Commands in them, but you can generally work around this limitation using just @Functions.

I use background macros quite a lot for automatically moving documents between databases (for workflow and archiving purposes). Background macros are the only type of macro that allows documents to be deleted without user intervention. Any other type of macro that uses the @DeleteDocument function just marks documents for deletion, and no matter what you do, the user will be prompted to verify the deletion. When @DeleteDocument is used in background macros, however, the documents are deleted without any prompt. This feature is very useful when you want to move old documents or resolved issues to an archive type of database, because your background macro simply needs to use @MailSend to mail a document to the archive database, and the @DeleteDocument to remove the document from the current database.

> **TIP**
>
> When using @DeleteDocument in a background macro on a server, you need to add the database's replica ID to the database's access control list as at least an editor (see the example in Figure 14.33). Simply naming the server's name in the ACL is not adequate.

**FIGURE 14.33.**

*A database's ACL with the database's replica ID listed as an editor.*

# Numbering Documents

One of the most common problems that Notes application developers face is convincing users that documents do not necessarily have to be sequentially numbered, as in traditional database applications that they might be used to. Users like numbers that are sequential and short, such as bug number 4563, case number 10989, and purchase requisition number 34543.

The problem is that Notes is a distributed database, so there is no easy way to sequentially number documents with *unique* sequential numbers. If you are using only one Notes server in your organization, you can sequentially number documents by using a document number field that is computed when composed and that uses a formula similar to this one:

```
1 + @Subset(@DbColumn("Notes" : "NoCache"; ""; "vwByDocNumber"; 1); -1)
```

The idea here is to get lookup into a view whose first column is sorted (ascending) by document number, and add one to the last value in the view. I don't recommend using this approach, however, because when you add a second Notes server, this technique creates duplicate document numbers, and you have to use a different numbering scheme.

What's better is to convince your users that document numbers mean less and less in a Notes application. In fact, they are mostly useful for communicating reference numbers between Notes and non-Notes users (for example, giving a customer a bug reference number for him to refer to when checking on the status of a bug report).

Depending on how the document numbers will be used, there are several document numbering schemes to choose from. Many of the numbering schemes come with the benefit of conveying additional information about the document, such as who originally composed it, or when the document was composed.

The easiest number scheme involves concatenating parts of the date and time when a document was composed. For instance, in the Bank Investigation Tracking Environment sample database, cases are assigned numbers using the following formula:

```
YearString := @Right(@Text(@Year(@Now)); 1);
MonthString := @Select(@Month(@Now); "01"; "02"; "03"; "04"; "05"; "06"; "07";
  "08"; "09"; "10"; "11"; "12");
DayNumber := @Day(@Now);
DayString := @Select(DayNumber; "01"; "02"; "03"; "04"; "05"; "06"; "07"; "08";
  "09"; @Text(DayNumber));
HourNumber := @Hour(@Now);
HourString := @If(HourNumber = 0; "00"; @Select(HourNumber; "01"; "02"; "03";
  "04"; "05"; "06"; "07"; "08"; "09"; @Text(HourNumber)));
MinuteNumber := @Minute(@Now);
MinuteString := @If(MinuteNumber = 0; "00"; @Select(MinuteNumber; "01"; "02";
  "03"; "04"; "05"; "06"; "07"; "08"; "09"; @Text(MinuteNumber)));
SecondNumber := @Second(@Now);
SecondString := @If(SecondNumber = 0;
  "00";
  @Select(SecondNumber; "01"; "02"; "03"; "04"; "05"; "06"; "07"; "08"; "09";
  @Text(SecondNumber)));
YearString + MonthString + DayString + "-" + HourString + MinuteString + SecondString
```

This formula produces a case number that looks like

```
40519-173523
```

which can be interpreted to be a case created on 5/19/94 at 5:35:23 p.m. The additional benefit of using a strategy similar to this is that a view sorted by document number is also sorted chronologically in terms of the date the document was composed. Depending on your application, you might be able to shorten the number by dropping the seconds designation, or by using the three-digit Julian-date designation *nnn* rather than the four-digit designation *mmdd*.

Another popular way to establish unique document numbers is to use a portion of the user's name in conjunction with a sequential number. This technique is used with the Notes environment variables. The following formula is useful for creating a document number when a user always uses the same computer, because it stores a user-specific number in the user's NOTES.INI file (Notes preferences file on a Macintosh computer):

```
TempPrefix := @Left(@UserName; 1) + @UpperCase(@Left(@RightBack(@UserName;
" "); 3));
TempSuffix := @If(@Environment("EnvPRNumber") = "";
                  "0000";
                  @Environment("EnvPRNumber"));
NextPRNumber := @TextToNumber(TempSuffix) + 1;
Zeroes := (NextPRNumber < 1000) + (NextPRNumber < 100) + (NextPRNumber < 10);
@SetEnvironment("EnvPRNumber"; @Repeat("0"; Zeroes) + @Text(NextPRNumber));
TempPrefix + @Repeat("0"; Zeroes) + @Text(NextPRNumber)
```

This formula, when used in Computed when composed fields, creates sequential document numbers *per user,* with the document numbers looking similar to ERAY2475. This technique is useful for creating numbers for documents such as customer problem reports and purchase requisitions because the number identifies who composed the original document.

> **TIP**
>
> It's a good idea to use document ID numbers in all applications that use response-type documents, even if the document ID numbers are hidden. Create a unique document ID number for every main document, and then inherit that number down to all response documents. The next section explains why these unique ID numbers are useful.

# Navigating Between Response-Only Views and Master Views

In many types of applications, you'll use views of response-only type documents to make it easy to find a particular record. For instance, in the software bug tracking sample application, customer records are response documents to the actual bug report, and a view of customer reports sorted by company name is quite useful. In a crime tracking system that I designed, suspects are response documents to the main case document, and it is very useful to have a view of suspect documents sorted by last name, to allow easy suspect searches.

But what happens when you find the response document you want? More often than not, it would be useful to be able to navigate to a master view that would show the response document in its response hierarchy. For instance, in the investigation tracking application, after you find a suspect's name in the view by suspect name, you probably want to know more information about the case.

To enable your users to easily navigate to a master view from a responses-only view, you can create a simple macro. For example, the execute-once macro in the bug tracking database is called Go To Main Bug Report doc. Its formula is simply this:

```
TempActionRequestID := ActionRequestID;
@Command([FileCloseWindow]);
@Command([OpenView]; "vwAllARID"; TempActionRequestID);
SELECT @All
```

This macro can be used from any view, but it's most useful in one of the Customer Reports views. For instance, suppose that you were in the view of customer reports sorted by company name. After you find the particular customer and bug that you are interested in (see Figure 14.34), you might want to see more information on the status of the bug, or which other companies had reported the bug. By running the macro 1. Go to Main Bug Report doc, you would be taken to a hierarchical view that would show you all documents associated with the particular bug, as in Figure 14.35.

**FIGURE 14.34.**

*The Customer Reports By Contact Name view in the bug tracking sample database.*

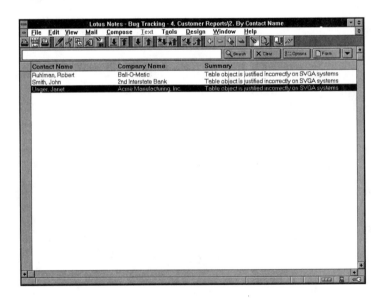

**FIGURE 14.35.**

*The view after the macro 1. Go To Main Bug Report doc is run from the location shown in Figure 14.34.*

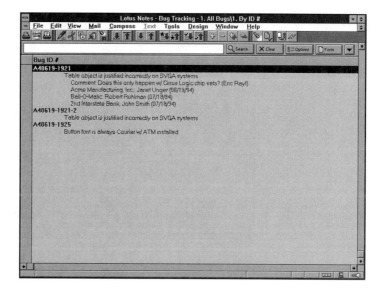

# Simulating Dynamic Multi-Row Tables in Forms

Dynamic multi-row tables are useful for tracking the previous states or status codes of a particular document and for accumulating numerical data, such as totals and balances.

For instance, in the sample software bug tracking application, the current state of the bug (To Be Determined, Confirmed, Fix Submitted, and so forth) could simply be a keyword field. But this method is not very elegant because it does not capture data such as who set the current state, what the bug's previous states were, and when the state was changed.

A more elegant approach is to use three multivalue text fields—State, StateSetBy, and DateStateSet—that are computed when composed (see Figure 14.36). When a bug is first reported (and a bug report is composed), the value in the State field defaults to "TBD" (To Be Determined), and the StateSetBy and DateStateSet values default to @UserName and @Now, respectively.

**FIGURE 14.36.**

*The bug report form in design mode showing the three fields State, StateSetBy, and DateStateSet.*

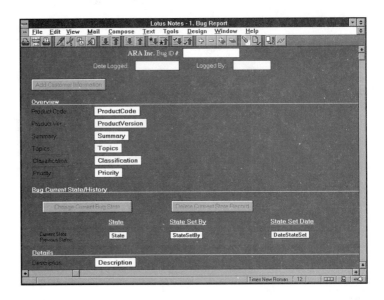

A button is then added to the form that allows the current state to be changed. When the button is clicked, the user is prompted for the state, which is then appended to the State field so that the first element of the State field will always be the most current state. In Figure 14.37, you'll see how the multivalued fields appear in use.

**FIGURE 14.37.**

*The bug report form with data.*

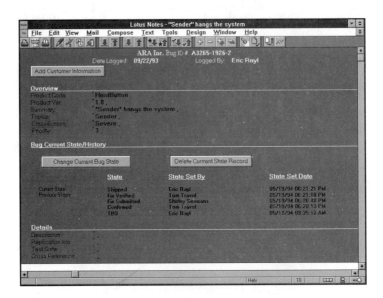

This is the formula for the Change Current Bug State button:

```
TempNewState := @Prompt([OKCANCELLIST]; "Changing An AR\'s State"; "Select the
  new state from the list below:"; "Confirmed"; ARStatesList);
@SetField("State"; TempNewState : State);
@SetField("StateSetBy"; @UserName : StateSetBy);
@SetField("DateStateSet"; @Now : DateStateSet)
```

Notice how the new values for State, StateSetBy, and DateStateSet are appended to the previous contents of the field using the colon operator. Thus the current values will always be the first (or left-most) values in the list. This means that the Notes formula

```
@Subset(State; 1)
```

can be used to compute the current state of the bug.

Notice the Delete Current State Record button in Figure 14.35. This button performs two functions. It first verifies that the current user is the person who set the current state—the user can delete the last "record" only if he was the one that changed the state. Second, if the user's name is correct, the macro deletes the last state "record." This is the formula for the Delete Current State Record button:

```
LastChangeBy := LastChangeBy;
NumberOfChanges := NumberOfChanges;
FIELD State := State;
FIELD StateSetBy := StateSetBy;
FIELD DateStateSet := DateStateSet;
@Set("NumberOfChanges"; @Elements(StateSetBy));
@If(NumberOfChanges = 0;
  @Do(@Prompt([OK]; "Error"; "There are no records to delete.");
      @Return(""));
  @Success);
@Set("LastChangeBy"; @Subset(StateSetBy; 1));
@If(@UserName != LastChangeBy;
  @Do(@Prompt([OK]; "Error"; "You are not authorized to delete the last status change
    because you did not set it.");
      @Return(""));
  @Success);
@If(NumberOfChanges = 1;
  @Do(@SetField("State"; "");
      @SetField("StateSetBy"; "");
      @SetField("DateStateSet"; ""));
  @Do(@SetField("State"; @Subset(State; -(NumberOfChanges - 1)));
      @SetField("StateSetBy"; @Subset(StateSetBy; -(NumberOfChanges - 1)));
      @SetField("DateStateSet"; @Subset(DateStateSet; -(NumberOfChanges - 1)))))
```

In a crime and investigation tracking application that I designed, a similar approach is used for entering a case's loss and recovery information. For any given case, many times there are multiple losses and perhaps loss types are associated with the case. Additionally, there is usually some sort of recovery or restoration. Initially, the application was architected such that all the different losses and recoveries were individual responses to the main case document, and a view was used to calculate the current balance. The problem was that many views, reports, and activities were driven by numbers such as the case's gross and net dollar loss, and these numbers were not available if individual documents were used for each loss and recovery.

Instead, a Loss/Recovery form was designed (see Figure 14.38).

**FIGURE 14.38.**

*A simulated multi-row table in a form with numerical calculations.*

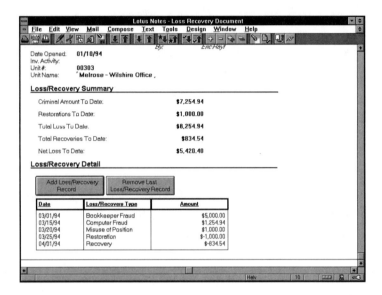

In this instance, the formula for adding a row to the simulated table was a little more complex because more prompts are required and more logic and mathematics must be evaluated. This is the formula for the Add Loss/Recovery Record button:

```
FIELD DateLossList := DateLossList;
FIELD LossTypeList := LossTypeList;
FIELD LossAmountList := LossAmountList;
FIELD CriminalAmountTotal := CriminalAmountTotal;
FIELD RecoveriesAmountTotal := RecoveriesAmountTotal;
FIELD RestorationsAmountTotal := RestorationsAmountTotal;
FIELD LossesOnlyList := LossesOnlyList;

TempDate := @TextToTime(@Prompt([OKCANCELEDIT]; "New Loss/Recovery"; "Type in
  the date in the box below- USE DATE FORMAT MM/DD/YY"; ""));

TempType := @Prompt([OKCANCELLIST]; "New Loss/Recovery"; "Select the type of
  loss/recovery from the list below"; ""; LossRecoveryKeywords);

TempAmount := @TextToNumber(@Prompt([OKCANCELEDIT]; "New Loss/Recovery"; "Type
  in the amount of the loss/recovery in the box below- NOTE: DO NOT USE NEGATIVE
  AMOUNTS"; ""));

@If(TempType = "Recovery" | TempType = "Restoration";
  @Set("TempAmount"; -1 * TempAmount);
  @Success);
```

```
@If(DateLossList = "";
  @Do(@SetField("DateLossList"; TempDate);
      @SetField("LossTypeList"; TempType);
      @SetField("LossAmountList"; TempAmount));
  @Do(@SetField("DateLossList"; DateLossList : TempDate);
      @SetField("LossTypeList"; LossTypeList : TempType);
      @SetField("LossAmountList"; LossAmountList : TempAmount)));

@If(TempAmount >= 0;
      @SetField("CriminalAmountTotal"; CriminalAmountTotal + TempAmount);
    TempAmount < 0 & TempType = "Recovery";
      @SetField("RecoveriesAmountTotal"; RecoveriesAmountTotal -
        TempAmount);
    TempAmount < 0 & TempType = "Restoration";
      @SetField("RestorationsAmountTotal"; RestorationsAmountTotal -
        TempAmount);
    @Success);

@If(TempType != "Recovery" & TempType != "Restoration";
  @SetField("LossesOnlyList"; LossesOnlyList : TempType);
  @Success);

@Command([ViewRefreshFields])
```

Note that if the user selects a loss/recovery type of either Recovery or Restoration, the dollar amount is made negative. Also note how the running total fields LossAmountList, CriminalAmountTotal, RecoveriesAmountTotal, and RestorationsAmountTotal are each individually updated, depending on the type of Loss/Recovery record (TempType) selected.

# Simulating Dynamic Column-Oriented Tables

In some forms, you might want to have data oriented in a columnar fashion, rather than a row-oriented fashion. For instance, in the crime and investigation system that I designed, there might be one or more suspects (response documents) per case (main document). When the case is closed, the critical fields on each suspect document are reverse inherited into the main case document. Due to the nature of the data, it made more sense to try to orient each individual suspect as a "column" of data. That way, for cases with three or fewer suspects (the majority of cases), all the information will fit on the computer screen without any scrolling (see Figure 14.39 and Figure 14.40).

**FIGURE 14.39.**

*A view in the investigation tracking application showing three suspects associated with one case.*

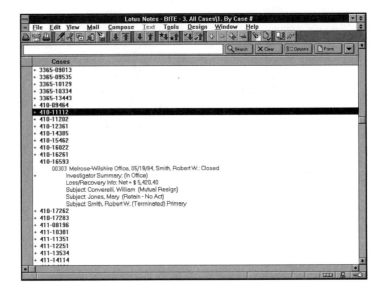

**FIGURE 14.40.**

*A closed-case (main) document showing the suspect information that has been reverse inherited into a simulated column-oriented table.*

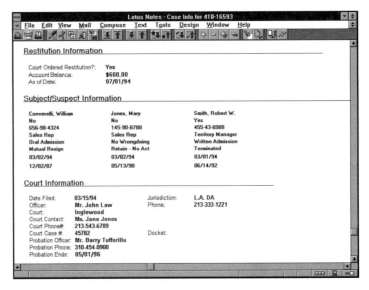

The key to formatting this table is to use @Implode, with @Char(9) (the tab character) as the separator. In design mode, the form looks like the one in Figure 14.41. Notice the tab stops on the ruler.

**FIGURE 14.41.**

*The form shown in Figure 14.40, in design mode.*

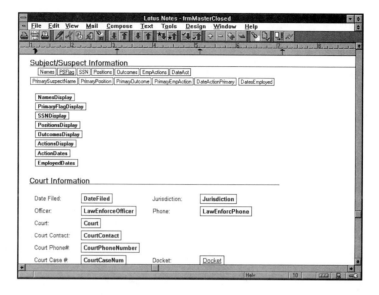

When a case is closed, information for all the case's suspects is reverse inherited into the hidden multivalued fields Names, SSN, Positions, and so forth. Then the table is created by using the computed fields NamesDisplay, PrimaryFlagDisplay, SSNDisplay, and so on. These fields all have a formula similar to the formula for NamesDisplay:

```
@Implode(Names; @Char(9))
```

When there are more than four suspects for a case, the information naturally scrolls off the right side of the screen. But in most instances, all suspect information is presented on one screen. Using a row-oriented table would have caused some of every suspect record to scroll off of the right side of the screen, which was not desirable.

# Moving Response Documents to Different Main Documents

In some of your applications, you might want to enable users to move response documents from one main document to another. Users can always take this action by cutting and pasting the response document, but the problem is that the data that the response document inherited from the main document when it was composed is incorrect after the document is pasted in as a response to another main document.

If your application truly needs the capability of moving response documents from one main topic to another, you will most likely have to simulate a response hierarchy.

Simulating a response hierarchy involves using a common field on the main document and response documents that contains that same data for all related documents (for example, company name, bug report number, and so on). Then views are created that are categorized on this common field, and column formulas are used that indent the response-type documents.

For instance, the architecture of the sample software bug tracking database is such that each bug report (main document) has perhaps one or more customer report documents associated with it. In the real world, it might turn out that several bug reports have been created that describe the same bug. When this is the case, the customer reports must be moved from the duplicate bug and associated with the original bug report document. To enable users to move customer reports from one bug report to another, a button was added to the customer report form (see Figure 14.42).

**FIGURE 14.42.**

*The software bug tracking database's customer report form, with the Re-Assign prompt that appears when the button is clicked.*

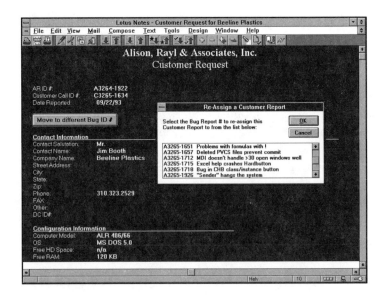

This is the formula for the Move button:

```
NewActionRequestString := @Prompt([OKCANCELLIST]; "Re-Assign a Customer
  Report"; "Select the Bug Report # to re-assign this Customer Report to from the
  list below:"; ""; @DbColumn("Notes" : "NoCache"; ""; "vwARIDSubjectLookup";
  1));
@SetField("ActionRequestID"; @Left(NewActionRequestString; 10))
```

In the bug tracking application, the only field that relates the customer's report with the main bug report is the field ActionRequestID. What the preceding button macro does is simply change the customer report document's ActionRequestID to match that of the selected bug report.

Making the customer report appear as a response to the bug report in views is handled by first categorizing on the ActionRequestID field, then using column formulas similar to this:

```
@If(Form = "frmActionRequest";
    Summary;
  Form = "frmCustomerRequest";
  "     " + CompanyName + ":  " + ContactName + " (" +
    @Text(@Date(DateReported)) + ")";
  Form = "frmInternalComment";
  "     " + Subject;
  "")
```

This column formula artificially indents documents that are composed with either the frmCustomerRequest or the frmInternalComment forms, making the documents appear as responses. This is not the most refined solution, but in the bug tracking application, the users needed the capability of moving responses from one document to another.

# Using Paste-In Macros

Mail-in and paste-in macros, although actually the same type of macros, are generally used in completely different contexts. Because many databases are not mail-in databases, a mail-in macro would never run, but all databases can have documents pasted into them. As a developer, you need to decide whether you want users to be able to paste in documents (you can use a paste-in macro to block users from pasting in documents too) and what results when a document is pasted into a database.

For example, in an audit application I designed, there was a document library type of database that contained all of a division's standard audit objective and test documents. When the division started a new audit, the people would create a new, empty audit database from the audit template. Then they would select the appropriate audit objectives from the audit library and copy-and-paste the documents into the new audit database. When the objectives and tests were pasted into the database, a paste-in macro would run that would update each objective and test with information specific to that audit, such as audit ID and audit name.

In the software bug tracking sample database, a paste-in macro is used for a slightly different purpose. The system was originally designed for a software company which had products that ran on several different platforms (Windows, OS/2, and Macintosh). When a bug was reported on one platform, the quality assurance personnel were responsible for determining whether the bug potentially existed in the products on the other platforms. Then they would have to "clone" the bug report to the other products if necessary.

One of the easiest ways to create "clones" of a bug report was to enable users to copy-and-paste the document. But a paste-in macro was needed that would prompt the user for the new product name, and that would change the bug report ID number accordingly. This is the formula for the paste-in macro:

```
TempProductCode := TempProductCode;
TempVersion := TempVersion;
TempARID := ActionRequestID;
@If(Form = "frmActionRequest";
  @If(@Prompt([YESNO]; "Cloning a Bug Report"; "You are about to copy a Bug
        Report to a new product code- do you wish to continue?");
    @Do(@Set("TempProductCode";
        @Prompt([OKCANCELLIST]; "Cloning a Bug Report"; "Select the Product
          Code to copy this Bug Report to from the list below:"; "";
            @DbColumn("Notes" : "NoCache"; "";
            "vwProductCodeVersionLookup"; 1)));
        @SetField("ProductVersion"; @Prompt([OKCANCELLIST]; "Cloning a Bug Report";
                                "Select the version number from the list below:"; "";
                                  @DbLookup("Notes" : "NoCache"; "";
                                "vwProductCodeVersionLookup"; TempProductCode; 2)));
        @SetField("ProductCode"; TempProductCode);
        @SetField("ActionRequestID";
    @If(@Length(ActionRequestID) = 10;
      ActionRequestID + "-2";
      @Left(ActionRequestID; 10) + "-" +
        @Text(@TextToNumber(@Right(ActionRequestID; 1)) + 1))));
      @Return(""));
    @Return(""));
SELECT @All
```

This macro first checks to see whether the Form field in the document that is being pasted in is equal to "frmActionRequest"; if it's not, the macro ends with an @Return(""). Next, the macro prompts the user to confirm that he really wants to clone the bug report—if the user clicks the No button, the macro execution ends with @Return("").

If the user clicks the Yes button, a prompt appears listing all the company's product codes (this is accomplished with an @DbColumn into a view of all the company's product documents). After the user selects the product code, a list of all of that product code's valid version numbers is presented via an @DbLookup using the selected product code as the key to determine which version numbers are valid.

One other key feature of this system is how the bug report ID number (the ActionRequestID field) is handled. A cloned bug has the same ID number as the bug it was cloned from, except it has a "-2" or "-3" or such after the number to designate that the bug was actually reported on a different platform. The limitation to the approach I used to generate this new bug ID number is that if you are going to clone a bug to two platforms, for example, you must copy-and-paste the bug with the "-2" ID number to create the "-3" bug ID. If you copy-and-paste the same bug twice, you will generate duplicate bug ID numbers. A fancier solution would use an @DbLookup to return a sorted list of the bugs with the same bug ID prefix, then add one to the highest suffix to create the new bug ID number.

# View "Deselection" Formulas

When you're designing an application that will involve a lot of forms, it makes sense to use form naming conventions that will allow you the easiest management when it comes to view selection formulas. For example, the crime and investigation tracking system I designed has more than 40 forms, and more than 60 views, and managing which forms appear in which views could be a nightmare if some thought was not given to the process.

The basic tenet of a view "deselection" formula is that in views that use response hierarchy, a response document cannot appear in the view unless its corresponding main document appears. This technique is very useful if used correctly.

For instance, in views of all open cases and their associated documents, I don't have to use long, complex selection formulas like this:

```
SELECT Form = "frmMain" ¦ Form = "frmInvestigatorSummary" ¦ Form =
  "frmInvStatus" ¦ Form = "frmLossRecoverySummary" ¦ Form = "frmSuspect" ¦ Form =
  "frmShortForm" ¦ Form = "frmLongForm" ¦ Form = "frmInvReport" ¦ Form =
  "frmInvReport2" ¦ Form = "frmInvReport3" ¦ Form = "frmInvReport4" ¦ Form =
  "frmInvReport5" ¦ Form = "frmRecMgmt" ¦ Form = "frmComment" ¦ Form =
  "frmAuditNotification" ¦ Form = "frmAC45" & Form != "frmMailingList" & Form !=
  "frmInvInfo" & Form != "Help" & Form != "frmQA"
```

Instead, I can use a much simpler formula that basically just *excludes* all closed main case documents (and the maintenance type forms). This formula additionally excludes all the other documents related to closed cases (since they are response-type documents) but lets all the open case response documents appear in the views. All the open case views use the following manageable selection formula:

```
SELECT Form != "frmMainClosed" & Form != "frmMailingList" & Form !=
  "frmInvInfo" & Form != "Help" & Form != "frmQA"
```

# Speeding Macro Processing Using Views

Many applications require macros that will process a main document and all of its related response documents. Traditionally, you would use a macro that processes all documents in the database and acts on those that match the main document's specific key or ID number. In large databases, this process can be very slow.

Using a technique similar to the view deselection formula, you can easily write macros that process only the response documents of a given main document. You need only have a "flag" type of field that is not set on all of your main documents. Then, when you are ready to process the responses of a given main document, set this flag field, and then switch to a hierarchical view that shows only main documents with the flag set and all the related response documents. Now you can run a macro on all the documents in the view, which should be only the documents you are interested in.

For instance, in the crime and investigation tracking system I designed, when a case closes, all the case's response documents need to have their form field changed to the appropriate closed-case type of form. You would not want to run a macro that processed every document in the database, looked for those with the correct case number, and then changed their form variables.

Instead, I added a computed-when-composed field called NeedToBeClosed to the main case form and defaulted its value to No. Next, I created a hidden view of "Need To Be Closed Cases" with the following selection formula:

```
SELECT NeedToBeClosed != "No" & Form != "frmInvInfo" & Form !=
"frmMailingList" & Form != "Help"
```

With this "deselection" formula, the view contains any main documents in which NeedToBeClosed has a value of Yes. It also contains all of its response documents.

Finally, I added a Close Case button macro to the main case document that, among other things, performs the following operations:

```
FIELD DateClosed := DateClosed;
TempCaseNum := CaseNum;
@SetField("CaseStatus"; "Closed");
@SetField("DateClosed"; @Today);
@SetField("NeedToBeClosed"; "Yes");
@Command([FileSave]);
@Command([FileCloseWindow]);
@Command([OpenView]; "vwNeedToBeClosedCases");
@Command([ToolsRunMacro]; "(ChangeFormToClosed)");
@Command([FileCloseWindow])
```

When the user clicks the Close Case button on the main case document, several fields are updated, and the NeedToBeClosed flag is set to Yes. Then the document is saved and closed, and the view vwNeedToBeClosedCases is opened. Lastly, a macro is called (ChangeFormToClosed) that runs on all documents in the view, and then the view is closed.

Using a similar technique, you should be able to avoid having macros that process all the documents in the database just to find several documents to act on.

# Form Override Printing Tricks

When documents are being printed, the Form Override... button appears on the File Print dialog box (see Figure 14.43).

**FIGURE 14.43.**

*The Notes File Print dialog box, with the Form Override... button.*

Clicking the For**m** Override... button causes a list of all the application's forms to appear, including hidden forms. The user can then choose a form to have the selected documents printed with.

Many sales and marketing types of applications can benefit from the form override option by using it to create mail-merged documents. For instance, suppose that your company has a leads-tracking Notes application, and you are about to introduce a new product. You can design a Notes form letter announcing the product and add fields to the form to include individual contact information. You can even create a Notes form to mail-merge envelopes if you have an envelope tray for your laser printer.

The Catalog Inquiry Tracking sample application uses a similar approach for creating mail-merged letters that are sent, along with a catalog, to potential customers who request catalogs. At the end of the day, all the day's catalog request documents are printed with the appropriate letter form using form override, and the catalogs are mailed out.

In other instances, you might need to have multiple Notes documents appear as one document when printed. For example, in the audit tracking application that I designed, each audit could have one or more findings, which were each individual response documents related to a test or an objective document. The problem was that the corporation's customary paper-based audit report contained a narrative section and then listed the findings in bulleted, numerical order. To print the findings correctly, I created an "audit report header" document that was part of the master audit template. Then, when the findings report needed to be printed, the auditor simply switched to the view 2. Findings\By Number (see Figure 14.44), reordered the findings as necessary by renumbering them, and then printed the documents using form override in conjunction with a finding report form. Additionally, the report was printed with the Document Se**p**aration option on the File Print dialog box (Figure 14.43) set to No Separation.

**FIGURE 14.44.**

*The view of an audit's findings—notice the Findings Header Text document.*

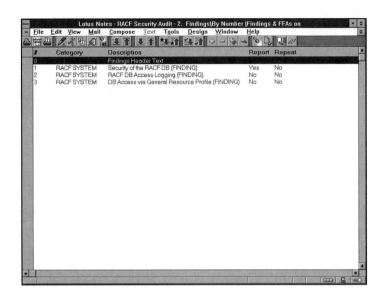

# Using OLE in Form Design

Using object linking and embedding (OLE) in form design is a way to leverage on Notes's "object container" capabilities. Although OLE is available only on the Windows platform, it is a very powerful tool that most major Windows programs support. Using OLE, you can integrate Notes with other Windows applications, such as word processors, spreadsheets, presentation/graphics products, and project management applications.

For instance, you might want to use Excel spreadsheets to track budgets within your organization. Each department might be required to submit an updated quarterly budget, complete with actual spending information. A Notes database makes an ideal "container" for these spreadsheets, enabling users to easily find departmental budget information and review previous budget information. And using OLE can make this process simple.

Here's a simple example of how this method could work. Suppose that you have a budget template in Excel, similar to the one in Figure 14.45. All you would need to do is copy and paste this Excel spreadsheet template into a Notes form at design time, using the Paste Special... option on the Notes **E**dit menu, and then select Rich Text and click the **E**mbed option in the Paste Special dialog box (see Figure 14.46).

**FIGURE 14.45.**

*An Excel spreadsheet template that has been selected and copied to the clipboard in preparation for pasting into a Notes form.*

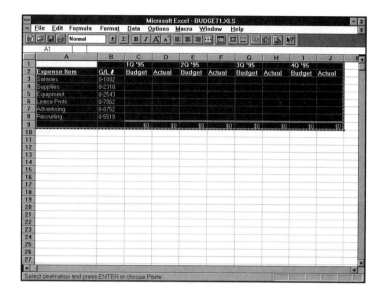

**FIGURE 14.46.**

*The Notes Paste Special dialog box. To use OLE, you click the Embed button.*

When you click the **Embed** button, the Excel spreadsheet is embedded into the Notes form, thus creating a true compound document (see Figure 14.47). I added one Notes field (Department) to allow the budget worksheets to be sorted by department.

**FIGURE 14.47.**

*The Notes form with the embedded Excel spreadsheet.*

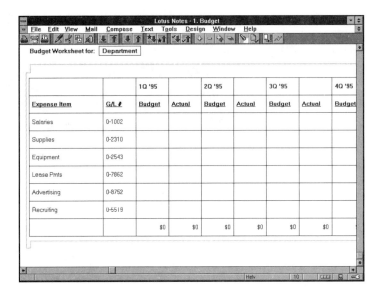

Now the form's attributes need to be set to handle the embedded object. One of the most important form attributes to set is the attribute called **S**tore forms in documents, which allows the embedded object to vary from document to document. (If you forget to check this option, Notes reminds you that there is an embedded object in the form and that you should select this option.)

The other important form attributes to consider when designing forms with embedded objects are accessed via the O**b**ject Activation... button on the Design Form Attributes dialog box. Clicking this button opens the Object Activations Options dialog box, shown in Figure 14.48.

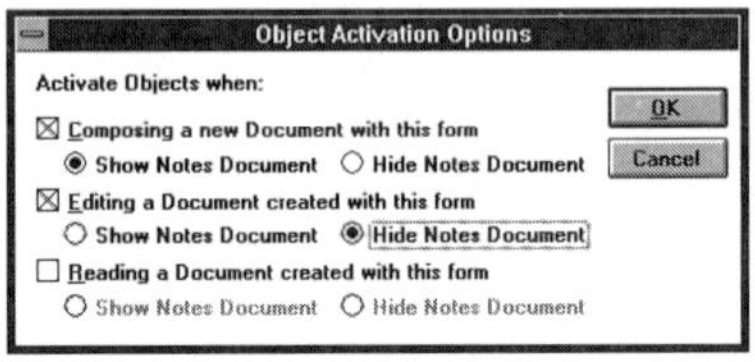

**FIGURE 14.48.**

*The various object activation options that are available for designing forms with embedded objects.*

For this example, I have selected to activate the object when a new document is composed. This selection means that when a new document is composed, Excel will automatically be launched if it is not running, and the embedded spreadsheet will be the active Excel window. I also selected the option Show Notes Document because the user will have to select the appropriate department on the Notes form. When the user is editing the document, I also want the spreadsheet to be activated so that the user actually updates the data in Excel, but this time, I do not need to show the Notes document because the user should not be editing the contents of the Notes department field. When the Notes document is being read, I don't want the object to be activated because the spreadsheet can be read fine in Notes.

Now, what would really be useful in an application similar to the preceding example would be to have the budget totals available in Notes fields. This feature would allow the Notes database to consolidate the budgets for the various departments using views. This is precisely the concept behind Lotus Notes Field Exchange (Notes F/X). Notes F/X is currently available only in Lotus products, such as 1-2-3, Ami Pro, and Freelance graphics, although Microsoft has announced that its suite of products will support Notes F/X. Notes F/X allows a very tight integration between Notes fields and fields or ranges of data in another product. The communications between the applications are two-way—changes made in Notes appear in the other application, and vice versa. You owe it to yourself to see Notes F/X in action—it is incredible. I think organizations using Notes should strongly consider using products that support Notes F/X.

To get you thinking about the types of applications you can build using Notes F/X, take a look at Figure 14.49, Figure 14.50, and Figure 14.51. These figures illustrate an expense report tracking application that uses Notes F/X to exchange data between Notes forms and an expense report template in Lotus 1-2-3. The important concept here is that the total dollar amount for each expense report is available in a Notes field, via field exchange, which allows views to contain and consolidate multiple expense reports, as in Figure 14.48. Many other types of applications can be created using F/X-enabled products such as Lotus Freelance, Ami Pro, and Improv.

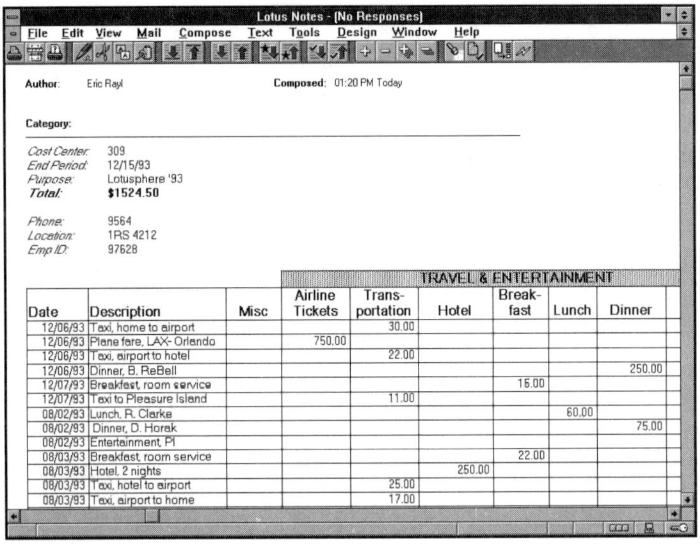

**FIGURE 14.49.**

*A Notes expense report form with an embedded Lotus 1-2-3 spreadsheet.*

**FIGURE 14.50.**

*When the embedded 1-2-3 spreadsheet is activated, fields such as Name, Emp #, and Dept # are automatically updated from the Notes document.*

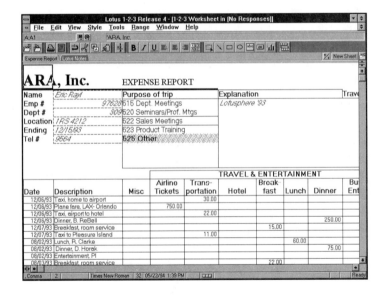

**FIGURE 14.51.**

*A view in the expense report database that uses the numerical information computed in each spreadsheet.*

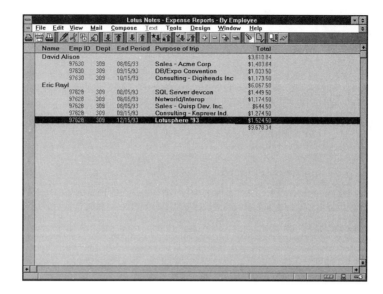

# Summary

This chapter should not only have shown you some techniques I've successfully used in Notes applications, but also made you think about some of your own new techniques that you will try to implement in your Notes applications. Next, I'm going to go over the various aspects of Notes security, including some tips on when and where to use the security options available in Notes.

# 15

## Advanced Security Issues

# Overview

One reason Lotus Notes makes such a worthy application development platform is that it has a multitude of security options. Security can be maintained from as high as the server level, through the database and document level, and right on down to the field level of individual documents.

Some types of Notes security are basically ironclad, such as certificates and encryption. Other types of security are based on the physical security of the server. And still other options are not really security features but options that create a perceived security that is useful in certain circumstances but that is open to hacking by advanced Notes users.

Because of the many kinds of security options in Notes, choosing the right security options for your application can be confusing. Additionally, excessive use of security features such as encryption keys can cause many administrative headaches in the long run. And when designing applications with advanced security requirements, do not forget that the application will require much more rigorous testing to ensure that the security is set up correctly.

In this chapter, I'll take a "top-down" approach to discussing the security features available in Notes, starting with server security and ending with field-level security techniques. In the conclusion of the chapter, I'll summarize the myriad security options available in Notes, and I'll also offer suggestions for implementing application-level security in Notes.

# Limiting Access to Databases

Limiting access to databases can be broken down into two types of security: the physical security of the Notes server, and the settings contained in each database's Access Control List. All of Notes security is based on the assumption that Notes servers must be physically secure, through the use of locked server rooms, keyboard locks, and perhaps even disabled floppy drives. When a Notes database is removed from a Notes server (by copying it to a floppy disk or to a file server), all of its security is broken (except for data that is contained in encrypted fields, which remains encrypted). Therefore, it is very important to first make certain that your Notes servers are physically secure and maintained by trusted employees.

Additionally, make certain that there are no problems with the network security. For instance, if you are running any file services on your Notes server, such as IBM Lan Server or NFS, the security needs to be examined to ensure that users cannot get to Notes databases by use of the file services, which effectively bypasses the Notes server security. But more for performance reasons than security reasons, I do not recommend using Notes servers additionally as file servers.

One of the most effective Notes security tools is a database's Access Control List (ACL), which is used to specify who can access a given database and what types of tasks users can perform in that database. The ACL is a powerful and effective first line of defense for protecting databases from unauthorized access, but you must be careful to ensure that the ACL is set correctly so that there are no "back doors" or "holes."

> **TIP**
>
> Most of the ACL problems I've encountered arise from carelessness. Many of the Lotus-supplied Notes templates give the Default user Designer access to the database, which generally should be changed immediately after a database is created. Additionally, the Notes group OtherDomainServers is referenced, many times with Designer access, in many of the Lotus templates. Many companies do not think twice about this situation until the company starts communicating with Notes servers at other companies, and they mistakenly list the external servers in the OtherDomainServers group when they really should create an External Servers group. I strongly suggest that you perform an ACL audit on your databases before you connect your Notes network with any external Notes servers.

ACLs are especially critical when databases are replicated between different divisions or companies. If the ACLs are set improperly, data can be lost, and design changes can quickly propagate to all replicas of the database. When determining how to set up ACLs for databases that will be distributed to either remote users or other servers, it helps to try to envision the replication process step-by-step. In server-to-server communications, picture the database on each server, along with its local ACL, and then think about what data will be exchanged when the servers replicate. You must think about how to set up the ACL to ensure that only the appropriate data is exchanged and that the database's design or ACL is not changed inadvertently.

For example, suppose that you want to use a Notes database as a method of distributing information to your customers. You could create a group called "All Customers" in your Notes Name & Address book and then add the names of your customers (if they are dialing in from a workstation) or the names of your customers' servers to this group. Then, in your shared database on your Notes server, you would add the group "All Customers" to the ACL with Reader access (or Author access if you want your customers to be able to compose information). Of course, you'll probably want to have your server listed in the ACL as a Manager (assuming that the database resides on more than one server within your organization).

Next, you can send out a "replica stub" of the database to your customers, with instructions on how they should modify the ACL. The main ACL modification they will need to make is to explicitly list your company's Notes server as a Designer, not a Manager. If they leave your server as a Manager, then every time the servers replicate, your database's ACL will overwrite theirs, which can cause problems. But with your server listed as a Designer, any design changes made to the database will replicate to your customer's database. At this point, your customer can set the ACL on the database as he likes, and he won't have to worry about having the ACL changed by your server. Additionally, the database on your server is secure, because no matter what changes your customer makes to the database's documents, design, or ACL, the changes will never be replicated to your server.

When setting a database's ACL, you have the additional option of creating Roles. Roles are essentially subgroups of the Notes user names, server names, or group names that appear in the ACL. They can act as Notes groups, but only within the database where the Role is defined. These Roles can be useful when setting up the security of forms, views, and sections.

To create a Role, you first must get the Database Access Control List dialog box by selecting **D**atabase|**A**ccess Control... from the **F**ile menu (see Figure 15.1).

**FIGURE 15.1.**

*The Database Access Control List dialog box, with the **R**oles... button in the lower-right corner.*

When the **R**oles... button is clicked, the Access Roles dialog box appears. Here you can add, edit, and delete the roles assigned to a given database (see Figure 15.2).

**FIGURE 15.2.**

*The Access Roles dialog box, where Roles can be created, and people, groups, or servers can be added to or taken out of a Role.*

For example, a role called Purchasing has been created, and "Michelle Mahler" and "Paul Nakamura" have been added to the role (as indicated by the plus signs next to the names). Then, when forms, views, and sections are being designed, this Purchasing role can be used to limit access without having to name each individual specifically.

> **TIP**
>
> Although Roles are useful in certain circumstances, I have found that it is much easier to manage a Notes system by using groups in the Name & Address book and getting the Notes administrator to create the groups as needed. Roles, especially in large Notes systems with many databases, can be confusing and hard to maintain.

# Securing the Design of a Database

Many new Notes developers and users are horrified to find out that not only do Notes users have access to the Notes development tools, but a user can view a database's underlying design. On a server, a user can be locked out of reviewing the design by not being allowed design access in the ACL, but the user simply needs to make a local copy or replica of the database. In local copies or replicas of a database, the database's design can be analyzed (although it still cannot be changed on the server, which is really what counts).

Notes 3.x has a feature that allows the **D**esign menu to be hidden for a given Notes database. To access this feature, you select **D**atabase|Information from the Notes **F**ile menu, click the Other **S**ettings... button, and check the **H**ide the design of this database check box (see Figure 15.3).

**FIGURE 15.3.**

*The Database Settings dialog box, where a database's design can be hidden.*

After the **OK** button is clicked, you will be warned, "Once this option has been set it can never be changed" (see Figure 15.4), which is not quite true (see the following Warning). If you select **Yes**, the **I**con..., **V**iews..., **F**orms..., **S**hared Fields..., **M**acros..., and S**y**nopsis... options are grayed out on the database's **D**esign menu, and this change affects all the database's replicas similarly.

**FIGURE 15.4.**

*The warning that appears when you are about to disable the design options in a specific database.*

---

### WARNING

Although this feature might be needed or useful in certain circumstances, it contains a major bug that occasionally causes a database's design to reappear when a replica or a copy of a database is made. Although this is not a repeatable phenomenon, it does happen frequently when you are creating new replicas or copies of databases with hidden designs, and you should be aware of the potential.

Additionally, use of this feature requires that you have a design template for the database in case you later need to make changes to the database's design.

---

# Limiting Access to Forms and Documents

When a form is designed, there are two special form attributes that can be set in the Design Form Attributes dialog box that are used to control who can use the form to compose documents and who can read documents composed with the form. In Figure 15.5, notice the **R**ead Access... and Com**p**ose Access... buttons.

**FIGURE 15.5.**

*The Design Form Attributes dialog box, with the **Read** Access... and Com**pose** Access... buttons.*

After you click either of these buttons, it is a simple matter to define what users, groups, or roles can either read or compose documents with a given form. As illustrated in Figure 15.6, if you are going to limit compose (or read) access to a form, you simply select the names of the users, groups, or roles from the add access list entry picklist (or you can type a new entry). This is because the picklist for adding access list entries is created from the members of the database's ACL.

If a user is not listed in the Compose Access Control List for a given form, that form will not appear on the **C**ompose menu for that database.

---

**TIP**

If you are using the Reader Access Control List feature for a form, be aware that all documents created with that form contain a $Readers field that controls the reader access to the document. If you subsequently update (or delete) the Reader Access Control List on the form, you will have to write a macro to manually update (or delete) the $Readers field on the already-existing documents.

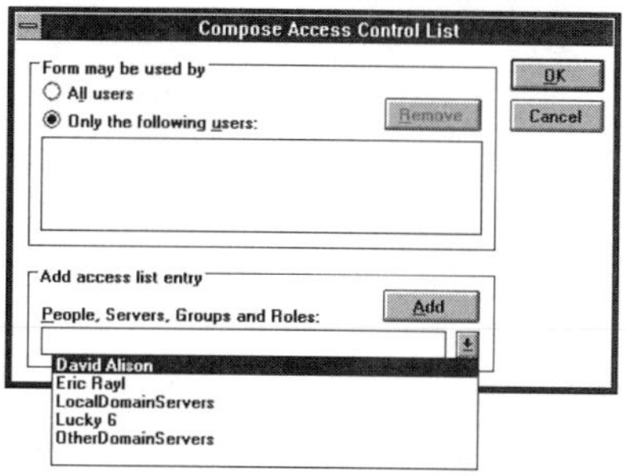

---

**FIGURE 15.6.**

*The Compose Access Control List for a form, showing the list of users, groups, and roles from the database's ACL.*

Another, slightly more flexible variation on controlling access to forms and documents is through the use of the special field data types called Author Names and Reader Names. When a field is added to the form, it can be specified as one of these data types. The contents of the field can include the names of people, groups, or roles that can either read a document or be considered authors of the document. (When a Reader Names type of field exists along with a Reader Access Control List, a user need only be listed in the Reader Names field or the Reader Access Control List to read a document, not in both.)

> **TIP**
>
> With just these four ways of controling access to forms and documents, many variations of security can be devised, and they can get quite confusing. I personally prefer using the Author Names feature, because it enables me to grant users Author access to the entire database and then list specific people as editors for certain documents by adding their names (or groups) to the Author Names field.

# Limiting Access to Views

From a security standpoint, limiting access to views is almost meaningless. Because users can always create private views, they could potentially create any view they want, including any documents they have access to. Limiting access to a view essentially means that the users will not see the view on the Notes **V**iew menu. There are a couple of ways to accomplish this task.

The easiest way to limit access to a view is to put parentheses around the view name, as in "(vwCategoryLookup)", but this technique hides the view for all users. If the view needs to be available only for a subset of the database's users, the view design attribute option **R**ead Access... can be used. To access this option when a view is in design mode, you select View **A**ttributes from the Notes **D**esign menu, then click the **R**ead Access... button (see Figure 15.7).

**FIGURE 15.7.**

*The Design View Attributes dialog box, where the **R**ead Access... button is located.*

When you click the **R**ead Access... button, you are presented with the view's Read Access Control List dialog box (see Figure 15.8).

**FIGURE 15.8.**

*A view's Read Access
Control List dialog box.*

If a user is not listed in a view's Read Access Control List, the view will not appear on the user's **V**iew menu. This feature is useful for making the **V**iew menu more user friendly, because many databases have views that are used only for administrative purposes, and there is no reason to clutter up the user's **V**iew menu. But again, it is not a security feature, and even a fairly unsophisticated user could gain access to documents contained in these hidden views simply by creating a private view.

# Limiting Access to Macros

Although Notes macros are very useful and powerful, they lack the security options that are available in forms and views. Macros observe the database security that is established by the database's ACL, but there is no way to have certain macros available only for a specific group of users and to have the macro not appear on the macro menu for other users.

Many of the macros that I use first authenticate that the current user is allowed to run the macro before the rest of the macro executes. Suppose, for example, that you have a certain type of database/application for which the general access level is Editor. This application additionally has a macro that is used to update a field in all the documents in the database based on certain conditions. If this macro could be run by any user with access to the database, it could cause problems.

The easy way to stop unauthorized users from running a macro, assuming that a small number of users are authorized to run the macro, is to start the macro's formula with an @If statement and check the current user's name against a list of authorized macro users. For example, the formula

```
@If(@IsNotMember(@UserName); "Eric Rayl" : "David Alison");
  @Do(@Prompt([OK]; "Error"; "You are not authorized
          to run this macro");
    @Return(""));
  @Success)
```

when used at the beginning of a macro can stop unauthorized users from running the macro. A slightly more complex but manageable version of the preceding idea is to see whether the current user's name is in a particular group in the Name & Address database using an @DbLookup. The only concern with using this approach is that remote users will need to have a copy of the Notes Group document in their personal Name & Address book database for this approach to work correctly.

All in all, Lotus needs to add a security feature to macros that is similar to the way forms and views are secured, which would allow certain macros to not appear on the macro menu. Also, the addition of "private macros," similar to private views, with the capability to create "shared, private on first use" macros could help in certain circumstances. But until then, about the best you can do is to validate the current user's name against either a list or a @DbLookup and not allow macro processing to continue if the user's name is not contained in the list.

# Encrypting, Sealing, and Signing Fields

The capability for Lotus Notes developers to selectively encrypt fields using sophisticated encryption algorithms is one of the most valuable tools, but one that is often not considered during evaluation of development platforms. Certainly, other third-party products are available that can be used to encrypt files, but I have not found any that work as unobtrusively or as seamlessly as the encryption systems built into Lotus Notes.

Lotus Notes includes two kinds of encryption: a shared-key methodology that is used to secure data in certain fields to only individuals who have access to the encryption key, and a public/private key encryption mechanism ("sealing") that is available to all documents mailed via the Notes mail engine.

## Shared-Key Field Encryption

The shared-key encryption mechanism is most often used by Notes application developers to secure data in selected fields within a form. One item worth noting is that documents are not encrypted, but the fields within the document can be encrypted.

> **TIP**
>
> You must seriously think about the ramifications of encrypting fields because an encrypted field cannot be displayed in a view. This limitation will certainly affect which fields you choose to encrypt.

Using encryption keys within an application is a four-step process. You must take the following actions:

1. Create the encryption key.
2. Enable encryption for the specific field(s) on a form.
3. Associate the encryption key with the form.
4. Distribute the encryption key to the correct users.

Consider the following example of how to design an encrypted field:

Your company has a human-resource type of application that contains a field with an employee's salary. This data is very sensitive, and you need a way to help ensure that this data is not misappropriated. The easiest approach is to encrypt the data in the Salary field. To accomplish this task, you first need to create a new shared encryption key. Shared encryption keys are part of a user's Notes ID file, and they can be created by any user.

To create a new encryption key, you select User **ID**...|**E**ncryption Keys... from the Notes **T**ools menu. This selection presents the User ID Encryption Keys dialog box, as in Figure 15.9.

**FIGURE 15.9.**

*The User ID Encryption Keys dialog box, which displays all the shared encryption keys contained in a user's ID file.*

To create a new encryption key, click the **N**ew... button, which opens the Add Encryption Key dialog box (Figure 15.10). Type the name of the encryption key and a description of where it is used, and select **I**nternational if the key will need to be used internationally.

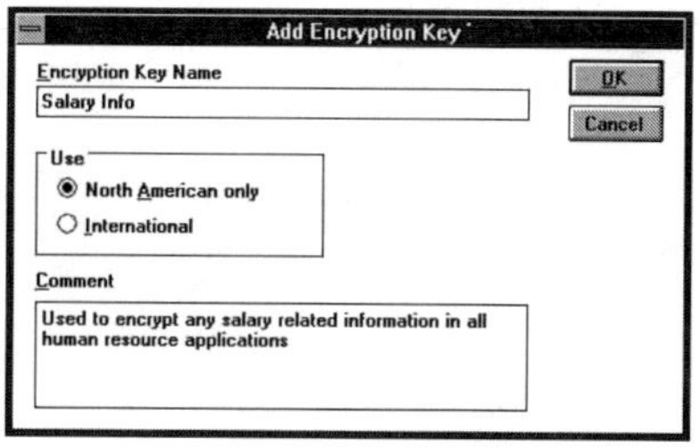

**FIGURE 15.10.**

*The Add Encryption Key dialog box, where a new encryption key's name is defined.*

Now that you have an encryption key defined, you need to enable encryption for the Salary field in your application. After opening the appropriate form in design mode, you double-click on the Salary field to set its attributes. Then you click the Security... button in the Field Attributes dialog box. This action presents you with the Design Field Security window, where you click the check box **E**nable encryption for this field (see Figure 15.11). You then click **O**K on the Design Field Security window, then **O**K on the Field Attributes window.

**FIGURE 15.11.**

*A field's Design Field Security dialog box, where encryption is enabled for the given field.*

Before exiting the form's design mode, you still need to associate the encryption key with the form. To do this, select Form **A**ttributes... from the **D**esign menu, and then click the Encryption... button. The Encryption Keys window appears. Here is where you associate an encryption key with this document, by clicking the **A**dd button. Now you can exit the form, saving the changes you've made to it.

All new documents composed with this form will have their Salary field encrypted, which means that the field will appear blank to any users who do not have the Salary Info encryption key as part of their Notes user ID. (If documents existed with unencrypted data in the field, you would have to refresh the fields in the documents in order to encrypt the data.)

The last task you must perform is distributing the encryption key to the authorized users. Notes makes this task exceptionally easy, because it allows encryption keys to be mailed between users (with some restrictions). All you need to do is select **M**ail|User ID|Encryption Keys... from the Notes menu, and then select the appropriate encryption key from the Mail Encryption Key window (see Figure 15.12).

After selecting the appropriate encryption key and clicking the **M**ail button, you are presented with the Mail Address Encryption Key dialog box, shown in Figure 15.13. Notice that the default subject explains to the user how to insert the key into his or her user ID file. Clicking the Se**n**d button completes the process of distributing the encryption key.

**FIGURE 15.12.**

*The Mail Encryption Key window is where an encryption key is selected for mailing to specified users.*

It's important to remember that more than one encryption key can be associated with a given form, but only one of the keys is needed to decrypt any of the fields on the form. The Notes "Internals: Security" database explains this situation very well by stating that you can think of it as being similar to a room with three doors, all of which are locked with different keys, only one key of which is required to gain entrance to the room.

## "Sealing" Fields When Mailing

In contrast to the shared-key method of encrypting data just illustrated, Notes also uses the public/private key encryption technology. This encryption method is built into the Notes mail system. Although sealing a mailed document is not really a database designer function, it is important to understand how the process works, because many companies will opt to change the design of the standard mail forms, or add new, mailable forms to the standard mail template.

When a document is mailed via the Lotus Notes mail engine, the user is presented with the option of encrypting the document (see Figure 15.13).

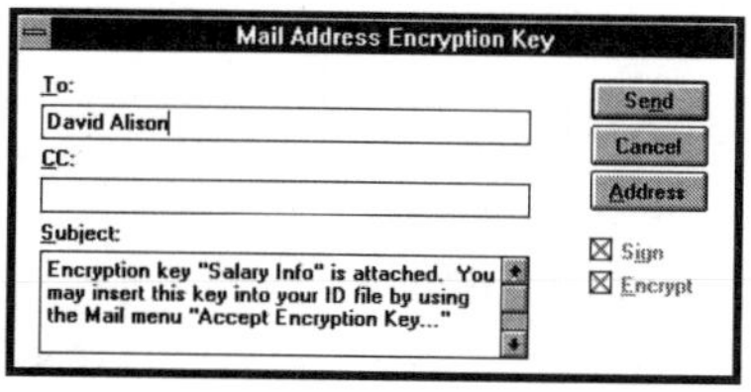

**FIGURE 15.13.**

*When a mailable form is about to be saved, the user is prompted with an Encrypt option.*

In one respect, the Notes mail encryption is similar to the shared key encryption in that only specified fields are encrypted within the document, and these fields must be specified by the database designer. If the user selects the **E**ncrypt option when mailing a document, Notes creates a random encryption key and encrypts the encryptable fields in the document. Then, it encrypts the key with the recipient's public key (which is stored in the Person document in the Name & Address book) and adds this encrypted key to the message as it is mailed, effectively *sealing* the document so that only the intended recipient can open it.

When the recipient receives the mail, his or her private encryption key (which is stored in the user's ID file) is used to decrypt the key, which in turn is used to decrypt the fields in the message.

Although this approach sounds time-consuming, in the Notes environment it is almost instantaneous, except when the encrypted fields are rich text and contain large objects or bit maps. When designing new forms for users' mail databases, you should consider what fields should be encryptable.

Additionally, you can force encryption on fields by adding a computed when composed field called Encrypt to the forms that you design, and setting its value to 1 (actually, any number other than 0). This move forces the encryptable fields on the form to be encrypted as the document is mailed.

> **TIP**
>
> The important idea to remember about encrypting mailed documents is that the fields on the form must still be flagged as "Encryptable" (by setting the Security attributes of the field). You also must remember that encrypted fields are not visible in views (that is one of the reasons why the Subject field on the standard mail memo form is not encrypted, because it could not be used in views).

# Electronically Signing Fields

Another unique development tool in Notes is the capability to electronically "sign" a document and then have users verify that the fields on the document have not been tampered with since it was signed. This feature is very useful in forms-routing types of applications in which you want to make sure that the contents of certain sensitive fields have not been altered since the form was electronically approved.

Electronically signing a document involves a lot of the encryption system I've already discussed, but it also involves the concept of Notes certificates. For electronic signing to be used effectively, users must have either a common certificate (in flat-certificate organizations) or a common ancestral certificate (for hierarchical certificates) for the electronic signing to be authenticated by the recipient. In most organizations, this is not a problem, but it does provide a dilemma for sending electronically signed documents between companies. It does not mean that signed documents cannot be sent between companies, but the user will see a message on the status bar at the bottom of the screen similar to this one:

> "You and signer have no Certificates in common; signer cannot be assumed to be trustworthy."

Signing has a little different twist than encryption in that either an entire document is signed, or fields *within a section* are signed. This allows for a document to have multiple signatures, each associated with a given section on the form.

---

**TIP**

Although a document can be signed by multiple people, it cannot have sections that are signed by the same person at different times. For example, a form cannot have an InitialApproval section and a FinalApproval section, each of which is signed by the same person at different times in the process. This is because when a user signs a Notes document, all fields that he has access to are signed. Some tricky section techniques can be used to work around this problem, but generally you should avoid designing forms that require multiple electronic signatures by the same individual.

---

To enable a form in an application to be signed, you first have to specify at least one field as signable. Generally, these fields would be the critical fields on the form, such as purchase requisition amount, travel itinerary, and so on—the fields that should not be tampered with. Next, the field's security attributes need to be set to allow the field to be signed. This task is accomplished by double-clicking on the field while the form is in design mode, and then selecting the check box **S**ign this field during mail signing or when saved within a section (see Figure 15.14).

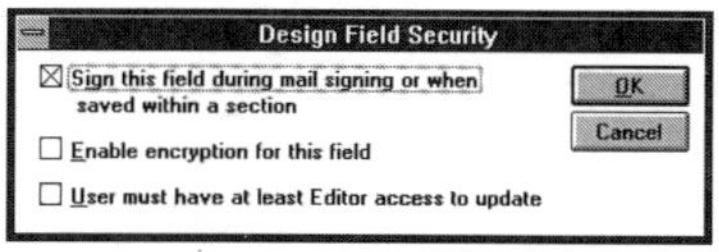

**FIGURE 15.14.**

*Electronically signing a field is enabled via the Design Field Security dialog box.*

Then, to force the fields to automatically be signed when the document is saved or mailed, you can add a computed when composed field called Sign to the form and set its formula to 1. This action forces the document to be signed when it is saved or mailed.

Although signing is a nice feature to add to your applications, especially for workflow applications with multiple approvals, many applications will not benefit from this additional level of complexity.

# Some Other Ways of Limiting Access to Fields

A couple of other methods can be used to limit access to the data contained in fields in documents. Notes sections are actually a special type of Notes field that is used to divide a form into areas that have different editors. Additionally, all Notes fields have a security attribute that can be set to block authors of documents from editing fields within documents they authored. Although not widely used, these two types of field-level security might be of use to you under certain circumstances.

## Sections

Fields of the Section data type are used to break a form into regions, with the edit access of the fields in the area being controlled by the contents of the section field. Sections are most commonly used on forms to allow the same document to be signed multiple times.

To see how sections are used, suppose that you want to create a purchase requisition system. Say that every purchase requisition requires the signature of the requester's immediate supervisor and the signature of the Controller of the company. Ideally, you want the completed form to look similar to the purchase requisition in Figure 15.15 (Figure 15.16 shows the form in design mode).

As you will notice, the requisition form has two section-type fields, called Section1 and Section2. The field Approver1Comments is considered to be in the first section, and the field Approver2Comments (and any fields below it) are in the second section of the form. Both Approver1Comments and Approver2Comments have their attributes set as **Sign** this field during mail signing or when saved within a section.

**FIGURE 15.15.**

*An example of a Notes form that uses sections to enable multiple electronic signatures.*

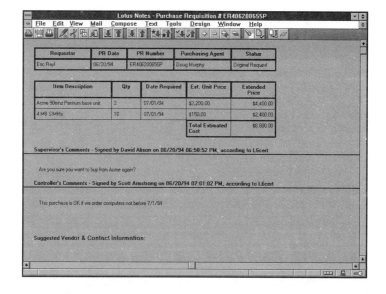

**FIGURE 15.16.**

*The purchase requisition form in design mode showing the two section fields.*

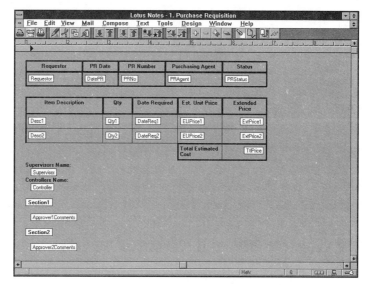

If Section1 and Section2 were just left as editable fields, users would have to specify who could edit (and thus sign) the section when they composed the document. This task is accomplished by double-clicking on the solid black line produced by the section field (labeled "Supervisor's Comments" in Figure 15.17) and then adding users, groups, or roles to the Edit Section dialog box using the Add access list entry listbox.

> **TIP**
>
> Personally, I like using computed and computed when composed sections as much as possible so that the users do not have to worry about setting the editors for a given section. For example, in the actual purchase requisition system I designed for a client, I used the Personal Defaults form technique (described in the Workflow example in Part IV of this book), with fields for the user's supervisor and controller's names. Then I used a @DbLookup to compute the values for the section fields, which automatically set the section editors when the form was composed.

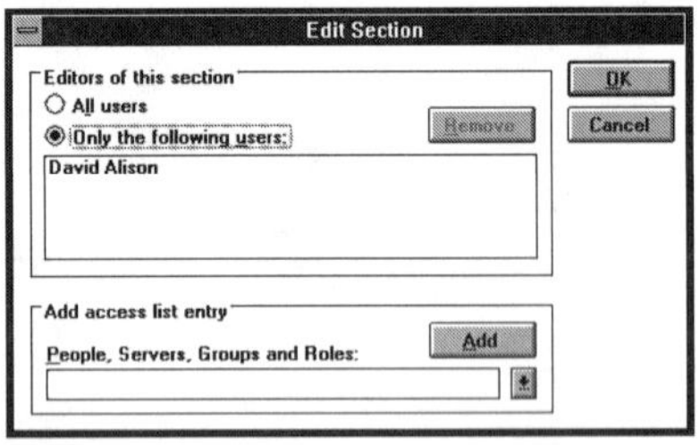

**FIGURE 15.17.**

*An editable section-type field enables users to select editors for a given section when composing a document.*

Although sections are not a true security feature because they can be "hacked" into by sophisticated users, they can often be used to create a perceived secure area of a form.

## The "User must have at least Editor access" Option

This field attribute, located by clicking the Security... button on the Field Definition dialog box (see Figure 15.14), is simply used to keep users with Author access to a database from changing the contents of a field after a document has been saved. Only people listed with at least Editor access in the database's ACL can modify the contents of the field.

I personally find this approach a little extreme in most cases. It's extreme because many users like to (and should!) save their work periodically, particularly when entering large amounts of text in fields, and this method prevents them from doing so. What I have found to be a rather effective deterrent most of the time is to use the Edit History technique to discourage users from changing documents that were previously composed.

# Testing Security

If you design a Notes application that uses many levels of security access, and particularly when you use combinations of Read and Compose access lists for forms, in conjunction with Author and Reader Names field data types, you must plan on doing extensive testing to verify that you have designed the security correctly. Testing Notes applications with high security demands can be very confusing for people not used to the Notes environment, and it should not be performed by inexperienced Notes users.

To test the security of Notes applications, you have to use the application exactly as it will be used in the real world, including having the database on servers, replicating the database between servers, and adding remote users who create replicas of the database from servers. Most important, you need to create several "test" user IDs and list them as users that would appear in the ACL, and additionally assign them to the appropriate groups, roles, and so forth.

Several times I've designed complex applications, and they were to be tested by project managers who had hardly any Notes experience. Many so-called "bugs" were found that really were caused because the application was not being used as it would be in the real world. For example, a tester would be using a Notes ID that had relatively high-level access to the database, then make a local replica of the database, then switch to a low-security level ID, and the tester would wonder why he could see certain documents, and so forth. Or in another situation, the tester would be testing features locally, rather than actually on the server.

---

**TIP**

When testing applications that require a high level of security, make sure to use several different Notes IDs and to perform tests using the database in as close to a real-world scenario as possible. When you change user IDs, make certain that you completely close the database (to the point that the icon for the database is not highlighted on the desktop) before you change IDs to ensure that the Notes server is forced to open a new session for you when you reopen the database as the new user. Many security "bugs" that arise during testing can be attributed to not fully closing a database before switching IDs.

# Summary

Although Notes version 3.x offers a very impressive array of security tools, I strongly advise you not to get carried away with trying to integrate all the various security possibilities into one application. Too often people try to over-design the security of an application, and not only does it become hard to test and maintain, but it can be overly restrictive to users if taken to the extreme.

> **TIP**
>
> When designing systems that are replacing paper-based workflows, you should give some thought to what security and audit trails existed in the paper-based world. I think you'll find that many times, the electronic version of the system will have vastly more security and auditing capabilities, without too many sophisticated Notes security techniques being implemented in one application.

It's my experience that probably 75 percent of Notes applications can get by with not much more than a good solid ACL strategy. And the extra effort put into overly secure applications can take as long if not longer than the actual database design itself, especially when testing and maintenance issues are concerned. But when you do need the utmost in security, Notes has the integrated tools to enable you to design a "bullet-proof" application.

# IV

## Real-World Examples

LOTUS
NOTES

# 16

## Inquiry Tracking System

# Overview of the System

A plastics company in Los Angeles needed a way to leverage the information it gathered from its advertising, convention, and direct marketing activities. The company, Beeline, manufactures advertising and point-of-purchase displays, and it runs large advertising campaigns in trade journals. Additionally, it places advertisements in direct-mailed "card decks," and it gathers leads at industry tradeshows. The company needed a way to track the effectiveness of its advertising, and at the same time, it needed an efficient way to process the 50-plus daily catalog requests and sample requests it receives from potential customers. Additionally, the West Coast–based company used a marketing consultant based in Colorado, and the consultant would from time to time conduct direct-mail marketing campaigns for the company.

A Notes system was designed that allowed the company's customer service employees to process requests for catalogs while a potential customer was on the phone. While entering the company, contact, and address information into a Notes form (see Figure 16.1), the customer service employee would also ask the requestor where he heard about "Beeline Plastics." Then the "Catalog Request due to:" field in Figure 16.1 would be updated to reflect what advertisement generated the request.

**FIGURE 16.1.**

*A catalog request being entered into the Inquiry Tracking system.*

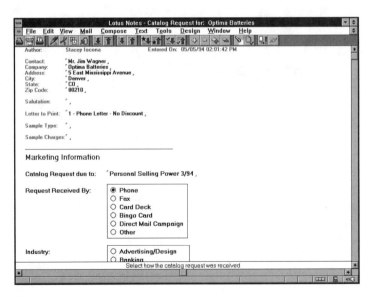

The "Letter to Print:" keyword field determined what type of form to use later when actually printing the mail-merged requests. Figure 16.2 shows the types of letters that were available.

**FIGURE 16.2.**

*The keyword list for the LetterToPrint field.*

This keyword list is based on a `@DbColumn` formula and allows values that are not in the list. From time to time, Beeline purchases a mailing list or enters leads from trade shows into this database. The customer service reps enter the leads in their spare time, and they assign a new letter type to these leads so that they don't get mixed in with the other requests when it comes time to print the mail-merged letters.

Other information on the Catalog Request form was a field to capture how the request was received (phone, fax, bingo card, and so on) and a field to be used later to track whether the company or individual places an order.

After the system was in use for several months, I decided to add one more field to the form. This field would flag companies that were in certain key industries so that Beeline could occasionally send out industry-specific advertisements. I also wrote a query macro to help Beeline search for types of companies that it could then generate mail-merged letters for.

At the end of the day, each customer service agent switched to a view that would allow the agent to print the mail-merged letters (see Figure 16.3).

**FIGURE 16.3.**

*A view used for selecting and printing the catalog request letters.*

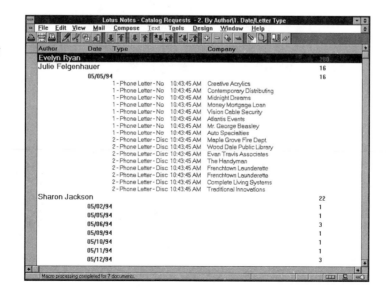

All the documents of the same type would then be selected in the view. The documents would be printed using form override, selecting the appropriate hidden mail-merge form from the form-override menu (as in Figure 16.4 and Figure 16.5).

**FIGURE 16.4.**

*After catalog requests are selected in the view, they are printed as a letter using form override.*

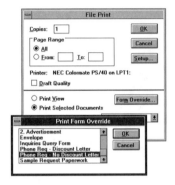

**FIGURE 16.5.**

*An example of a document printed with the Phone Req - No Discount form.*

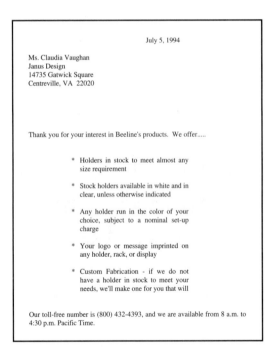

The phone request letters would then be stuffed into 9- by 12-inch window envelopes, where they would additionally serve to address the letter.

In the system, views were created that could help gauge the effectiveness of advertisements by categorizing on the Advertisement field and adding a column to count the number of catalog requests for each advertisement (see Figure 16.6).

**FIGURE 16.6.**

*A view of catalog requests categorized By Advertisement.*

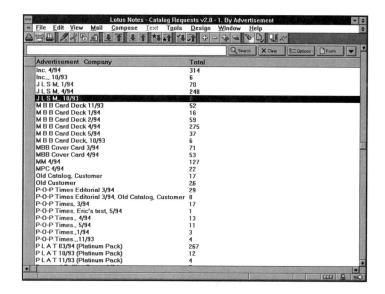

This same system is used for handling both leads from tradeshows and leads that the company purchases from mailing list vendors. The lead information is entered into the system. Then a custom Notes form letter is designed and used to mail-merge the lead information into a cover letter.

Two other features help the company make the most of the lead information it gathers in the Inquiry tracking system. One is the capability to track which leads actually place orders. This feature not only provides a more accurate idea of how qualified the leads are from a given source, but also allows the company to capitalize its advertising costs under new tax laws.

The other feature that has made the system pay for itself is the capability to export the leads generated and sell or trade these files with list brokers. At first, this process was not automated, but it became hard to track which leads had been sold to which list broker, so the system was automated to allow a history of exports to be maintained.

# The System's Architecture

The system uses a very simple architecture, with no response hierarchy. There are essentially two forms that drive the entire application: the 1. Catalog Request | frmRequest and the 2. Advertisement | frmAdvertisement, both of which are main documents. The Advertisement code on the Advertisement form was used in an @DbColumn to build the keyword list of Advertisement choices on the Catalog Request form.

The system was originally designed in Notes 2.1a. After the system was used for a while, the database had more than 30,000 catalog requests and leads. When Notes 3.0 shipped, the system was split into two separate databases—the current database and an archive database. A background macro was written that would automatically move catalog requests older than 30 days to an archive database. The archive database had almost the same structure as the original database, but it was full text indexed.

As mentioned earlier, after the system was in use awhile, we added the Industry keyword field to allow Beeline to send industry-specific letters to the companies. But there were already tens of thousands of requests that did not have this field. Because the database was fully text indexed, I was able to write several query macros to perform searches for specific types of companies based on certain words in the companies' names. These query macros were used to select the documents that would be printed.

# Setting Up the System

The databases can be used locally, but to see how documents are automatically moved from the main database to the archive database, the databases must be put on a Notes server. After both the Catalog Request and the Request Archive database are put on a Notes server, the background macro needs to be modified to reference your server's name.

Select **M**acros... on the Notes **D**esign menu, and then edit the Mail Old Requests macro. In the Edit Existing Macro window, you need to change value in the box labeled **S**erver/ workstation on which to run: to reflect either your Notes user name or the name of one of your servers (see Figure 16.7).

**FIGURE 16.7.**

*Specifying the server/workstation where the Mail Old Requests background macro runs.*

If you want to have the background macro run on the server, you must add the database's replica ID to the database's ACL. The easiest way to do this is to cut and paste the database's replica ID from the **R**eplication Information generated by the **D**esign|**Sy**nopsis menu option. The replica ID needs to have at least Editor access to be able to delete the documents from the database (see Figure 16.8).

**FIGURE 16.8.**

*The Catalog Request database's replica ID needs to be set to at least an Editor in the database's Access Control List.*

A mail-in database document needs to be composed in the Name and Address book database. Figure 16.9 shows an example of a Mail-In Database document.

---

**TIP**

Remember that the Mail-In Name on the Mail-In Database document is the name that must appear in the SendTo field on a document (or as the SendTo argument of @MailSend). It is not the actual title of the mail-in database.

**FIGURE 16.9.**

*An example Mail-In Database document for the Request Archive database.*

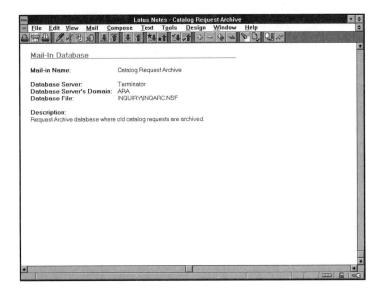

Finally, the Request Archive database should be full text indexed so that you can see how the query macros work. Simply select the icon for the Request Archive database, select **F**ull Text Search|**C**reate Index from the **F**ile menu, and the index will be created.

# The System's Key Formulas and Macros

There really aren't any complex formulas or macros in this application. The Advertisement form has only four fields (see Figure 16.10). The main purpose of this form is to provide a place where each advertisement can be described. The Advertisement field is used to generate the keyword list when a customer service agent is composing a catalog request. This means that an Advertisement document must exist before a Catalog Request can be associated with it. But because no response hierarchy is being used, if the correct Advertisement document does not exist, the service rep can just assign the Catalog Request temporarily to a "dummy" advertisement. Then when the potential customer is off the phone, the service rep can compose the appropriate Advertisement document and associate the request with the new advertisement simply by editing the keyword field on the request.

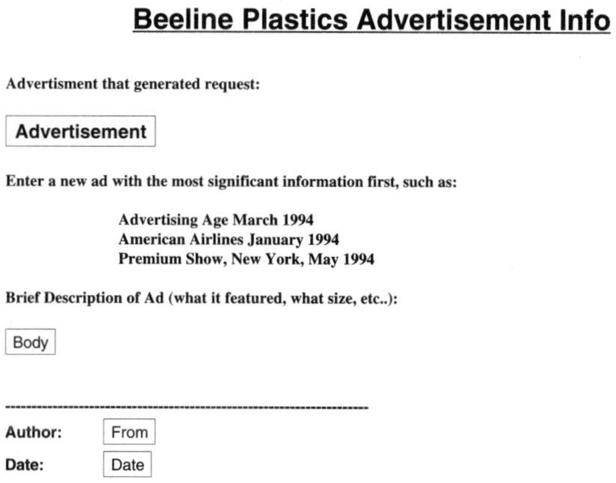

**FIGURE 16.10.**

*The fields on the Inquiry Tracking system's Advertisement form.*

**Beeline Plastics Advertisement Info**

Advertisment that generated request:

Advertisement

Enter a new ad with the most significant information first, such as:

Advertising Age March 1994
American Airlines January 1994
Premium Show, New York, May 1994

Brief Description of Ad (what it featured, what size, etc..):

Body

-------------------------------------------------------------------

**Author:**     From

**Date:**     Date

The Catalog Request form looks like Figure 16.11.

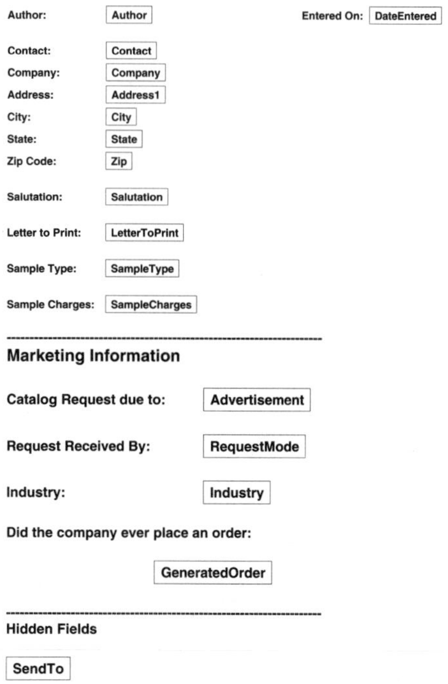

**FIGURE 16.11.**

*The Catalog Request form in design mode.*

Author:     Author                     Entered On:  DateEntered

Contact:     Contact
Company:     Company
Address:     Address1
City:     City
State:     State
Zip Code:     Zip

Salutation:     Salutation

Letter to Print:     LetterToPrint

Sample Type:     SampleType

Sample Charges:     SampleCharges

-----------------------------------------------------------------
**Marketing Information**

**Catalog Request due to:**     Advertisement

**Request Received By:**     RequestMode

**Industry:**     Industry

**Did the company ever place an order:**

GeneratedOrder

-----------------------------------------------------------------
**Hidden Fields**

SendTo

The Catalog Request form is simple also—it has two keyword fields (Advertisement and LetterToPrint) that both use @DbColumn to generate dynamic pick lists. It also has a hidden, computed when composed field, SendTo, that simply has this formula:

```
"Catalog Request Archive"
```

The background macro, Mail Old Requests, runs daily on the server and "prunes" the main database, keeping its performance relatively fast. The macro's formula is simply:

```
@If(Form = "frmRequest" & DateEntered < @Adjust(@Today; 0; 0; -30; 0; 0; 0);
    @Do(@MailSend; @DeleteDocument);
    @Success);
SELECT @All
```

> **TIP**
>
> The technique used in the preceding discussion for automatically moving documents between databases can be useful in many other situations. For instance, you can keep discussion databases from getting too unwieldy by archiving resolved issues or old messages. Or in a project management database, when projects are completed, after a certain period they might be moved to an archive database. This method keeps the size of the day-to-day database down and keeps its performance up.

In the archive database, the forms and views are the same as in the Catalog Request database, except that there is one additional form, the 1. Mailing List Request | frmExportRequest (see Figure 16.12).

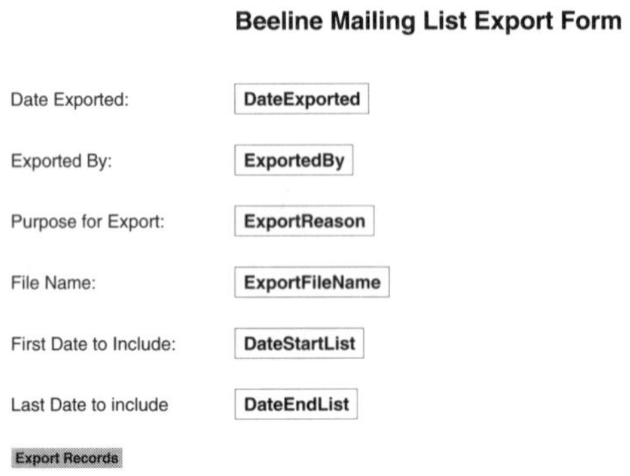

**FIGURE 16.12.**
*The Mailing List Request form in design mode.*

**Beeline Mailing List Export Form**

| | |
|---|---|
| Date Exported: | **DateExported** |
| Exported By: | **ExportedBy** |
| Purpose for Export: | **ExportReason** |
| File Name: | **ExportFileName** |
| First Date to Include: | **DateStartList** |
| Last Date to include: | **DateEndList** |

**Export Records**

This form is used to help track what portions of the database were sold to which companies, and it contains the Export Records button macro that helps automate the export process. When a company would want to purchase a portion of the Beeline database—for example, the last three months of leads—a user would compose a Mailing List Request form and fill in the DateStartList and DateEndList fields. The form automatically computed what the export file name would be by using the following formula for the field ExportFileName:

```
LastFileNumber := @Right(
                    @LeftBack(
                      @Subset(
                        @DbColumn("Notes" : "NoCache"; "";"vwExportFileName"; 1);
                      1);
                    4);
                  2);

NewFileNumber := @Text(@TextToNumber(LastFileNumber) + 1);

@If(@Length(NewFileNumber) = 1;
  @Set("NewFileNumber"; "0" + NewFileNumber);
  @Success);

"c:\\notes\\data\\inqexp" + NewFileNumber + ".txt"
```

This formula needs to be modified in order for you to try the Export button on the Mailing List Request form. It's best to change the file path to point to a shared directory on the network. That will help ensure that the exported files are named correctly.

After a user enters the reason for the export, and the starting and ending catalog request dates to include, the user saves the document and then clicks the Export Records button. This button macro has the following formula:

```
EnvDateStartList := EnvDateStartList;
EnvDateEndList := EnvDateEndList;
EnvExportFileName := EnvExportFileName;

@If(@IsNewDoc;
  @Do(@Prompt([OK]; "Error"; "You must save this
        document first before you can export records.
        Press <Ctrl>-S to save this document, then press
        the Export button again");
      @Return(""));
  @Success);

@SetEnvironment("EnvDateStartList"; @Text(DateStartList));
@SetEnvironment("EnvDateEndList"; @Text(DateEndList));
@SetEnvironment("EnvExportFileName"; ExportFileName);
@Command([FileCloseWindow]);
@Command([OpenView]; "(vwExport)"; 1);
@Command([ToolsRunMacro]; "(Select Records To Export)");
@Command([ToolsRunMacro]; "(Export Selected Requests)")
```

This macro first checks to see whether the document has been saved, and it terminates with a prompt if the document has not been saved (the contents of the DateStartList and DateEndList fields are not available until the document is saved). Next, the macro sets three Notes environment variables, `EnvDateStartList`, `EnvDateEndList`, and `EnvExportFileName`, that are used within the macro (Select Records to Export).

Then the form is closed, and the (vwExport) is opened. At this point, one selection macro is called that processes all the documents in the view and selects the catalog requests that meet the export criteria. The formula for the (Select Records To Export) is this:

```
TempDateStartList := @Environment("EnvDateStartList");
TempDateEndList := @Environment("EnvDateEndList");
SELECT DateEntered >= @TextToTime(TempDateStartList)
        & DateEntered <= @TextToTime(TempDateEndList)
```

This macro recovers the starting and ending dates from the environment variables and then proceeds to select the documents within the range of dates.

After the selection macro is complete, an execute-once type of macro is called, (Export Selected Requests), which has the following formula:

```
Filename := @Environment("EnvExportFileName");
@Prompt([OK]; "Reminder"; "At the next prompt,
                select \"Selected Documents\" and do
                not check the \"Include View Titles\" box");

@Command([FileExport]; "Tabular Text"; Filename);

@Command([FileCloseWindow]);

@Command([Execute]; "WRITE"; Filename);


SELECT @All
```

Unfortunately, no matter what I tried, `@Command([FileExport])` always caused a dialog box to appear, as in Figure 16.13. Therefore, I added the `@Prompt` as a reminder of how to respond to the dialog box.

**FIGURE 16.13.**

*The Tabular Text Export dialog box that appears when the @Command([FileExport]) command is used.*

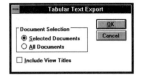

Currently, this macro is set up to export to a fixed-field text file and then launch the Windows's Write program so that you can examine the export file. At Beeline, the program was set to export in Lotus 1-2-3 format and then launch the file into Microsoft Excel. Excel was used to convert the file into a dBASE III file format.

When the Request Archive database is full text indexed, there are several query macros that can be run. To see how the macros run, pull down the full query bar by clicking the down-arrow button on the query bar. When the full query bar is open, you can click the Saved Queries button and select one of the queries. Notice the formulas that appear in the query criteria field and the Define Action area of the query bar. Figure 16.14 depicts the results of selecting Ad/Marketing/Design Query from the Saved Queries and then clicking the Search button. (The Execute button sets the field on all documents that match the criteria, but it does not leave the documents that meet the criteria in the view window—you should click Search first, and if you are happy with the results, use the Execute button to make the changes to the industry field.) Notice that in addition to finding all the catalog requests that meet the search criteria

```
([Company] CONTAINS (Advertising,Graphics,Design,Ad ,Marketing))
```

the macro also performs the following formula:

```
FIELD Industry := "Advertising/Design";
```

This search macro was used to try to assign industries to the 30,000 or so catalog requests that were composed before the Industry field was added to the form.

**FIGURE 16.14.**

*The Full Query bar, with a saved query, after the query was executed using the Search button.*

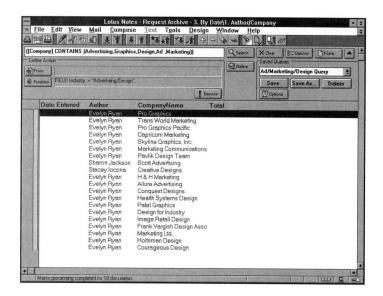

## Summary

The Inquiry Tracking system, with the Catalog Request database and the Request Archives database, represents a relatively simple Notes application. But this one application has paid for itself several times over just with its capability to capture names and addresses that can later be sold. Additionally, there is a return on investment due to its capability to track the number of responses generated by individual advertisements and the capability to quickly process requests for catalogs while generating a respectable cover-letter/letter address at the same time.

This example illustrates how even simple Notes applications can be very useful. The next two real-world applications will be much more complex and will employ more of the techniques that were explained in Part III.

# 17

## Bug Tracking System

# Overview

This Notes application was designed to help software developers track bugs in the various versions of their products. It also tracks who reported the bug so that when the bug is fixed, the customer service department can send "fix disks" to the individuals who reported the bug.

For many small and medium-sized software companies, not to mention in-house development departments, Notes is an ideal platform for creating bug tracking applications. Although it does not have all the relational capabilities of a system that uses a traditional database management system, there are many benefits to the Notes free-form approach of enabling developers to add comments and pose questions in the bug tracking application. The other major benefits are its immediate support for multiple platforms (Windows, OS/2, Macintosh, and UNIX), its support for distributing the database to many development sites using replication, and the potential for allowing customers access to certain areas of the database via remote access.

# Architecture of the System

There were two main factors that drove the underlying architecture of the application:

■ Many software companies have just a few products, but each product is available on several platforms (generally Windows, Macintosh, and maybe OS/2). The products generally share some parts of the code or documentation across the various platforms, and therefore a bug that is reported on one platform could potentially exist on the other platforms. When a bug is reported, it should be the responsibility of the QA (quality assurance) department to determine whether the bug could exist in the same product on a different platform. If there is the potential for the bug, then the bug report needs to be "cloned" to a different platform, where testing would determine whether the bug exists.

■ Sometimes, a customer will call technical support and report a problem, and a new bug report will be opened. Later, after closer inspection of the bugs in the database, it will turn out that the problem had already been reported and was already being worked on. At this point, the customer report needs to be associated to the actual bug report, and the duplicate bug needs to be deleted.

To solve the "cloning" issue, I decided that the copy-and-paste process, at the view level, was the most efficient way of creating new bug reports. Almost all the fields in the cloned report would contain the same information as in the original report, so a simple copy-and-paste of a bug report in a view made sense. To distinguish cloned reports, a hyphenated bug-numbering scheme was used to identify reports that were cloned. For example, the original bug ID number might be A4144-2105, and clones of this bug would appear as A4144-2105-2, A4144-2105-3, and so on. When a bug was copied and pasted, a paste-in macro would be activated that would prompt the user for the new product name and version number, and then the macro would update the fields accordingly.

The Notes database was architected such that each bug report was a main document, and every customer report of that bug was a response document to the bug report. This architecture was developed because many bugs were discovered internally and did not require associated customer information.

Additionally, when it was determined that the problem a customer reported had been previously identified as a bug, the customer reports needed the capability to be moved from one bug report to another. The easiest approach to moving response-type documents from one main topic to another is cutting and pasting, but another useful approach is to simulate a response hierarchy. This simulation is accomplished by using a common field in both the bug report and the customer report—the bug ID number. Then views could be built that were categorized on the bug ID number, which would cause all of a particular bug's customer reports to appear related to the appropriate bug report.

Many larger software companies could use a design similar to this application's, but use a separate database for each product type or category to keep the size of the database down and the performance high. If needed, a central management database could be created that contained summaries of all the open bugs per product and their various states.

# Setting Up the Bug Tracking Application

The software bug tracking application relies heavily on lookup documents for building product code and version number keyword lists, as well as for company and contact information. For instance, products and customers/contacts cannot be created "on the fly" as a bug report is being composed; they must be created first before a bug report or customer report is entered. This is not a major limitation because all product documents should be created when the system is set up, and they should be maintained as new products and versions are added. Additionally, because many software companies sell support on a yearly, per-individual basis, company and contact documents should already exist for valid customers, and the customer service department should be responsible for creating and maintaining the company/contact documents. However, if a customer calls in and uses the support ID number for another individual within his company, a temporary contact profile can be set up for the person, and this exception can be noted.

When the system is being set up, a Product Description document should be created for each product/version combination that is currently supported (see Figure 17.1 and Figure 17.2).

**FIGURE 17.1.**

*Setting up a new product description.*

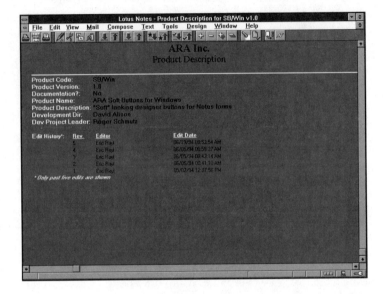

**FIGURE 17.2.**

*The product description form in design mode.*

**ARA Inc.**
Product Description

| Product Code: | ProductCode |
| Product Version: | ProductVersion |
| Documentation?: | DocumentationProduct |
| Product Name: | ProductName |
| Product Description: | ProductDescription |
| Development Dir: | ProductDevDirector |
| Dev Project Leader: | DevProjectLeader |

| Edit History*: | Rev. | Editor | Edit Date |
|---|---|---|---|
| | E1 | A1 | D1 |
| | E2 | A2 | D2 |
| | E3 | A3 | D3 |
| | E4 | A4 | D4 |
| | E5 | A5 | D5 |

* Only past five edits are shown

Hidden Fields

| TimesModified |
|---|
| PastAuthors |
| PastEditDates |
| SortOrder |

On the Product Description form, both the product code and the product version number fields are keyword fields that use @DbColumn to generate valid picklists (but they also allow new values to be entered). The form also contains the DocumentationProduct keyword field, which can be used to flag the product as a documentation component of a product (although the value contained in the product code should reflect whether the bug is a documentation product or actual software). This field allows product codes to be created for the individual documentation components of a product. For instance, an example or a tutorial within a product's manual could be reported as a bug, and the documentation department could then look for any documentation-specific bug reports. The DocumentationProduct is then used to set a flag on the Bug Report form identifying whether the bug report is documentation related, which in turn drives the selection formulas for the documentation-only bug report views.

Additionally, each product/version has an associated development director and development project leader. In the system as it currently exists, the development director name is also a computed field on bug reports that looks up the current assigned development director for each product as the bug report is filled out. This allows views to be developed that are categorized by the development director. Currently, neither the development director nor the development project leader fields are used in any views, however.

In addition to the Product Description type of document, there are two other administrative types of forms: the Customer Master Record and the Contact Profile (see Figure 17.3 through Figure 17.6).

**FIGURE 17.3.**

*The Customer Master Record form.*

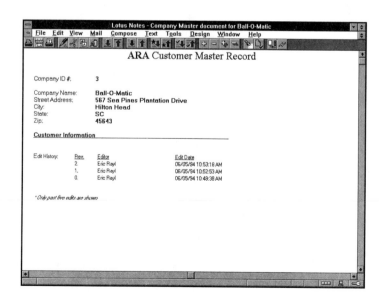

**FIGURE 17.4.**

*The Customer Master Record form in design mode.*

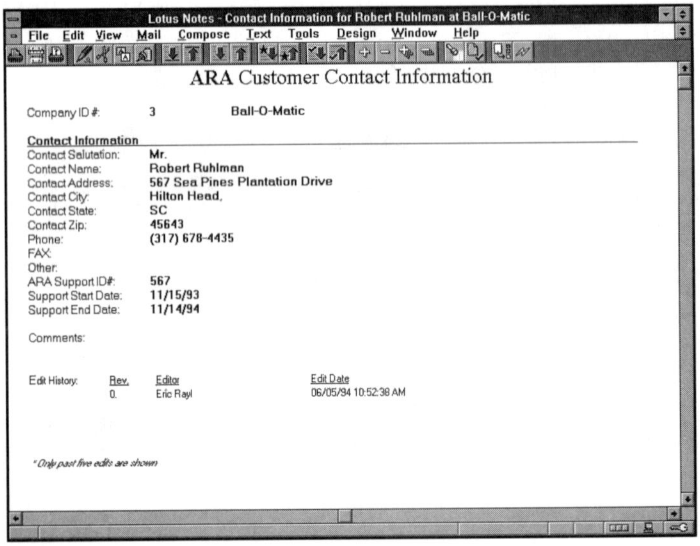

TimesCustomerButtonPressed

**ARA** Customer Master Record

Company ID #:         CompanyID

Company Name:         CompanyName
Street Address:       CustomerAddress1
City:                 CustomerCity
State:                CustomerState
Zip:                  CustomerZip

**Customer Information**

CustomerInfo

| Edit History: | Rev. | Editor | Edit Date |
|---|---|---|---|
| | E1 | A1 | D1 |
| | E2 | A2 | D2 |
| | E3 | A3 | D3 |
| | E4 | A4 | D4 |
| | E5 | A5 | D5 |

*\* Only past five edits are shown*

Hidden Fields

TimesModified

PastAuthors

PastEditDates

**FIGURE 17.5.**

*The Customer Contact Information form.*

Lotus Notes - Contact Information for Robert Ruhlman at Ball-O-Matic

File  Edit  View  Mail  Compose  Text  Tools  Design  Window  Help

**ARA** Customer Contact Information

Company ID #:        3          Ball-O-Matic

**Contact Information**
Contact Salutation:    Mr.
Contact Name:          Robert Ruhlman
Contact Address:       567 Sea Pines Plantation Drive
Contact City:          Hilton Head,
Contact State:         SC
Contact Zip:           45643
Phone:                 (317) 678-4435
FAX:
Other:
ARA Support ID#:       567
Support Start Date:    11/15/93
Support End Date:      11/14/94

Comments:

| Edit History: | Rev. | Editor | Edit Date |
|---|---|---|---|
| | 0. | Eric Rayl | 06/05/94 10:52:38 AM |

*\* Only past five edits are shown*

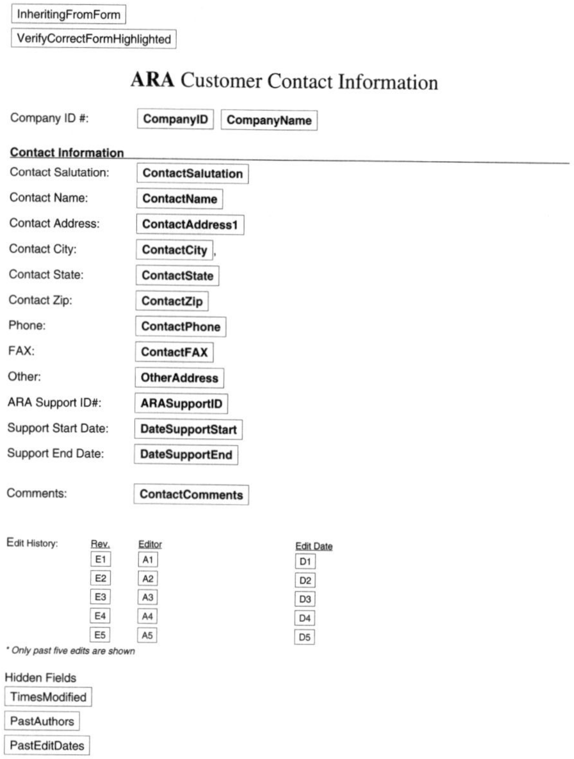

**FIGURE 17.6.**

*The Customer Contact Information form in design mode.*

The Customer Master Record form was designed to be composed by a software company's Customer Service department. When an individual purchases a technical support contract, his company and contact documents are composed at that time.

This form has a CompanyID field that generates a unique number for each customer. Generally, I would use some sort of a date/time stamp to generate this ID number, but this example assumes that all individuals within the customer service department use the same Notes server and that the number of new companies being set up is not very large. Therefore, a sequential numbering system was used for assigning Company ID numbers. The computed-when-composed field CompanyID on the Customer Master Record has the following formula:

```
@If(@Elements(@DbColumn("Notes" : "NoCache"; ""; "vwLookupCompanyID"; 1)) = 0;
  1;
  @Subset(@DbColumn("Notes" : "NoCache"; ""; "vwLookupCompanyID"; 1); 1) + 1)
```

The first part of the formula uses @DbColumn to return the first column of the view vwLookupCompanyID, which is sorted by CompanyID in descending order. If the @DbColumn returns no elements, the CompanyID is set to 1; otherwise, the first element of the list that the @DbColumn returns is extracted using @Subset, and 1 is added to that element, creating the new company ID number.

> **TIP**
>
> In most circumstances, I do not recommend trying to create sequential numbers in Notes applications. If, however, you can ensure that all documents that need to be numbered will be created on one server, and if the volume of documents is sufficiently low, this approach might be useful.

The Customer Contact Information form is a response document that must be composed with the appropriate Customer Master Record highlighted. To ensure this, two hidden fields, InheritingFromForm and VerifyCorrectFormHighlighted, are used at the top of the form. InheritingFromForm is an editable field that has a Default Value Formula of Form, causing it to inherit the value in the Form variable of the document that was highlighted when the document was composed. In addition, the field has the following Input Validation Formula:

```
@If(InheritingFromForm != "frmCompanyMaster";
   @Do(@Prompt([OK]; "Error"; "You must have a Company Master Profile highlighted
          before you compose this Contact Profile.  Close this document now without
          saving it.");
      @Return(""));
   @Success)
```

This formula does not allow the Customer Contact document to be saved if a valid Company Master document was not highlighted when the form was composed. Additionally, the computed-when-composed field VerifyCorrectFormHighlighted has the following formula:

```
@If(InheritingFromForm = "frmCompanyMaster";
   @Return("");
   @Prompt([OK]; "Error"; "You must highlight a Company Master document to compose
          this form. Close this document without saving it and highlight a
          Company Master document before composing the Contact Profile"));
```

This formula causes the user to be prompted immediately when a Customer Contact document is composed incorrectly, instead of waiting for the InheritingFromForm's input validation formula to prompt the user when the document is saved.

This design might or might not be ideal for the types of companies and contacts a given software company deals with. In some instances, the company and contact information would be better maintained in one document, rather than in two documents. However, many software companies have a relatively small number of actual customers, whereas these companies had a large number of individuals that had technical support contracts.

# Composing/Editing Bug Reports

After all the product descriptions have been loaded into the system and valid customers/contacts documents have been loaded, actual bug reports can be composed. The bug report form (see Figure 17.7) is where most of the action happens within the bug tracking application.

**FIGURE 17.7.**
*The Bug Report form.*

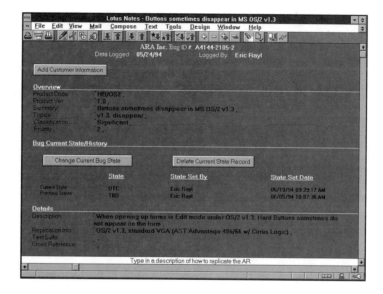

## The Overview Area of the Bug Report Form

When a bug report is first composed, it is assigned a bug ID number based on the date and time the bug is reported. As in almost all the Notes applications that I design, I need to have a unique number that identifies a particular document, whether it is a bug report, an investigation case, or a project. As mentioned before, ID numbers in Notes take on a different role than in traditional systems, because they are rarely used for searching for a particular document. In the bug tracking application, the main purpose for the bug ID number is to allow a relationship between the bug report and subsequent customer reports of the bug. In the real world, bugs are not referenced as much by bug ID numbers as by the problem's description. For instance, a conversation between a technical support person and a quality assurance person within the software company would probably not include the question, "Have you found out any more information on the bug number 3456?" The conversations I've often heard are more likely to include a question like this: "Have you found out any more information on the Hard Button/OS2 disappearing problem under OS/2 v1.3?"

Therefore, the bug ID number was not made a sequential number, as it would be with traditional database development systems. Instead, the bug ID number is a semi-significant number (meaning that it conveys more information than simply sequential numbers). Here is the formula for the computed-when-composed ActionRequestID (bug ID) field:

```
YearString := @Right(@Text(@Year(@Now)); 1);
MonthString := @If(@Month(@Now) >= 10; @Text(@Month(@Now));
  "0" + @Text(@Month(@Now)));
DayString := @If(@Day(@Now) >= 10; @Text(@Day(@Now)); "0" + @Text(@Day(@Now)));
HourString := @If(@Hour(@Now) >= 10; @Text(@Hour(@Now));
  "0" + @Text(@Hour(@Now)));
MinuteString := @If(@Minute(@Now) >= 10; @Text(@Minute(@Now));
  "0" + @Text(@Minute(@Now)));

"A" + YearString + MonthString + DayString + "-" + HourString + MinuteString
```

This formula creates a bug ID number that is in the format

*AYMMDD-hhmm*

in which

- ■ *A* is a constant that indicates that this is a bug ID number, as opposed to a customer report ID number.
- ■ *Y* is the last digit of the year (for example, 4 for 1994).
- ■ *MM* is the two-digit month value (for example, 06 for June).
- ■ *DD* is the two-digit date value (for example, 09 for the 9th).
- ■ *hhmm* is the hours and minutes value of the function @Now, when the report was composed.

The first field on the bug report form is the keyword field ProductCode. This keyword field uses a @DbColumn to provide a picklist of valid product codes to the user—only existing product codes can be selected. After a product code has been selected, the ProductVersion keyword field presents the user with a list of valid version numbers based on the ProductCode selected. This is accomplished through the use of the contents of the ProductCode field, in conjunction with a hidden, categorized version-number lookup table and the @DbLookup function. @DbLookup is used in the keyword formula, rather than the conventional @DbColumn, to return a picklist of version numbers specific to a given ProductCode. This is the keyword formula for the ProductVersion field:

```
@If(@IsDocBeingLoaded & !@IsNewDoc;
  @Unavailable;
  @DbLookup("Notes" : "NoCache"; ""; "vwProductCodeVersionLookup"; ProductCode; 2))
```

As with many of the other keyword fields within my Notes applications, I use the @IsDocBeingLoaded & !@IsNewDoc/@Unavailable combination to speed the loading of forms because the lookup does not have to check for keyword synonyms when an existing document is being opened. But additionally, the `@DbLookup` function returns a list of version numbers that correspond to the value in ProductCode field. For example, data in the hidden lookup view (vwProductCodeVersionLookup) looks like the data in Figure 17.8.

**FIGURE 17.8.**

*Product data as it is arranged in the hidden lookup view (vwProductCodeVersion Lookup).*

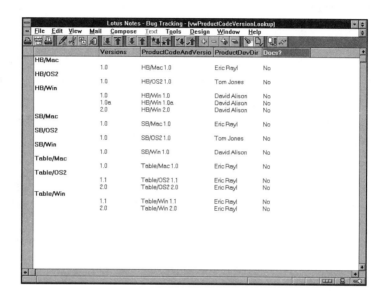

Thus, when the ProductCode field contains "HB/Win," the keyword formula for the ProductVersion field returns a list that represents the contents of the second column of the view shown in Figure 17.8, namely "1.0, 1.0a, 2.0." This list is used as the field's keyword picklist.

The Summary field is nothing special; it is intended to be a one-line description of the bug report that would appear not only in Notes views but as the subject for bulletin board and CompuServe postings of bug reports.

The Topics field has turned out to be more problematic. This field was intended to be used as the basis for the keywords associated with a bug report that was uploaded on CompuServe. It was a multivalued keyword field that would contain several very specific words associated with the essence of the reported bug. But at one company, this field was not used with discretion, and each bug report was assigned a multitude of Topics. For example, 1,000 bug reports contained more than 15,000 unique topic identifiers. This caused serious performance problems, because building a 15,000-entry keyword list was not fast.

The easy solution to this problem was to simply make the Topics field a multivalued Text field, not a keyword field, which was similar to the old bug tracking system the company used. A better solution, however, was to educate the technical support personnel on how to use the field properly. For example, if the problem was similar to the one shown in Figure 17.7, the Topics field often would contain information such as "OS/2 v1.3," "HB OS/2," "1.0," and "disappearing buttons." To fix this problem, the users needed to be instructed on how to judiciously select items for the Topics field, and the CompuServe upload routine needed to be modified to add items such as product code, version, and operating system to the Topics keyword list as new bug reports were uploaded.

The other two fields in the bug report form's overview section, Classification and Priority, were both keyword fields, but with fixed keyword lists. Because the definition of each field's possible keywords was open to interpretation, Notes PopUps for each field were designed into the form (see Figure 17.9 and Figure 17.10). The PopUps included more verbose field definitions than could be allowed with the simple field help text.

**FIGURE 17.9.**

*The PopUp associated with the Classification static text during design mode.*

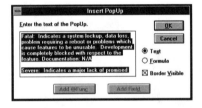

**FIGURE 17.10.**

*The Classification PopUp as it appears when a bug report is being composed.*

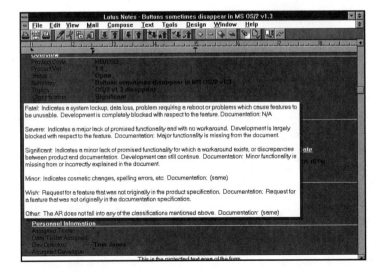

# The Bug Current State/History Area

In the bug tracking system, a bug report is considered to be in one of 12 possible states:

TBD (To Be Determined)

Confirmed

Integrated

Fix Submitted

Fix Verified

Failed

Postponed

No Issue

CNR (Could Not Replicate)

UTC (Unable to Confirm)

WNI (Will Not Implement)

Shipped

A simple keyword field could have been used to control the state of the bug, but I wanted to capture more information about the bug's state, such as when the current data was set and what previous states the bug had been in. For that reason, a dynamic, three-column, multirow table was simulated using three multivalued, computed-when-composed fields, State, StateSetBy, and DateStateSet (see Figure 17.7 and Figure 17.8). These fields all had the multivalue display separator set to New Line. The formulas for the three fields were "TBD", @UserName, and @Now, respectively. To change the state, the Change Current Bug State button was clicked, which had the following formula:

```
TempNewState := @Prompt([OKCANCELLIST]; "Changing An AR\'s State"; "Select the
                new state from the list below:"; "Confirmed"; ARStatesList);
@SetField("State"; TempNewState : State);
@SetField("StateSetBy"; @UserName : StateSetBy);
@SetField("DateStateSet"; @Now : DateStateSet)
```

This button macro would prompt the user to select a new state from a list of states (the field ARStatesList was a hidden, computed-when-composed field that contained the values of the possible states). Then the contents of the three state-related fields were updated, with the new state values being added to the extreme-left position in the multivalued lists State, StateSetBy, and DateStateSet. Therefore, a bug's current state was always the extreme-left element of the State list, and so on.

In case an error is made when selecting a state, a Delete Current State Record button was added to the form, and its formula was as follows:

```
LastChangeBy := LastChangeBy;
NumberOfChanges := NumberOfChanges;
@Set("NumberOfChanges"; @Elements(StateSetBy));
@If(NumberOfChanges = 0;
  @Do(@Prompt([OK]; "Error"; "There are no records to delete.");
      @Return(""));
  @Success);
@Set("LastChangeBy"; @Subset(StateSetBy; 1));
@If(@UserName != LastChangeBy;
  @Do(@Prompt([OK]; "Error"; "You are not authorized to delete the last
        status change because you did not set it.");
      @Return(""));
  @Success);
@If(NumberOfChanges = 1;
  @Do(@SetField("State"; "");
      @SetField("StateSetBy"; "");
      @SetField("DateStateSet"; ""));
  @Do(@SetField("State"; @Subset(State; -(NumberOfChanges - 1)));
      @SetField("StateSetBy"; @Subset(StateSetBy; -(NumberOfChanges - 1)));
      @SetField("DateStateSet"; @Subset(DateStateSet; -(NumberOfChanges - 1)))))
```

This button macro first checks to ensure that there is at least one element in the field StateSetBy. If not, the user is prompted that there are no records to delete, and the macro ends processing. Then the macro checks to see whether the current state was set by the current user, and it stops executing if the extreme-left value in the StateSetBy field is not equal to the value returned by @UserName. If the user is the person who set the current state, the macro then deletes the leftmost entry from the three list variables State, StateSetBy, and DateStateSet.

## The Details Area

The Details area of the Bug Report form contains only four variables, Description, TestSuite, Replication, and CrossReference. These are just basic test fields for describing the bug, the QA test suite that encountered the bug, and how to replicate the problem. The CrossReference field is actually rich text, which allows DocLinks to be pasted into the field.

## The Personnel Area

Although the Personnel area of the Bug Report form contains seven fields, only two fields appear editable in edit mode: NewAssignedTester and NewAssignedDeveloper. The NewAssignedTester field is used with the computed field CurrentAssignedTester and the computed-when-composed field DateTesterAssigned to track the date a Tester is assigned to a given bug report. This is the formula for the CurrentAssignedTester:

```
FIELD DateTesterAssigned := DateTesterAssigned;
@If(NewAssignedTester != CurrentAssignedTester;
  @SetField("DateTesterAssigned"; @Now);
  @Success);
NewAssignedTester
```

This formula checks to see whether the value in NewAssignedTester is the same as the value in CurrentAssignedTester. If it's not, the DateTesterAssigned field is updated to @Now. A similar approach is used for tracking the date that the current developer was assigned to the bug.

As for the computed field ARDevManager, this is a computed field that uses @DbLookup to determine the name of the individual listed in the ProductDevDirector field on the appropriate Product Description form. (The individual listed in the DevProjectLeader field on the Product Description form is not currently used anywhere.)

## The QA Configuration Area

The fields in the QA Configuration area were used either when a bug was found during QA testing or after a bug that was reported by a customer was confirmed. The names of the fields all correspond to the same fields on the Customer Report form, with the intention that queries could be constructed that use a similar format to obtain, for example, all bug reports and customer reports in which CustComputerModel contained IBM.

## The Resolution Information and Availability Areas

The Resolution Information area contained fields that were used for tracking how the bug was fixed, what version the bug was fixed in, and perhaps the actual code that fixed the bug, or a suggested workaround technique. Additionally, the Visibility keyword field was used to determine whether the details of the bug and related information should be made available on the company's bulletin board and on CompuServe.

The Availability area currently only tracked the bug's status on the CompuServe forum. The CompuServeStatus keyword field had four possible choices: New, Changed, Uploaded, Deleted. These values had to be set manually, and the users had to be sure to update this field when appropriate to ensure that the information on CompuServe was accurate.

## Other Hidden Fields on the Bug Report Form

One of the most important hidden fields is the Status field. This field is a computed field that checks the current state of the bug report and either sets itself to "Open" or "Closed." The formula for the Status field is as follows:

```
@If(@IsMember(@Subset(State; 1); "TBD" : "Confirmed" : "Integrated" :
        "Fix Submitted" : "Fix Verified" : "Failed" : "Postponed");
  "Open";
  "Closed")
```

This approach was used to help view performance by moving the computation for a bug's status to the form, rather than to the view's selection formula.

Three other of the form's hidden fields, TimesModified, PastAuthors, and PastEditDates, are used to build the now-familiar edit history table that I almost always use on forms.

The computed-when-composed field TimesCustomerButtonPressed field starts at zero, and each time the Add Customer Info button macro is run, it adds one to the value of this field. This information is then used to create an appropriate Customer Report ID number.

The computed-when-composed ARStatesList field is used by the Change Current Bug State button. It simply contains a list of the valid state names. This technique is used primarily to make the button macro as readable as possible.

SortOrder is a computed-when-composed field that is set to 1. This field is used in some views to ensure that bug reports are always listed before customer reports. Using this technique improves view performance over having a computed, hidden column in the view that is used for creating the sort order.

The computed DocProblem field was added to allow views to be created that contained documentation-specific bug reports. This is the formula for the field:

```
@If(ProductCode = "" | ProductVersion = ""; "";
  @DbLookup("Notes" : "NoCache"; ""; "vwPersonnelLookup"; ProductCode + " "
        + ProductVersion; 4))
```

Essentially, the DocProblem field is set to the value of the DocumentationProduct field (either Yes or No) on the Product Description document for the specified product code and version number.

The Subject field is a computed field that helps views perform better by moving another of the computations from the view to the form. For the Bug Report form, the formula for the Subject field is simply Summary.

# The Customer Report Form

The customer report form is the place where information specific to the customer's site (such as CPU type, memory available, and video drivers) is captured for later analysis by developers and QA analysts. This form also allows views to be easily created that are sorted by customer name, contact name, and so on. These views are very helpful for the technical support personnel who must check on the status of a given bug report.

## Composing a Customer Report for a Specified Bug Report

To add customer-specific information to a bug report, a bug report must have already been composed. One of the easiest ways to enforce this is to not show the Customer Report form on the Compose menu, and to allow it to be composed only by clicking the Add Customer Information button on the Bug Report form. The formula for this button macro is simply this:

```
FIELD TimesCustomerButtonPressed := TimesCustomerButtonPressed + 1;
@Command([FileSave]);
@Command([Compose]; ""; "frmCustomerRequest")
```

This formula just increments the counter TimesCustomerButtonPressed, saves the Bug Report form to ensure that its fields are available for inheritance, and then composes a new Customer Report form ("frmCustomerRequest"), as shown in Figure 17.11.

**FIGURE 17.11.**

*A new customer report being composed.*

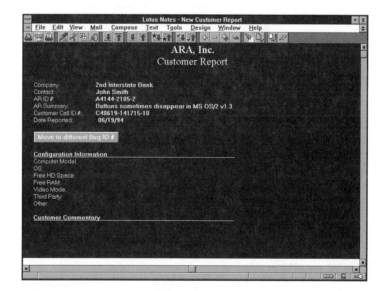

## The Fields on the Customer Report Form

The Customer Report form is shown in design mode in Figure 17.12 (the text color was changed from white to black so that the field names were visible).

**FIGURE 17.12.**
*The Customer Report form in design mode.*

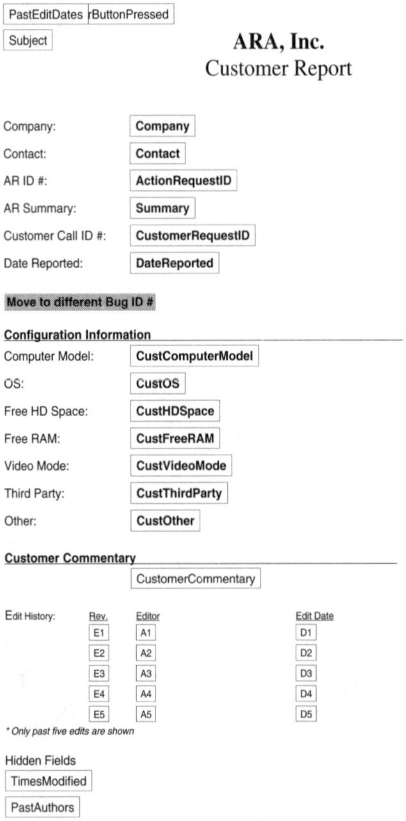

| PastEditDates | ButtonPressed |
| --- | --- |

| Subject |
| --- |

**ARA, Inc.**
Customer Report

| Company: | Company |
| --- | --- |
| Contact: | Contact |
| AR ID #: | ActionRequestID |
| AR Summary: | Summary |
| Customer Call ID #: | CustomerRequestID |
| Date Reported: | DateReported |

**Move to different Bug ID #**

**Configuration Information**

| Computer Model: | CustComputerModel |
| --- | --- |
| OS: | CustOS |
| Free HD Space: | CustHDSpace |
| Free RAM: | CustFreeRAM |
| Video Mode: | CustVideoMode |
| Third Party: | CustThirdParty |
| Other: | CustOther |

**Customer Commentary**

| CustomerCommentary |
| --- |

| Edit History: | Rev. | Editor | | Edit Date |
| --- | --- | --- | --- | --- |
| | E1 | A1 | | D1 |
| | E2 | A2 | | D2 |
| | E3 | A3 | | D3 |
| | E4 | A4 | | D4 |
| | E5 | A5 | | D5 |

\* Only past five edits are shown

**Hidden Fields**

| TimesModified |
| --- |
| PastAuthors |

The first field on the Customer Report form is a hidden, computed-when-composed field called TimesCustomerButtonPressed. This field just inherits the value of the similarly named field on the bug report form, and it is then used to compute the value for the CustomerRequestID field.

Both the Company and the Contact fields are computed when composed, and the Company field prompts the user to select the company name from a list of company names that is created by an @DbColumn. This is the formula for the field:

```
FIELD Company := Company;
@SetField("Company"; @Prompt([OKCANCELLIST]; "Select a Company"; "Select the
                Company from the list below:  (if the company is not
                listed, you must cancel and create a new company
                document)"; ""; @DbColumn("Notes" : "NoCache"; "";
                "(vwLookupCompany)"; 1)))
```

Next, the computed-when-composed Contact field presents the user with a list of the contact names for the company that was selected. Here is the Contact field's formula:

```
FIELD Contact := Contact;
@SetField("Contact"; @Prompt([OKCANCELLIST]; "Select a Contact"; "Select the
                    Contact\'s name from the list below:  (if the contact
                    is not listed, you must cancel and create a new
                    contact document)"; ""; @DbLookup("Notes" : "NoCache";
                    ""; "(vwLookupContact)"; Company; 2)))
```

The ActionRequestID field is a computed-when-composed field that simply inherits the ID number from the bug report form. The Summary field is also a computed-when-composed field that inherits the summary from the bug report form.

The CustomerRequestID field is computed when composed, and it uses an approach similar to the bug report ID number for computing CustomerRequestID number. This is the formula:

```
YearString := @Right(@Text(@Year(@Now)); 1);
MonthString := @If(@Month(@Now) >= 10;
                    @Text(@Month(@Now));
                    "0" + @Text(@Month(@Now)));
DayString := @If(@Day(@Now) >= 10;
                    @Text(@Day(@Now));
                    "0" + @Text(@Day(@Now)));
HourString := @If(@Hour(@Now) >= 10;
                    @Text(@Hour(@Now));
                    "0" + @Text(@Hour(@Now)));
MinuteString := @If(@Minute(@Now) >= 10;
                    @Text(@Minute(@Now));
                    "0" + @Text(@Minute(@Now)));
"C" + YearString + MonthString + DayString + "-" + HourString + MinuteString
   + "-" + @Text(TimesCustomerButtonPressed)
```

This formula creates a customer request number that is in the same format as the bug report ID number, except that the number begins with a *C* to identify it as a customer report and has the contents of the TimesCustomerButtonPressed field appended to the end of the field.

The DateReported field is an editable field, but it defaults to @Now.

The fields in the Configuration area of the form are used for gathering information about the customer's computer setup. This information can later be used for searches and by the Quality Assurance department to help those personnel duplicate the problem. The Customer Commentary area, and its related field, is for comments or suggestions that the customer might make while talking with the technical support personnel.

## Moving a Customer Report to a Different Bug Report

If a Customer Report form needs to be "moved" or "associated with" a different bug report, the Move to different Bug ID # button is pressed. Here is the formula for this button macro:

```
FIELD ActionRequestID := ActionRequestID;
FIELD Summary := Summary;
NewActionRequestString := @Prompt([OKCANCELLIST]; "Re-Assign a Customer Report";
                          "Select the Bug Report # to re-assign this
                          Customer Report to from the list below:"; "";
                          @DbColumn("Notes" : "NoCache"; "";
                          "vwARIDSubjectLookup"; 1));
@SetField("ActionRequestID"; @Trim(@Left(NewActionRequestString; ":")));
@SetField("Summary"; @Trim(@RightBack(NewActionRequestString; ":")))
```

When the user clicks the button, the user is presented with a listbox that contains the bug ID number and the Summary information. Although not all the Summary can fit within the listbox, generally there is enough information to enable the user to select the correct bug to move the customer request to. Additionally, the column number 1 in the view vwARIDSubjectLookup has this formula:

```
ActionRequestID + " : " + Summary
```

This formula allows for the ActionRequestID and the Summary fields to be extracted from the temporary variable NewActionRequestString, which holds the value that the user selected. This extraction uses the @Left and @RightBack functions and assumes that the colon (:) character will not be used in the contents of the Summary field.

Then, because there is a "simulated response hierarchy" between the bug reports and the customer reports that is derived by the column formulas in the views, the customer report appears associated with the new bug report because they both have the same ActionRequestID number.

---

**TIP**

In this application, as in most of my Notes applications, I try to design the forms and views such that the forms do most of the computational work. Instead of having a view column formula that is similar to

```
@If(Form = "frmActionRequest";
      Summary;
   Form = "frmCustomerReport";
        "     " + Company + ": " + Contact +
      " (" + DateEntered + ")"
etc...
```

I do all the computing in each form by using a hidden Subject field, then I simply have a Subject column in the view. This method makes maintenance much easier, and it increases the "snappiness" of views.

# "Cloning" Bug Reports

When a bug is reported and it is suspected that a similar bug could exist within another of the company's products, it is up to the Quality Assurance department to open up a new bug report, with the same information but for the new product and version number. Instead of requiring the QA personnel to compose an entirely new report, I decided that copying-and-pasting the original bug report document (the whole document from the view level, not just the contents of a field) would be a good method to help create a new, "cloned" bug report.

The problem was that several fields needed to be updated after the document was pasted into the database, particularly the ProductCode and ProductVersion fields. Additionally, the bug ID field needed to be changed, but it was an uneditable (computed when composed) field. A paste-in macro was designed that prompted users for the new product code and version information, and additionally updated the bug ID number with a numerical suffix (–2, –3, and so on) to indicate that the bug was cloned, while including the original bug ID number for reference.

The application's paste-in macro has the following formula:

```
TempProductCode := TempProductCode;
TempVersion := TempVersion;
TempARID := ActionRequestID;
@If(Form = "frmActionRequest";
  @If(@Prompt([YESNO]; "Cloning a Bug Report"; "You are about to copy a bug
        report to a new product code- do you wish to continue?");
    @Do(
        @Set("TempProductCode";
          @Prompt([OKCANCELCOMBO]; "Cloning an AR"; "Select the Product
                  Code to copy this AR to from the list below:";
                  @Subset(@DbColumn("Notes" : "NoCache"; "";
                  "vwProductCodeVersionLookup"; 1); -1);
                  @DbColumn("Notes" : "NoCache"; "";
                  "vwProductCodeVersionLookup"; 1)));

        @SetField("ProductVersion";
          @Prompt([OKCANCELCOMBO]; "Cloning a Bug Report"; "Select
                  the appropriate version of " + TempProductCode +
                  ":"; @Subset(@DbLookup("Notes" : "NoCache"; "";
                  "vwProductCodeVersionLookup"; TempProductCode;
                  2); -1); @DbLookup("Notes" : "NoCache"; "";
                  "vwProductCodeVersionLookup"; TempProductCode; 2)));

        @SetField("State"; "TBD");
        @SetField("StateSetBy"; @UserName);
        @SetField("DateStateSet"; @Now);
        @SetField("ProductCode"; TempProductCode);
        @SetField("ActionRequestID";
          @If(@Length(ActionRequestID) = 11;
            ActionRequestID + "-2";
            @Left(ActionRequestID; 11) + "-"
              + @Text(@TextToNumber(@Right(ActionRequestID; 1)) + 1))));
```

```
        @Return(""));
    @Return(""));
SELECT @All
```

Essentially, this macro first checks to ensure that the user realizes he is about to paste in a bug report (Form = "frmActionRequest") by prompting with a Yes/No prompt. If the user selects No, @Return("") stops the document from being pasted into the database.

Then the temp variable TempProductCode is set by using an @Prompt([OkCancelCombo]) that presents a list of the product codes using an @DbColumn. (The first @DbColumn, used in conjunction with the @Subset, is used to present a default value in the @Prompt window—it looks better than an empty listbox.)

The next @Prompt([OkCancelCombo]) is used to prompt the user for the correct version number, and the picklist is based on versions that exist for the product in the TempProductCode variable.

Finally, the three "state table" variables (State, StateSetBy, and DateStateSet) are reset, and the ProductCode field is set based on the contents of the TempProductCode variable.

Last, but not least, the ActionRequestID field is updated to reflect that it is a cloned bug report. The logic for this update is that if the new bug report is being cloned from the original report, a "–2" should be added to the ActionRequestID field. Otherwise, if it is already a cloned report, take the suffix ("–2," "–3," and so on) and add one to it to create the new ID number. This technique has the limitation that all bug reports must be cloned "sequentially"; that is, the second cloned bug report must be copy-and-pasted from the first clone, and so on, or else duplicate IDs will occur. But if this limitation is deemed too serious, it should be an easy matter to change this into a formula that does an @DbLookup, returns a list of all the bug IDs with a given bug ID prefix, and then using @Subset to get the last value in the list, extracts its suffix and adds one.

For you to be able to visualize the cloning process better, look at Figures 17.13, 17.14, and 17.15, which illustrate what the user sees when this paste-in macro is executed.

**FIGURE 17.13.**

*When a user pastes a bug report into the database, the user is asked to confirm whether to clone the bug report.*

**FIGURE 17.14.**

*If the user wants to clone the bug report, a listbox is presented with all the valid product codes.*

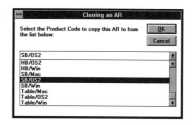

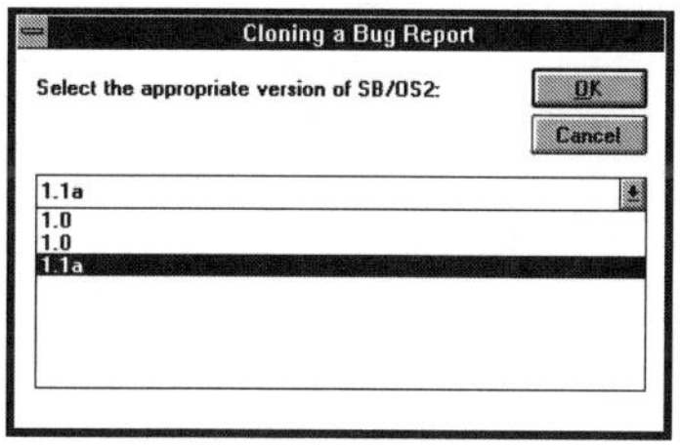

**FIGURE 17.15.**

*After a product code is selected, the user is prompted with a list of the possible versions of that product code.*

# Summary

This application, although it has some rough edges on it that need to be ironed out and tailored to a specific organization, still illustrates some very useful Notes techniques that you should be able to integrate into your applications. One change I would consider is to move the company/contact records to a separate database, because this information could also be used for tracking customer service contacts and creating "tickler" files for salespeople. I could also see mail-enabling the application with the use of a background macro that would send development directors memos when a bug report stayed in a given state too long. But all in all, this application is a useful example of a technical support application.

# 18

## The Travel Authorization Request Workflow System

# Overview

Workflow and forms-routing systems have received a lot of attention and hype lately, and rarely is Notes mentioned as a platform for developing workflow applications. Since its inception, however, Notes has been able to support workflow applications. Its integrated database/mail environment, along with its electronic "signing" capability and background macro processing, makes it an excellent platform for developing workflow applications.

When you are designing a workflow system in Notes, it is important to remember that the success of the system largely depends on how strictly the workflow is defined—the stricter the better. Many companies that try to replace relatively undefined paper-based processes with a Notes system run into problems in the development process because there are too many exceptions to rules that the system must account for. For instance, in a paper-based approval system, something like the following scenario might occur:

> "I fill out the form, take it to Mr. X's office, and put it in his in-basket. Later that afternoon, I find out that Mr. X is not going to be in the office for the rest of the week. So I go retrieve my request from Mr. X's in-basket and then put it in Mr. Y's basket (Mr. X's appointed approver)."

Notes systems that are flexible enough to handle this situation can be designed, but every step of the process needs to be specifically analyzed. For instance, in an electronic form routing system, exactly how long should a form remain "stalled" at a given status within the system (that is, unapproved in a user's mail database). One of the biggest concerns that needs to be addressed is how to ensure that duplicate requests are not processed. Many times, if systems are not designed correctly, users will submit the same request several times, perhaps with different routing lists, and the forms will be processed twice. In an electronic forms routing system, this practice has to be minimized to avoid confusion.

# The System and the Workflow

This system is similar to a system that I designed for a large international corporation that used a paper-based travel authorization/approval system. Corporate policy stated that any person who needed to travel would fill out a standard form, which would then have to be signed by the employee's immediate supervisor (and perhaps the supervisor's supervisor) and finally by the overall department manager. After the form was signed by the department manager, a copy would be sent to the accounting department, and a copy would be returned to the employee so that he would know that the request was approved and could make travel reservations.

One large department within the corporation enlisted me to automate the paper-based process using Notes. Additionally, these personnel decided to centralize the reservation process by creating a departmental "Travel Bureau" and appointing a staff to this new function.

First, I resolved the application's architecture. I decided to add a Travel Authorization form to the Notes mail database template, which would enable users to compose Travel Authorization requests from their mail database. The form would contain a field called NextApprover that would contain the name of the user's immediate supervisor. Because this was a very large department, different groups within the department had slightly different approval requirements. Depending on the job grade of the supervisor, the user might need to forward the request to another manager before the request would be routed to the Travel Bureau. But we did not require the original recipient to know the exact routing order when the request was composed.

The system is based on the assumption that at the time a Travel Request is composed, the user knows at least the next person who must approve the request; he or she might not know whether multiple approvals are required. When an approval request is received, the recipient has, in addition to the option of denying the request, the option of entering an additional approver's name (the next approver field). If the next approver field is blank, the system assumes that the request is fully approved and routes the approved request to the Travel Bureau database. There the travel bureau personnel make the required travel arrangements, and then they click a Mail Confirmation button, which sends a memo back to the traveler with the specifics of the reservations that were made.

I used the Notes electronic signature feature to "sign" travel requests when approved. Then travel bureau personnel are responsible for noting that the traveler's supervisor's electronic signature was verified, then for printing the approved Notes travel request document. At this point, the printed version, which looks almost exactly like the standard corporate paper-based form, is signed by the department's Vice President (or CFO, for international travel), and the paper form is sent to the accounting department (they were not Notes users, unfortunately).

Throughout each step of the process, the requester is kept informed of the progress of the travel request. Each time the travel request is approved, an approval confirmation memo bearing the approver's name is sent back to the requester stating that the request was approved. When the travel bureau personnel process the travel request, they enter the actual reservation times, dates, hotel information, and so forth on the form and then click a Confirm button, which mails a confirmation report back to the original requester. If a request is denied at any point in the process, the request is mailed back to the requester. It has the status "Denied" and includes a field for an explanation.

One item that made the workflow slightly more complex was that the system needed to allow a travel request for one individual to be composed by another individual (generally an administrative assistant or secretary). I solved this problem by having a computed Originator field based on the user's Notes ID and having an editable traveler name field. By default, only the actual traveler received notification of the approvals and reservation confirmation, but I added a check box to enable the originator to be copied on these approvals and confirmations.

To make the system easy to use, I didn't want to have the users always enter the same information, such as department name/number, and particularly travel preferences such as frequent flyer numbers, seating preferences, and so forth. I looked at several approaches but decided to add a new form to each user's mail database called a "Personal Preferences" form. This form would contain information pertinent to the Travel Request system, but it also could contain fields that other Notes applications looked up. I chose this approach mainly because of the security of each user's mail database—some information in a user's Personal Preferences document could be confidential and should not be in the public Notes Name & Address book.

Other information, such as title and department name, already existed in the Name & Address book, but the fields on the printed travel request form had length limitations to ensure that the form printed correctly. For instance, because of the layout of the corporate-standard travel request form, the data in the Title field on a travel request could be no longer than 20 characters, or the text on the form would wrap, creating a problem. If the title for travel authorizations was just looked up from the Notes Address Book database every time a document was composed, a user with a long title would have to abbreviate his title every time he composed a request—not very user friendly.

---

**TIP**

If your Notes applications, particularly forms-routing systems, need some types of user-specific information, such as credit card numbers or Social Security numbers, consider adding a Personal Preferences form (and a corresponding lookup view) to the mail database template. This form can have fields that several different applications look up data from.

---

One other approach used for the travel request system was to make a separate form for printing the request versus viewing the request. This was done mainly because the actual printed form used very small fonts and was hard to see on a Macintosh PowerBook's screen, but also because the travel request form contained much more information that was used to convey information to the travel bureau, such as traveling preferences.

# The System in Action

To illustrate the preceding process graphically, Figures 18.1 through 18.14 show travel authorization requests as they appear at various stages of the workflow process.

**FIGURE 18.1.**

*Composing a Personal Defaults document in the mail database.*

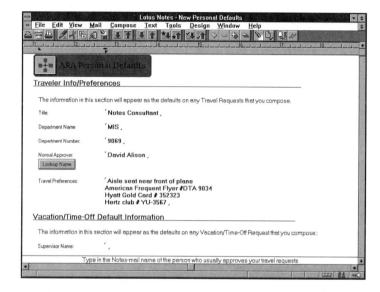

**FIGURE 18.2.**

*A new travel authorization request being composed.*

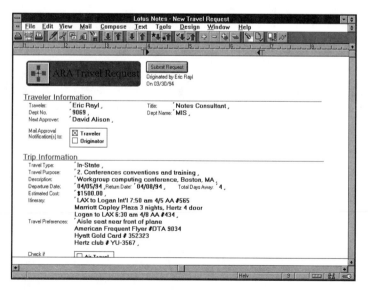

**FIGURE 18.3.**

*The mail database's All by Category view showing a submitted travel request in a user's mail database.*

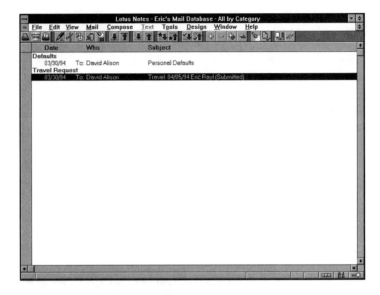

**FIGURE 18.4.**

*The view All by Category in the approver's database showing a new travel approval request form that has not been read or acted on.*

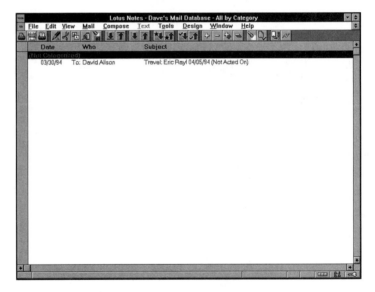

**FIGURE 18.5.**

*A travel authorization request as it appears in an approver's mail database (in edit mode).*

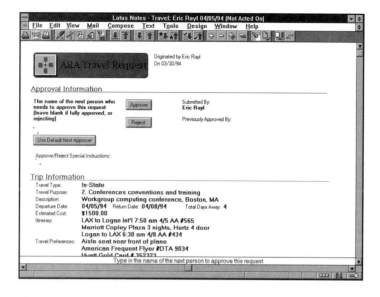

**FIGURE 18.6.**

*An (unread) approval confirmation as it appears in the requester's mail database view All by Category.*

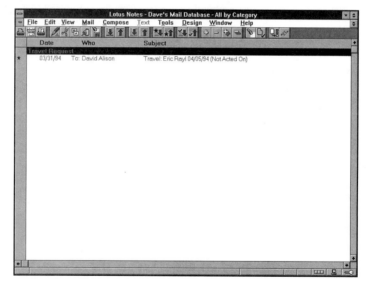

**FIGURE 18.7.**

*The approval
confirmation notice
displays using the mail
database's default form.*

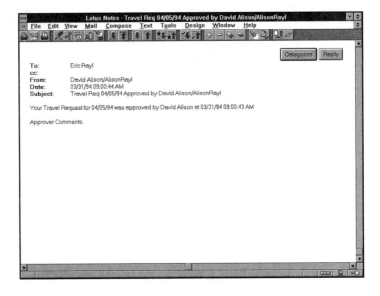

**FIGURE 18.8.**

*An unread travel
request rejection notice
as it appears in the
traveler's mail database
view All by Category.*

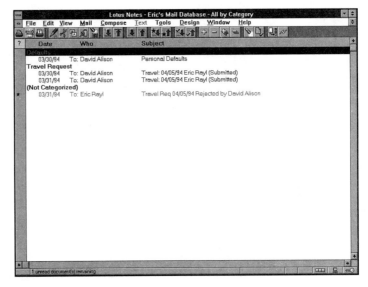

**FIGURE 18.9.**

*The rejection notice, like the confirmation notice, displays with the mail database's default form.*

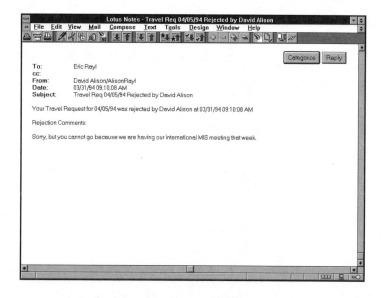

**FIGURE 18.10.**

*The Travel Bureau database's view of travel requests that have not been confirmed (sorted by departure date).*

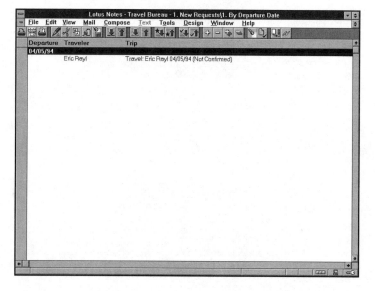

**FIGURE 18.11.**

*The Travel Bureau
database's view of
travel requests that have
not been confirmed
(sorted by traveler).*

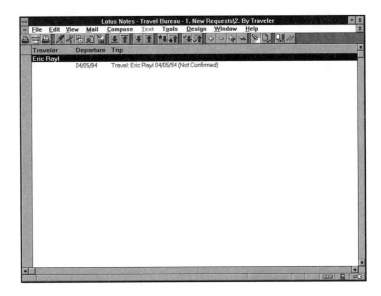

**FIGURE 18.12.**

*An approved travel
authorization request as
it appears in edit mode
in the Travel Bureau
database. Notice the
electronic signing
information at the
bottom of the screen.*

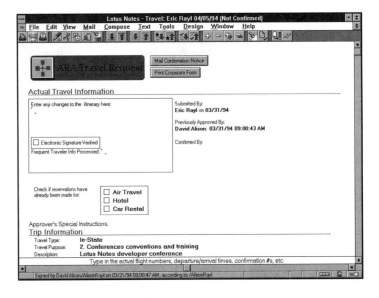

**FIGURE 18.13.**

*A new travel confirmation notice in a traveler's mail database. Notice that it appears to be from the "Travel Bureau."*

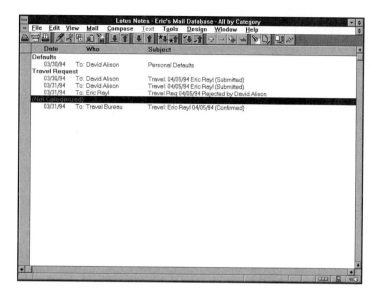

**FIGURE 18.14.**

*The travel confirmation document contains an area in which the travel bureau can convey important reservation information to the traveler.*

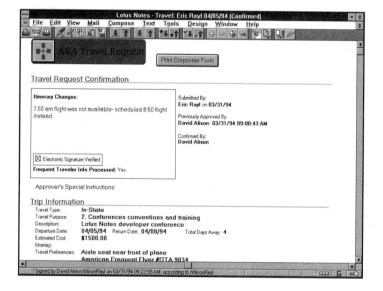

# Setting Up the System

## Adding the New Design Elements to the Mail Databases

To use this workflow system, several new design elements need to be added to the user's mail databases. These include the following design elements:

New Forms

>2. Admin Forms\1. Personal Defaults | frmDefaults
>
>2. Admin Forms\2. Travel Auth. Request Form | frmTravAuth2
>
>frmTravAuthSubmitted
>
>frmTravelConfirm
>
>Trav Auth Override | frmTravAuth

New Views

>All by Category
>
>(vwDefaults)

New Macro

>Mail-In Macro

These new design elements can be added either by cutting and pasting the documents into your mail database template and then refreshing the design of the user's mail databases, or simply by copying and pasting the design elements from the sample database into the user's mail databases. Note that the view All by Category already exists in most mail templates/databases, and the new view is identical to the one that comes with Notes except for a couple of modifications to the column formulas that allow travel request approvals and confirmations to appear correctly in the view. You should delete the original view All by Category before you paste the new view into your template/database.

If you are just interested in experimenting with the system and do not want to modify the standard mail template, there is one caveat: you probably should turn off the design template for your mail database after you paste in the new design elements (using **File|Database|Information|Design** Template...). Otherwise, the automatic nightly database redesign process could remove all the changes you've made to the database. When you are done experimenting with the system, you can reset your mail database's design template and then refresh your database's design to restore your mail database to its original design.

Additionally, the Travel Bureau database should be placed on a Notes server, and an appropriate mail-in database document needs to be composed in the Notes Address book, similar to that in Figure 18.15.

**FIGURE 18.15.**

*An example of a mail-in database document for the Travel Bureau database.*

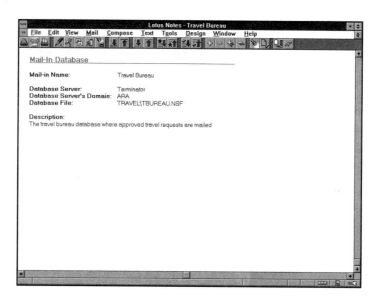

Now you are ready to start using and experimenting with the system.

# The Macros and Views That Control the Workflow

After the proper forms, views, and macros have been added to a user's mail database, the user should compose a Personal Defaults document before composing a Travel Request Authorization form. This is not mandatory, but the user is prompted (see Figure 18.16) if a travel request is composed before a Personal Defaults document exists. The user can still complete the request manually and submit it.

**FIGURE 18.16.**

*The prompt warning a user that he has not composed a Personal Defaults document.*

Checking for the Personal Defaults document is accomplished by using a hidden, computed-when-composed field on the travel authorization request form called CheckForDefaultsDoc, which has the following formula:

```
@If(@IsError(@DbLookup("Notes" : "NoCache"; "";  "vwDefaults";
  "Personal Defaults"; 4));
  @Prompt([OK]; "Warning"; "You have not composed and saved your Personal
    Defaults document. Please exit this form w/o saving and compose a
    Personal Defaults form before composing a Travel Authorization Request");
  @Success)
```

Additionally, if a user tries to compose a second Travel Preferences document, he is warned that one already exists, and the second preferences document cannot be saved. This task is accomplished through two fields on the defaults form. The first field is a computed-when-composed field, CheckIfPreferencesExist, with the following formula:

```
@If(@IsError(
    @DbLookup("Notes" : "NoCache"; ""; "vwDefaults"; "Personal Defaults"; 2));
  "1";
  "0")
```

A second, hidden, editable field, DoNotAllowSaving, has the following input validation formula:

```
@If(CheckIfPreferencesExist = "1";
  @Success;
  @Failure("A Personal Defaults document already exists for you
    - you must exit this document without saving and edit the
    existing defaults document"))
```

The combination of these two fields effectively blocks a second preferences document from being saved.

## The Submit Button on the Travel Authorization Request

After a user composes a new travel request in his or her mail database, the Submit button macro is used to start the workflow in motion. The Submit button macro's actions are outlined in the flowchart in Figure 18.17.

**FIGURE 18.17.**

*An outline of the
actions within the
Submit button macro.*

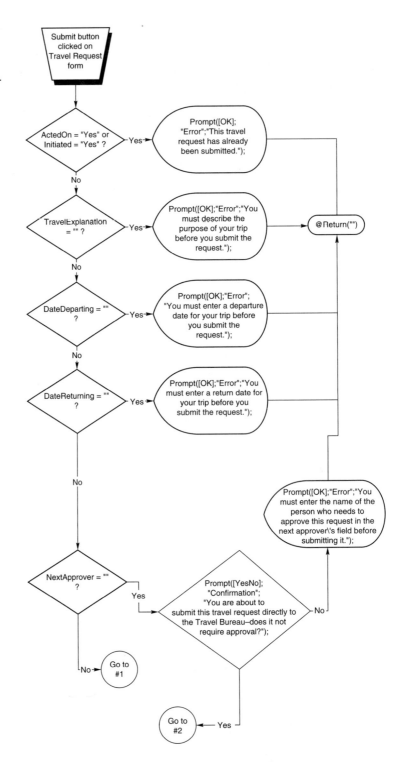

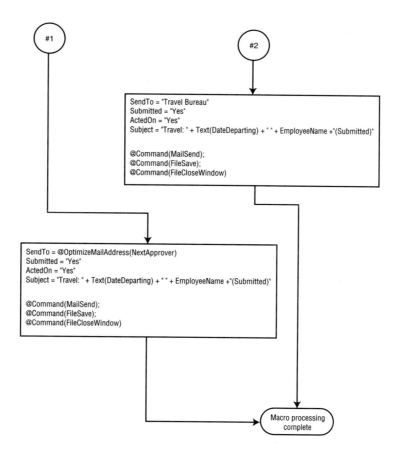

## The Submit Button Macro Formula

```
FIELD ActedOn := ActedOn;
FIELD Submitted := Submitted;
FIELD SendTo := SendTo;
FIELD Form := Form;
FIELD CopyTo := CopyTo;
FIELD Subject := Subject;
TRName := TRName;
TRTitle := TRTitle;
TRDept := TRDept;
TRPreferences := TRPreferences;

@If(ActedOn = "Yes" ¦ Initiated = "Yes";
   @Do(@Prompt([OK]; "Error"; "This travel request has already
         been submitted.");
      @Return(""));
   @Success);
@If(TravelExplanation = "";
   @Do(@Prompt([OK]; "Error"; "You must describe the purpose
         of your trip before you submit the request.");
      @Return(""));
   @Success);
@If(DateDeparting = "";
   @Do(@Prompt([OK]; "Error"; "You must enter a departure
         date for your trip before you submit the request.");
      @Return(""));
   @Success);
@If(DateReturning = "";
   @Do(@Prompt([OK]; "Error"; "You must enter a return date
         for your trip before you submit the request.");
      @Return(""));
   @Success);
@If(NextApprover = "";
   @If(@Prompt([YESNO]; "Confirmation"; "You are about to
         submit this travel request directly to the Travel
         Bureau- does it not require any approval?");
      @Do(@SetField("SendTo"; "Travel Bureau");
         @SetField("Submitted"; "Yes");
         @SetField("ActedOn"; "Yes");
         @SetField("Subject"; "Travel: " + @Text(DateDeparting)
            + " " + EmployeeName + " (Submitted)");
```

```
        @Command([MailSend]);
        @Command([FileSave]);
        @Command([FileCloseWindow]));
    @Do(@Prompt([OK]; "Error"; "You must enter the name of
        the person who needs to approve this request in
        the next approver\'s field before submitting it.");
        @Return("")));
@Do(@SetField("SendTo"; @OptimizeMailAddress(NextApprover));
@SetField("Submitted"; "Yes");
@SetField("ActedOn"; "Yes");
@SetField("Subject"; "Travel: " + @Text(DateDeparting) + " "
  + EmployeeName + " (Submitted)");
@Command([MailSend]);
@Command([FileSave]);
@Command([FileCloseWindow])))
```

## Important Points of the Submit Button Macro

The Submit button macro performs a couple of important validations before it allows the document to be mailed and saved. This macro validates that the request has not been already submitted, and then it validates that the necessary fields (TravelExplanation, DateDeparting, and DateReturning) have data in them. Additionally, it warns the user if he is submitting a travel request directly to the travel bureau without any approvals (some people within the organization are allowed to do this).

If the macro passes all the validations, it sets the fields Submitted and ActedOn to Yes, and it sets the Subject field to reflect that the travel request has been submitted already.

Finally, the @MailSend command is used to mail all the form's fields to the person listed in the SendTo field (either the NextApprover or the Travel Bureau database).

# The Mail-In Macro in Users' Mail Databases

For the system to work properly, each user's mail database must have a mail-in macro that checks for certain types of documents being mailed in and that acts on the documents accordingly. A graphical description of the events in a user's mail database mail-in macro is shown in Figure 18.18.

**FIGURE 18.18.**

*An outline of the actions within a mail-in database macro in a user's mail database.*

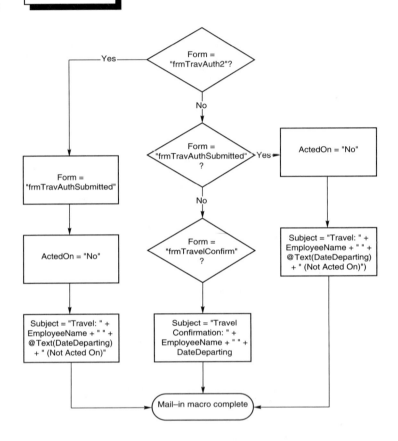

## The Formula for the Mail-In Macro in Users' Mail Databases

```
FIELD ActedOn := ActedOn;
FIELD Subject := Subject;
FIELD CurrentSubject := CurrentSubject;
FIELD CopyTo := CopyTo;

@If(Form = "frmTravAuth2";
  @Do(@SetField("Form"; "frmTravAuthSubmitted");
      @SetField("ActedOn"; "No");
      @SetField("NextApprover"; "");
      @SetField("Subject"; "Travel: "
        + EmployeeName + " "
        + @Text(DateDeparting) + " (Not Acted On)"));
@Success);
```

```
@If(Form = "frmTravAuthSubmitted";
  @Do(@SetField("ActedOn"; "No");
      @SetField("NextApprover"; "");
      @SetField("Subject"; "Travel: " + EmployeeName
        + " " + @Text(DateDeparting)
        + " (Not Acted On)"));
  @Success);

@If(Form = "frmTravelConfirm";
  @SetField("Subject"; "Travel Confirmation: "
    + EmployeeName + " " + DateDeparting);
  @Success);
SELECT @All
```

## Important Points of the Mail-In Macro

This macro checks to see whether the document being mailed into the user's mail database is one of three types: frmTravAuth2, frmTravAuthSubmitted, or frmTravelConfirm.

If the Form field contains frmTravAuth2, this is a new request that has not been approved yet. The Form field is changed to frmTravAuthSubmitted, which is the form where the traveler's information is "locked" and there are Approve and Reject buttons, and so on. The ActedOn and NextApprover fields are reset, and the Subject field is updated to reflect that it is a new travel authorization approval request.

If the Form field contains frmTravAuthSubmitted, the form is an approval request that has already been approved by at least one person, and the same steps are taken as if the form were a frmTravAuth2, but the Form field does not need to be changed.

If the Form field contains frmTravelConfirm, only the Subject field needs updating to reflect that it is a travel confirmation from the travel bureau.

# The Approve Button Macro

On the form frmTravAuthSubmitted, there is an Approve button that electronically "signs" the travel authorization request and then forwards the document either to the next required approver or directly to the Travel Bureau database.

Figure 18.19 outlines the events that occur when the Approve button is clicked.

**FIGURE 18.19.**

*An outline of the actions of the Approve button macro on the frmTravAuthSubmitted form.*

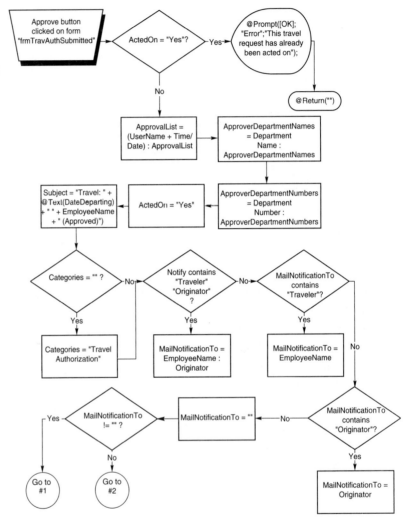

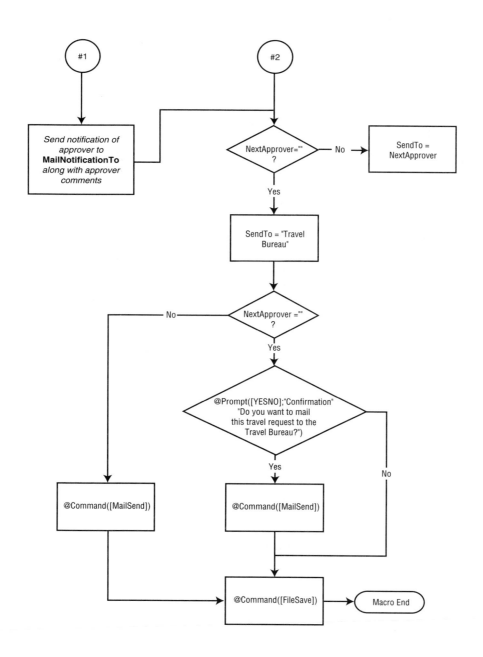

## The Approve Button Macro Formula

```
FIELD ApprovalList := ApprovalList;
FIELD ActedOn := ActedOn;
FIELD SendTo := SendTo;
FIELD Subject := Subject;
FIELD Categories := Categories;
FIELD ApproverDeptNames := ApproverDeptNames;
FIELD ApproverDeptNumbers := ApproverDeptNumbers;
MailToTravelBureau := MailToTravelBureau;
MailNotificationTo := MailNotificationTo;

@If(ActedOn = "Yes";
  @Do(@Prompt([OK]; "Error"; "This travel request has already
          been acted upon");
      @Return(""));
  @Success);

@SetField("ApprovalList"; (@Name([CN];@UserName) + ": " + @Text(@Now))
    : ApprovalList);

@SetField("ApproverDeptNames"; @DbLookup("Notes" : "NoCache"; "";
              "(vwDefaults)"; "Personal Defaults"; 3)
            : ApproverDeptNames);

@SetField("ApproverDeptNumbers"; @DbLookup("Notes" : "NoCache";
              ""; "(vwDefaults)"; "Personal Defaults"; 4)
            : ApproverDeptNumbers);

@SetField("ActedOn"; "Yes");

@SetField("Subject"; "Travel: " + @Text(DateDeparting) + " "
            + EmployeeName + " (Approved)");

@If(Categories = "";
  @SetField("Categories"; "Travel Authorization");
  @Success);

@If(@Contains(@Implode(Notify); "Traveler")
      & @Contains(@Implode(Notify); "Originator");
    @Set("MailNotificationTo"; EmployeeName : Originator);

  @Contains(@Implode(Notify); "Traveler");

    @Set("MailNotificationTo"; EmployeeName);

  @Contains(@Implode(Notify); "Originator");

    @Set("MailNotificationTo"; Originator);

  @Set("MailNotificationTo"; ""));
```

```
@If(MailNotificationTo != "";
   @MailSend(MailNotificationTo; ""; ""; "Travel Req " + @Text(DateDeparting)
      + " Approved by " + @Name([CN];@UserName); "Your Travel Request for "
      + @Text(DateDeparting) + " was approved by " + @Name([CN];@UserName) + " at "
      + @Text(@Now) + @NewLine + @NewLine + "Approver Comments:"
      + @NewLine + @NewLine + ApproversInstructions; ""; "");
   @Success);

@If(NextApprover = "";
   @SetField("SendTo"; "Travel Bureau");
   @SetField("SendTo"; NextApprover));

@If(NextApprover = "";
   @If(@Prompt([YESNO]; "Confirmation"; "Do you want to mail this travel
         request to the Travel Bureau?");
      @Command([MailSend]);
      @Success);
   @Command([MailSend]));
@Command([FileSave]);
@Command([FileCloseWindow])
```

## Important Points of the Approve Macro

As with many of the other macros in the Travel Authorization Request system, the Approve macro checks to see whether the request has previously been approved or rejected, and macro execution is stopped if the contents of the ActedOn field equal Yes.

Additionally, three multivalued fields (ApprovalList, ApproverDepartmentNames, and ApproverDepartmentNumbers) are used to hold the names of all the previous approvers and approval times, along with their department names and numbers. Currently, this information is captured, but only the ApprovalList field is being displayed. I am anticipating that the other information might be required at some later point, so I went ahead and designed the system to capture the data in case I need it later.

Again, the Subject field is changed so that in the approver's mail database, the subject reflects that the request has been approved.

Then a simple approval confirmation needs to be sent to the traveler, the originator, or both, depending on the contents of the multivalue Notify field. The @MailSend function is used here (as opposed to the @Command([MailSend]) function, which sends a simple document to the persons listed in the MailNotificationTo field, along with the contents of the ApproversInstructions field.

Then the contents of the NextApprover field are tested. If there is a name in the NextApprover field, it is assumed that the request needs further approval, and the request is mailed to the NextApprover. If NextApprover is blank, it is assumed that the request is fully approved, and the user is prompted as to whether to send the request to the Travel Bureau (some overseas units within the organization did not use the Travel Bureau function but simply printed approved requests).

# The Reject Button Macro

The Reject button macro is much simpler than the Approve button macro because its main task is to send a document to the traveler (and originator, if requested) that states that a certain travel document has been rejected, along with the rejecter's comments, as appropriate. A flowchart of the Reject macro is shown in Figure 18.20.

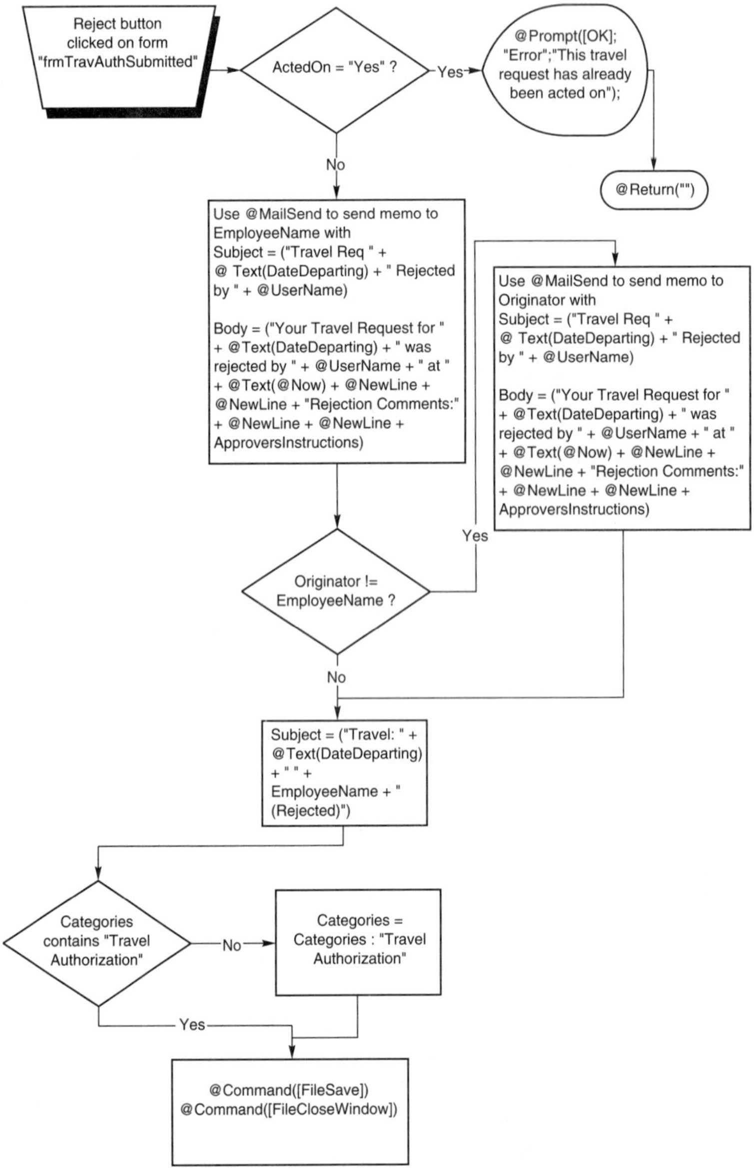

**FIGURE 18.20.**

*An outline of the actions within the Reject button macro.*

## The Reject Button Macro Formula

```
FIELD Subject := Subject;
FIELD SendTo := SendTo;
FIELD CopyTo := CopyTo;

@If(ActedOn = "Yes";
  @Do(@Prompt([OK]; "Error"; "This travel request has already
        been acted upon");
      @Return(""));
  @Success);

@MailSend(EmployeeName; ""; ""; "Travel Req " + @Text(DateDeparting)
    + " Rejected by " + @Name([CN];@UserName); "Your Travel Request for "
    + @Text(DateDeparting) + " was rejected by " + @Name([CN];@UserName) + " at "
    + @Text(@Now) + @NewLine + @NewLine + "Rejection Comments:"
    + @NewLine + @NewLine + ApproversInstructions; ""; "");

@If(Originator != EmployeeName;
  @MailSend(Originator; ""; ""; "Travel Req " + EmployeeName
      + @Text(DateDeparting) + " was rejected by " + @Name([CN];@UserName) + " at "
      + @Text(@Now) + @NewLine + @NewLine + "Rejection Comments:"
      + @NewLine + @NewLine + ApproversInstructions; ""; "");
  @Success);

@SetField("Subject"; "Travel: " + @Text(DateDeparting)
      + " " + EmployeeName + " (Rejected)");

@If(@Contains(@Implode(Categories); "Travel Authorization");
  @Success;
  @SetField("Categories"; Categories : "Travel Authorization"));

@Command([FileSave]);
@Command([FileCloseWindow])
```

### Important Points of the Reject Macro

The Reject button macro is fairly straightforward. After checking that the request has not already been acted on, it sends a document to both the traveler and the originator (if they are different) with the subject stating that the specified request was denied. The contents of the ApproversInstructions field are mailed along as a Body argument in @MailSend, which enables the rejecter to convey the reason that the request was rejected. Like the approval confirmation, the rejection notice that is mailed to the traveler is displayed using the mail database's default form. Additionally, the rejected request is categorized automatically in the Travel Authorization category, in addition to any other categories that the user has selected.

# The Mail-In Macro in the Travel Bureau Database

The Travel Bureau database has a mail-in macro used for changing the contents of the Form and Subject fields. In the Travel Bureau database, an approved travel request is displayed using the form frmTravelConfirm, which has no Approve or Reject buttons, but a button that is used to send a confirmation memo to the traveler. To switch a mailed-in document to the appropriate Form and Subject, a mail-in macro is used, as outlined in Figure 18.21.

**FIGURE 18.21.**

*An outline of the actions within a mail-in database macro in the Travel Bureau database.*

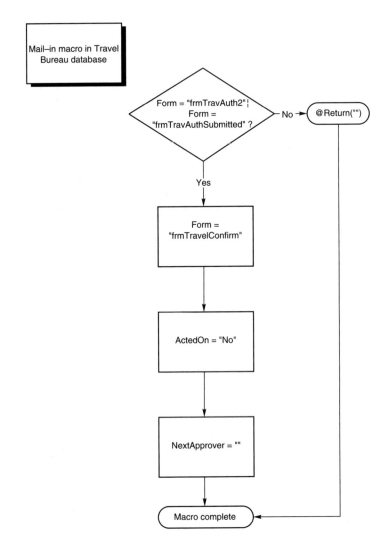

## Travel Bureau Database Mail-In Macro Formula

```
FIELD ActedOn := ActedOn;
FIELD NextApprover := NextApprover;
FIELD Subject := Subject;
FIELD Form := Form;

@If(Form = "frmTravAuth2" ¦ Form = "frmTravAuthSubmitted";
  @Do(@SetField("Form"; "frmTravelConfirm");
      @SetField("ActedOn"; "No");
      @SetField("Subject"; "Travel: " + EmployeeName + " "
          + @Text(DateDeparting) + " (Not Confirmed)"));
      @SetField("NextApprover"; ""));
   @Return(""));

SELECT @All
```

## Important Points of the Travel Bureau Database Mail-In Macro

This macro is simple, but its design allows many other types of documents to be mailed in to the Travel Bureau database because it checks for each form type. Eventually, different types of documents, such as "Travel Itinerary Change Requests," might be mailed to the travel bureau, and these types of forms can be handled by the user of additional `@If` statements.

# The Mail Confirmation... Button in the Travel Bureau Database

The form frmTravelConfirm has a button macro titled Mail Confirmation Notice to Traveler/Originator. It allows the Travel Bureau to confirm that reservations have been made, and it conveys information about itinerary that has been set, and so forth. In the Travel Bureau database, approved travel requests are in one of two states, Confirmed or Not Confirmed. As such, the documents appear in either the New Requests... or the Confirmed Requests... views, and the view selection formula is based on the contents of the Subject field.

When the Mail Confirmation... button is clicked, the chain of events shown in Figure 18.22 takes place.

**FIGURE 18.22.**
*An outline of the Mail Confirmation... button macro in the Travel Bureau database.*

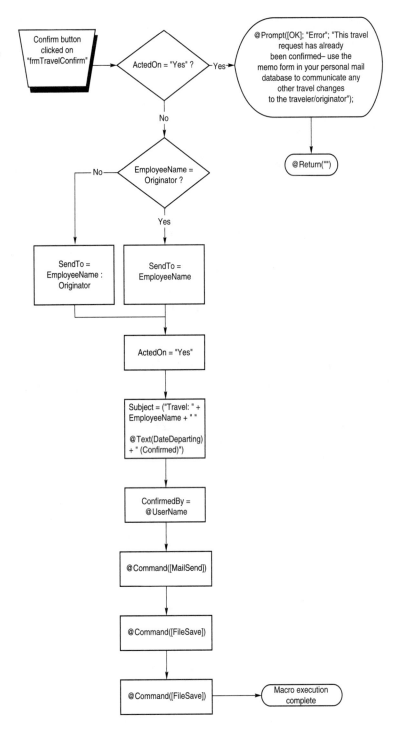

## The Mail Confirmation Macro Formula

```
FIELD SendTo := SendTo;
FIELD From := From;
FIELD ConfirmedBy := ConfirmedBy;
FIELD ActedOn := ActedOn;
FIELD Subject := Subject;

@If(ActedOn = "Yes";
  @Do(@Prompt([OK]; "Error"; "This travel request has already
        been confirmed- use the memo form in your personal mail
        database to communicate any other travel changes
        to the traveler/originator");
      @Return(""));
  @Success);

@If(SignatureVerified = "";
  @Do(@Prompt([OK]; "Error"; "You must verify the electronic
        signature and click the verify box before confirming this
        request");
      @Return(""));
  @Success);

@If(FrequentTravVerified = "";
  @Do(@Prompt([OK]; "Error"; "You must select whether or not the
        frequent traveler information was processed before you
        confirm this request");
      @Return(""));
  @Success);

@If(EmployeeName = Originator;
  @SetField("SendTo"; EmployeeName);
  @SetField("SendTo"; EmployeeName : Originator));

@SetField("ActedOn"; "Yes");
@SetField("Subject"; "Travel: " + EmployeeName + " "
   + @Text(DateDeparting) + " (Confirmed)");
@SetField("ConfirmedBy"; @Name([CN];@UserName));
@Command([MailSend]);
@Command([FileSave]);
@Command([FileCloseWindow])
```

## Important Points of the Mail Confirmation Macro

This macro is very similar to all the other button macros within this workflow system in that it first checks to see whether the travel request has already been processed. Then it determines whether to send the confirmation to both the originator and the traveler or to just the traveler. Finally, the subject of the document is changed to reflect that the request has been confirmed, and then, using @Command([MailSend]), the confirmation is mailed to the appropriate people.

One item worth noting is that @Command([MailSend]) is used here rather than @MailSend because the form frmTravelConfirm is included in the user's mail database. But this is not exactly like the frmTravelConfirm in the Travel Bureau database—its fields are "locked," and it does not have a Mail Confirmation... button.

## The Print... Button Macro

The main item worth noting about the Print Corporate Form button is the approach it takes to essentially help a user print the travel authorization form using the Notes form override function. But instead of making the user remember the steps necessary for printing using a different form, along with which form to select, this button macro basically composes a new document and inherits the necessary information from the open travel request document. The @Command([FilePrint]) is invoked.

The button appears on several forms, at different locations in the workflow, but its formula is always this:

```
@Command([FileSave]);
@Command([Compose]; ""; "Trav Auth Printing");
@Command([FilePrint]);
@Command([FileCloseWindow])
```

This technique can be used in many form-override situations to help users print the correct form.

## The View by Category

Two columns needed to have their formulas updated in order to display travel documents correctly in the All by Category view. Without the corrections, both approval confirmations mailed to the traveler and confirmations mailed to the traveler from the travel bureau would appear incorrectly in this view.

The two columns that needed to be modified were the column immediately before the Who column (the one that displays "To:" if a message was mailed, as opposed to received), and the Who column. The To: column's formula was changed from

```
@V2If(DeliveredDate != ""; ""; "To:")
```

to

```
@If(Form = "frmTravAuthSubmitted" & ActedOn = "Yes";
    "To";
  DeliveredDate != "";
    "";
  "To:")
```

The Who column's formula was changed from

```
REM "use @Name([CN]; ) here";
Person := @Trim(@Word(@Word(@Subset(@V2If(DeliveredDate != "";
  From;
  @Subset(SendTo; 1)); 1); "/"; 1); "="; -1));

@V2If(Form = "Delivery Report" : "NonDelivery Report";
  "Mail Router";
  Person)
```

to

```
Person := @Trim(@Word(@Word(@Subset(@V2If(DeliveredDate != "";
  From;
  @Subset(@Name([CN]; SendTo); 1)); 1); "/"; 1); "="; -1));
@V2If(Form = "Delivery Report" : "NonDelivery Report";
  "Mail Router";
  Form = "frmTravelConfirm"; "Travel Bureau";
  Form = "frmTravAuthSubmitted" & ActedOn = "Yes";
  @Name([CN]; SendTo);
  Person)
```

## The Personal Defaults Lookup View

This is a simple, hidden view used for looking up information from a user's Personal Defaults document. This view can easily be modified to include columns that contain data used in other applications, such as expense report forms or help bureau requests.

This program has evolved quite a bit and has gone through several changes to the workflow. Initially, the system was basically just one form in the user's mail database that was composed and then mailed around, and eventually printed. The problem was that duplicate requests were being mailed and approved, and it was not always clear what state the requests were in when they were in your mail database.

# Summary

The techniques used in this system outline some of the important concepts that can be used to create workflow applications in Notes. The main concepts are to minimize the chances that individuals will perform actions on documents that already have been acted on, and to use mail-in macros to switch the form types and subjects of documents, depending on the contents of their fields. Additionally, the use of the `@MailSend` function is contrasted with the command `@Command([MailSend])`, with each approach being used in different circumstances.

As with any real-world Notes application, a lot of changes and improvements can still be made to this application. The most important feature that I'm working on implementing is the capability to automatically "reroute" travel authorization approval requests that have remained untouched in an approver's mail database for longer than a certain period. Additionally, I want a user to be able to compose and submit a "reroute" or "delete" request to a database on the server that would in turn cause a "stalled" request to either simply be deleted or be rerouted and then deleted.

Workflow applications are fun to create in Lotus Notes, and no special add-on tools or products are required. All that is required is a relatively well-defined business process that can easily be described or visualized, and then a powerful Notes application can be developed.

# I

## Index

# Add to Your Sams Library Today with the Best Books for Programming, Operating Systems, and New Technologies

## The easiest way to order is to pick up the phone and call

# 1-800-428-5331

## between 9:00 a.m. and 5:00 p.m. EST.
## For faster service please have your credit card available.

| ISBN | Quantity | Description of Item | Unit Cost | Total Cost |
|---|---|---|---|---|
| 0-672-30382-5 | | Understanding Local Area Networks, Fourth Edition | $26.95 | |
| 0-672-30473-2 | | Client/Server Computing, Second Edition | $40.00 | |
| 0-672-30173-3 | | Enterprise-Wide Networking | $39.95 | |
| 0-672-30481-3 | | Teach Yourself NetWare in 14 Days | $29.95 | |
| 0-672-30209-8 | | NetWare Unleashed (Book/Disk) | $45.00 | |
| 0-672-30326-4 | | Absolute Beginner's Guide to Networking | $19.95 | |
| 0-672-30448-1 | | Teach Yourself C in 21 Days, Bestseller Edition | $24.95 | |
| 0-672-30388-4 | | Souping Up Windows (Book/Disk) | $29.95 | |
| 0-672-30380-9 | | Windows NT Unleashed | $39.95 | |
| 0-672-30402-3 | | UNIX Unleashed (Book/CD) | $49.99 | |
| 0-672-30466-X | | The Internet Unleashed (Book/Disk) | $44.95 | |
| 0-672-30519-4 | | Teach Yourself the Internet: Around the World in 21 Days | $25.00 | |
| 0-672-30520-8 | | Your Internet Consultant: The FAQs of Online Life | $25.00 | |
| 0-672-30485-6 | | Navigating the Internet, Deluxe Edition (Book/Disk) | $29.95 | |
| ❏ 3½" Disk | | Shipping and Handling: See information below. | | |
| ❏ 5¼" Disk | | TOTAL | | |

Shipping and Handling: $4.00 for the first book, and $1.75 for each additional book. Floppy disk: add $1.75 for shipping and handling. If you need to have it NOW, we can ship product to you in 24 hours for an additional charge of approximately $18.00, and you will receive your item overnight or in two days. Overseas shipping and handling adds $2.00 per book and $8.00 for up to three disks. Prices subject to change. Call for availability and pricing information on latest editions.

### 201 W. 103rd Street, Indianapolis, Indiana 46290

**1-800-428-5331 — Orders     1-800-835-3202 — FAX     1-800-858-7674 — Customer Service**

0-672-30500-3

# GO AHEAD. PLUG YOURSELF INTO MACMILLAN COMPUTER PUBLISHING.

## Introducing the Macmillan Computer Publishing Forum on CompuServe®

Yes, it's true. Now, you can have CompuServe access to the same professional, friendly folks who have made computers easier for years. On the Macmillan Computer Publishing Forum, you'll find additional information on the topics covered by every Macmillan Computer Publishing imprint—including Que, Sams Publishing, New Riders Publishing, Alpha Books, Brady Books, Hayden Books, and Adobe Press. In addition, you'll be able to receive technical support and disk updates for the software produced by Que Software and Paramount Interactive, a division of the Paramount Technology Group. It's a great way to supplement the best information in the business.

## WHAT CAN YOU DO ON THE MACMILLAN COMPUTER PUBLISHING FORUM?

Play an important role in the publishing process—and make our books better while you make your work easier:

- Leave messages and ask questions about Macmillan Computer Publishing books and software—you're guaranteed a response within 24 hours

- Download helpful tips and software to help you get the most out of your computer

- Contact authors of your favorite Macmillan Computer Publishing books through electronic mail

- Present your own book ideas

- Keep up to date on all the latest books available from each of Macmillan Computer Publishing's exciting imprints

## JOIN NOW AND GET A FREE COMPUSERVE STARTER KIT!

To receive your free CompuServe Introductory Membership, call toll-free, **1-800-848-8199** and ask for representative **#597**. The Starter Kit Includes:

- Personal ID number and password

- $15 credit on the system

- Subscription to CompuServe Magazine

## HERE'S HOW TO PLUG INTO MACMILLAN COMPUTER PUBLISHING:

Once on the CompuServe System, type any of these phrases to access the Macmillan Computer Publishing Forum:

| | |
|---|---|
| **GO MACMILLAN** | **GO BRADY** |
| **GO QUEBOOKS** | **GO HAYDEN** |
| **GO SAMS** | **GO QUESOFT** |
| **GO NEWRIDERS** | **GO ALPHA** |

Once you're on the CompuServe Information Service, be sure to take advantage of all of CompuServe's resources. CompuServe is home to more than 1,700 products and services—plus it has over 1.5 million members worldwide. You'll find valuable online reference materials, travel and investor services, electronic mail, weather updates, leisure-time games and hassle-free shopping (no jam-packed parking lots or crowded stores).

Seek out the hundreds of other forums that populate CompuServe. Covering diverse topics such as pet care, rock music, cooking, and political issues, you're sure to find others with the same concerns as you—and expand your knowledge at the same time.

# Installing Your Disks

# What's on the Disk

The disk for *Lotus Notes Developer's Guide* contains complete databases with examples of the techniques explained in the book:

- *The Catalog Request/Inquiry Tracking System* helps a company judge the effectiveness of its advertising campaigns. It also provides a way to easily generate mail-merged form letters to be sent out with catalogs, literature, and so on. Additionally, the system collects a history of the names and addresses of people who request information, which can later be exported and sold to mailing-list companies.

- *The Software Bug Tracking System* provides a way to track bugs associated with the various software programs that a company might develop. These bugs may be reported either internally or by a company's customers. Additionally, this program illustrates many of the techniques discussed in Chapter 14.

- *The Travel Authorization Workflow System* enables users to compose a Travel Authorization request in their Notes mail database and route the system to the necessary approvers. The approved request ultimately ends up at a central Travel Bureau database, where the specific reservation information can be entered for a given request. Throughout the approval process, the traveler/originator is kept abreast of the approval status.

# Installing the Disk

The software on the disk should be installed to your hard drive using the installation program, which runs from within Windows.

> **NOTE**
>
> To install the files, you'll need at least 3.5 MB of free space on your hard drive.

1. From File Manager or Program Manager, choose **R**un from the **F**ile menu.
2. Type `<drive>\INSTALL` and press Enter. `<drive>` is the letter of the drive that contains the installation disk. For example, if the disk is in drive B:, type `B:\INSTALL` and press Enter.

Follow the on-screen instructions in the installation program. The files will be installed in the \LNOTES directory, unless you choose a different directory during installation. Be sure to look at the README.TXT file in the root directory of the disk, as well as the file displayed at the end of the installation process. They contain information on the files and programs that were installed.